Victorian Appropriations
of Shakespeare

Victorian Appropriations of Shakespeare

George Eliot, A. C. Swinburne, Robert Browning, and Charles Dickens

Robert Sawyer

Madison • Teaneck
Fairleigh Dickinson University Press
London: Associated University Presses

Associated University Presses
2010 Eastpark Boulevard
Cranbury, NJ 08512

Associated University Presses
Unit 304, The Chandlery
50 Westminster Bridge Road, London SE1 7QY, England

Associated University Presses
P.O. Box 338, Port Credit
Mississauga, Ontario
Canada L5G 4L8

The paper used in this publication meets the requirements of the American National Standard for Permanence of Paper for Printed Library Materials Z39.48-1984.

Library of Congress Cataloging-in-Publication Data

Sawyer, Robert, 1953–
    Victorian Appropriations of Shakespeare : George Eliot, A.C. Swinburne, Robert Browning, and Charles Dickens / Robert Sawyer.
        p. cm.
    Includes bibliographical references and index.
    ISBN 0-8386-3970-4 (alk. paper)
    1. Shakespeare, William, 1564–1616—Adaptations—History and criticism. 2. Shakespeare, William, 1564–1616—Criticism and interpretation—History—19th century. 3. Shakespeare, William, 1564–1616—Appreciation—England. 4. English literature—19th century—History and criticism. 5. Shakespeare, William, 1564–1616—Influence. I. Title.
PR2880.A1 S29 2003
820.9'008—dc21

                                                            2002153644

For my brothers, James Joel Sawyer and Jonathan David Sawyer, and in memory of our mother, Katherine Ann Sawyer

Contents

Acknowledgments   9

Introduction   13

1. George Eliot and the Art of Dramatic
   Realism   18
2. Characterizing Shakespeare:
   A Study of Algernon Charles Swinburne   49
3. The Shakespeareanization of Robert Browning:
   The Objective and Subjective Poet   84
4. "An Eminently Practical Father":
   Dickens, *Hard Times,* and the Family   114

Afterword   138
Notes   146
References   155
Index   167

Acknowledgments

I owe many debts of gratitude to the numerous people who helped me accomplish this project. I need to thank, first, Christy Desmet and Tricia Lootens, who read early, middle, and late versions of this manuscript. Many others provided encouragement and camaraderie: Fran Teague, Ann and Terry Hawkes, Marianne Novy, Lydia Whitt, Dorothy Fink, Jim Nicholl, Gayle Miller, Phil Wade, Linda and Cary Cato, John Kennedy, Don Shipman, Judith Slagle, and Julianne Harper. Most importantly, I want to thank my best friends—Mary Anne O'Neal and George Fink—who stood by me through every phase of this work as well as all the other major projects in my life. I would also like to acknowledge my colleagues at East Tennessee State University for their most recent support, and I want to express my gratitude for an ETSU Research Development Grant that allowed me the time to finish this work. Christine Retz's erudition, wit, and editorial advice helped to make an occasionally challenging task much less so. My dog, Hallie, proved to be an excellent source of pleasant distraction during the years I worked on this book, while my new goddaughter, Madeleine, expressed her approval by cooing.

Part of the Swinburne chapter was published earlier in *Harold Bloom's Shakespeare*. Palgrave Press has kindly allowed me to reprint excerpts here. Routledge Press published an earlier, condensed version of the Browning chapter in *Shakespeare and Appropriation*. It has also graciously allowed me to reprint portions of that essay in this book.

Victorian Appropriations
of Shakespeare

Introduction

In the first critical essay published on Shakespeare (1664), Margaret Cavendish, the Duchess of Newcastle, attempted to defend Shakespeare from neoclassical "Dispraise." Proclaiming that Shakespeare's "Eloquence" diffused itself "upon all Subjects" and arguing that Shakespeare's "Wit and Language" were overwhelming, "so much he had above others," Cavendish concluded "that those, who Writ after him, were Forced to Borrow of him, or rather to Steal from him." The Duchess ends her critique by adding that although she "could mention Divers Places, that others of our famous Poets have Borrow'd or Stol'n" from Shakespeare, she decides instead to leave it to those that "Read his Playes, and others, to find them out" (Cavendish 1997, 13).

Two hundred years after Cavendish's pronouncement, Shakespearean "borrowing" and cultural influence reached its summit during the Victorian period. Agreeing with Gary Taylor, who argues that "Shakespeare's reputation peaked in the reign of Queen Victoria" (Taylor 1999, 197),[1] I take up Cavendish's challenge by examining the appropriation of Shakespeare's plays in the middle-Victorian period, roughly 1850 through the early 1880s. Concentrating on the "famous Poets" who have "Borrow'd or Stol'n" from Shakespeare, I focus on the "Divers Places" where George Eliot, Algernon Charles Swinburne, Robert Browning, and Charles Dickens draw upon Shakespeare in their own work.

These thirty-some years also mark an important transition in English culture and politics. In 1866, the same year that Swinburne published his first volume of poetry, the Hyde Park riots signaled a serious uprising against the limited enfranchisement. These demonstrations culminated in the passing of the Second Reform Bill in 1867, a bill that gave the vote to virtually all middle-class males as well as to most town workers. With the passage of the first Married Women's Property Act in 1870, a movement championed by George Eliot, significant changes for women also began to occur.

In addition, the universities were experiencing change. In 1871, the religious tests for university teachers and officials were abolished, and a decade later women were admitted to degree programs at the University of London, the same institute where Browning briefly studied. In politics, the 1880s witnessed the founding of the Fabian Society, the National Socialist League, and passage of the Third Reform Bill. Moreover, the 1870s and 1880s provided the fertile ground for the birth of the fin de siècle of the 1890s. Walter Pater, who also wrote extensively on Shakespeare, published his *Studies in the History of the Renaissance* in 1873; J. A. Symonds's *Male Love: A Problem in Greek Ethics* was composed the same year (although not published until ten years later). Indeed, Michel Foucault argues that the 1870s mark a time when gender roles were being expanded and modified, producing for some "a certain way of inverting the masculine and the feminine in oneself" (Foucault 1990, 43), a phrase that may call to mind Cavendish's earlier claim that in his writing, Shakespeare "had been Metamorphosed from a Man to a Woman" (Cavendish 1997, 13). Recently, other critical studies have also suggested that the Victorian period was one of sexual revolution, including those of Richard Dellamora, James Adams, and Linda Dowling.[2]

Representing a time in history when a society, individually and collectively, was redefining itself, these three decades then prove to be pivotal ones, particularly in terms of gender, culture, subjectivity, and the family. These vital years also propelled the English nation from heady nationalism—demonstrated by the Crystal Palace exhibition of 1851—to the cultural upheaval of the last decade of the century. While the religious controversy during this period has become a critical commonplace,[3] many critics ignore the other cultural changes, and no one has considered the role "Shakespeare" plays during this period in the competing ideological disputes.[4] Indeed, Shakespeare and his works were also being redefined during this period, and these multiple interpretations and uses of "Shakespeare" demonstrate Cavendish's claim for Shakespeare's ability to be "[t]ransformed into every one of those Persons he hath Described" (Cavendish 1997, 12). While my focus will consider the appropriation of various Shakespearean plays, including *1 Henry IV*, *The Tempest*, and others, *Hamlet* and *King Lear* will serve as central examples.

Both the theater audience and the culture that produced it were diverse in the nineteenth century. As Michael Booth argues, "If the Queen were the apex of the English audience, the working class was its broad, strong base" (Booth 1991, 5). At the center of this structure was the middle class, a group that became particularly important to the theater in the second half of the century due to the growing prosperity of England. Other factors that brought increasing numbers of the middle class to the more elite theaters included the growth of the railroads (to bring audiences from the provinces), the invention of gas lighting, and a unified police force (to keep the playgoers safe). At theaters like Drury Lane, the upper, middle, and lower classes shared the same building, although not the same sections within the theater. The urban working class, for instance, sat in the most affordable seats—the gallery—alongside soldiers, servants, and the socially marginalized. The Victorian theater was, therefore, a microcosm of English society in general, a society increasingly concerned with its national image. More important, as growing numbers of middle-class patrons attended Shakespearean productions, those advocates of a private, cultural Shakespeare on the page, such as Charles Lamb at the beginning of the century and A. C. Bradley at the close, grew more and more disillusioned with public Shakespeare on the nineteenth-century stage, so that in one sense, Shakespearean appropriation in novels, poetry, and criticism was not only the most political but also the most successful "Shakespeare" produced during the mid-Victorian period.

The distinction between Shakespeare on page and stage quickened in the early nineteenth century, partly due to the romantic championing of unmediated access to the "author's" mind, and this notion may further explain why Shakespeare on the page predominates over dramatic Shakespeare during this time. Borrowing from M. H. Abrams, Jonathan Arac refers to this movement as the "romantic shift from audience-centered to author-centered poetics" (Arac 1987, 215).[5] In fact, it is only in the second half of the twentieth century, according to critics such as J. L. Styan, that the prejudice against staged Shakespeare has been overcome (Styan 1977). Looking at Charles Lamb's and other romantic readings of Shakespeare will help to bring into focus the received notions of Shakespeare inherited by Eliot, Swinburne, Browning, and Dickens.

Lamb's influence on dramatic criticism and practice is more striking than most critics admit, and in his letters and essays, he disparagingly distinguishes between private Shakespeare and public Shakespeare. In fact, Lamb dismisses all dramatic interpretations of Shakespeare, comparing the playwright's "absolute mastery over the heart and soul of man" to the "low tricks upon the eye and ear" to which actors of his work resort, and to which the "common auditors" respond (Lamb [1812] 1980, 86, 91). Frustrated by this notion, Lamb claims that the "pleasure which Shakspeare's plays give in the acting" becomes no different from those "which the audience receive from those of other writers" (93). Therefore, Lamb "must conclude that there is something in the nature of acting which levels all distinctions" (93). Even the diction here—"common auditors," "low tricks," and a "level[ing]" of "distinctions"—intimates that Lamb may well be criticizing the attempt by some performers to appeal to the new, heterogenous theater audiences. Unfortunately, some critics have oversimplified Lamb's bias against the acting of Shakespeare, by blaming his assessment solely on the poor staging conditions in the nineteenth century; however, one must consider the theaters a minor factor at best, as Lamb was an inveterate playgoer who praised a number of contemporary productions. He even proposed marriage to one of the actresses whom he admired, proving that he did not look down on all actors and actresses, just those, it seems, who attempted to perform his beloved Shakespeare.

Other romantic critics also championed Shakespeare in print over Shakespeare in production. As Jonathan Bate points out, Coleridge's "best Shakespearean criticism is in the most private of forms, the personal marginal annotation," and even when Coleridge did lecture in public "it was to a socially élite audience" (Bate 1989, 133). In a comment he makes on *The Tempest*, Coleridge seconds Lamb's assertions about Shakespearean drama. Referring to Shakespeare's last romance, Coleridge writes that "[i]t addresses itself entirely to the imaginative faculty; and although the illusion may be assisted by the effect on the senses of the complicated scenery and decorations of modern times yet this sort of assistance is dangerous" (Coleridge 1969, 224). In other words, any "assistance" by a performer is harmful at best, "dangerous" at worst, as it may misinterpret the author's "intention." This tension between Shakespeare on the page and Shakespeare on the stage continued throughout the nineteenth century, and fuels a debate that continues to generate much scholarly work even today.[6]

Toward the close of the twentieth century, numerous critics began to examine Shakespearean appropriation,[7] with many of the works focusing on the ideological and political uses of Shakespeare, a focus that reflects the assertion that all of Shakespeare's plays are "site[s] of cultural struggle and change" (Sinfield 1985, 131). My definition of "appropriation" focuses on the first sense of the word, the taking of "possession . . . for one's own" purposes, a seizure often without permission,[8] a sense close to Cavendish's notion of "borrowing" or "stealing." While I agree with Hans Robert Jauss, who argues that literary texts "can continue to have an effect only if those who come after it still or once again respond to it—if there are readers who again *appropriate* the past work of authors who want to imitate, outdo, or refute it" (Jauss 1989, 1201, italics mine), I focus instead on the way these authors use Shakespeare's works to question their culture's notions of gender, desire, identity, and the family. Moreover, all four writers employ Shakespeare to lend cultural currency to their own works: George Eliot, who explores gender issues in the novel; A. C. Swinburne, who uses

Shakespeare to examine homoerotic topics in his criticism; Robert Browning, who fashions his own Shakespearean identity in his poetry, and Charles Dickens, who in his readings, novels, and personal life blurs the distinction between public and private families.

The connection between intertextuality and historical contextualization is inescapable. As Jean Howard argues, "*both* social and literary texts are opaque, self-divided, and porous, that is, open to the mutual intertextual influences of one another" (Howard 1987, 15). The careful study of these spaces between authority and reality, the discontinuities, should produce a clearer understanding of a particular society's understanding of itself. Of course, this move grants real power to literature, so that instead of reflecting some transcendent reality, literature becomes a powerful force in creating a culture's sense of itself. Ultimately, I argue that mid-Victorian Shakespearean appropriation produces a dynamic intertext: the works reflect the cultural charge that produced them, but the works may go on to affect the culture once they are re-produced.

Finally, I demonstrate how a single cultural context may produce diametrically opposed readings of Shakespeare, particularly when Shakespeare's plays become ideological battlegrounds. At the same time that Shakespeare's cultural status may be used to subvert traditional ideas of politics and sexuality in Swinburne and Eliot, it may also be used to promote more conservative policies and literary interpretations in other writers such as Browning and Dickens. By "stealing" from Shakespeare, to return to the Duchess of Newcastle's term with which I began, these writers participate in the game of ideology by competing on the playing field of Shakespeare studies.

1

George Eliot and the
Art of Dramatic Realism

In Jane Austen's novel *Mansfield Park*, Henry Crawford exclaims that Shakespeare "is part of an Englishman's constitution" and that Shakespeare's "thoughts and beauties are so spread abroad that one touches them every where, one is intimate with him by instinct" (Austen 1980, 306). The intimacy that Crawford celebrates allows novelists of the Victorian period to appropriate Shakespeare into their works in order to valorize their own writings. This chapter focuses on how one nineteenth-century novelist, George Eliot, appropriates Shakespeare, specifically *Hamlet*, to examine gender issues.

Eliot's appropriation and her understanding of Shakespeare mediated between page and stage. For example, her reading of Charles Knight's edition of Shakespeare with George Henry Lewes is well documented, and their copy at the Folger Shakespeare Library is filled with marginalia and critical responses to the various plays. Yet the couple also attended Shakespeare's plays together, and Lewes wrote perceptively on them. Thus, Eliot's sympathy with both public and private performances allows her to negotiate between the two in borrowing from Shakespeare. Moreover, as primarily a novelist, Eliot appropriates Shakespeare as a means of commenting on Victorian society, particularly gender roles.

Eliot engages with a long-standing tradition of a feminized Shakespeare—a Shakespeare whose defining characteristic is sympathy—as a way to discuss and destabilize traditional gender roles. Specifically, Eliot draws on the notion of a feminized Hamlet, a stage tradition many actresses had followed, beginning with Sarah Siddons, who played Hamlet in 1775. In *Daniel Deronda*, Eliot's last novel (published almost exactly one hundred years after Siddons's innovation), Eliot appropriates and develops this feminized Hamlet as a model for her protagonist. While not as popular or well received as her previous novel, *Middlemarch*, this work constitutes Eliot's most important appropriation of Shakespeare.

Although praised by Jewish readers and critics, the overall reviews of *Deronda* were mixed.[1] One reviewer even called attention to Eliot's nearly Shakespearean status to condemn the book, while others used echoes from *Hamlet* to express their disappointment. According to the *Edinburgh Review*, although the book was "received with a respect which Shakespeare himself could scarcely equal," ultimately the critic pronounces the book "a disappointment, even a failure" (Review of *Daniel Deronda* 1876b, 450); the unsigned critique in the 16 September issue of *Saturday Review* lamented that the book was a great "falling off from *Adam Bede*, and *Middlemarch*" (Review of *Daniel Deronda* 1876c, 356). Part of the ambivalence of the other critics, however, may have resulted from Deronda's ambiguous character.

Eliot's feminized "Hamlet," Daniel Deronda, fares much better in his relations with others than most interpretations of Shakespeare's Hamlet would allow. Most important, Deronda-as-Hamlet successfully resolves his relations with women. The key difference between the overly virile eighteenth-century Hamlets and Eliot's protagonist is Deronda's ability to sympathize with points of view other than his own, "an activity of imagination on behalf of others," which Hamlet in most productions of Shakespeare's play never achieves (Eliot 1988, 151). This sympathy, I believe, parallels in some ways the imaginative state, a capacity that Eliot believed to be essential both for the creative artist and the successful human being. For the artist, according to Eliot, sympathy tempers the ego by projecting the ego into the creation of fictional characters, while withholding judgment about those characters' actions and motivations; for others, empathy fosters the ability to sympathize with points of view that one does not understand or with which one does not agree. In Eliot's conception of sympathy, this creative identification seems to be particularly aligned with the feminine. For Eliot, as Marianne Novy perceptively argues, the concept of sympathy "mediated between her culture's ideal of womanhood" and her "culture's ideal of art, associated at its highest with Shakespeare" (Novy 1994, 112).[2]

The power of sympathy that Eliot perceives in Hamlet and that she represents in Deronda also makes Eliot heir to the tradition of sympathetic character portrayal that critics trace from Shakespeare to Jane Austen to Eliot herself, a tradition carefully constructed by her companion G. H. Lewes. Even as Eliot recreates *Hamlet* in *Daniel Deronda*, Lewes is creating Eliot's own image in the Shakespearean tradition and ensuring her place in the canon. Therefore, two levels of appropriation occur simultaneously—

Lewes's of Eliot and Eliot's of Shakespeare. While Lewes constructs a "safe" traditional Eliot, with Shakespeare as her father and Jane Austen as her literary mother, Eliot creates a less monolithic Hamlet, opening up a space for discussion of gender and demonstrating that traditional categories of gender can be destabilized. While I am indebted to Novy's work on Eliot and *Hamlet*, she overlooks the dialectical function of Eliot's appropriation of Hamlet, a function that I believe will increase our understanding of Eliot's power as a novelist. Eliot appropriated Shakespeare, but she also influenced Shakespeare: her feminized Hamlet may represent a pivotal point in the conception of nineteenth-century Hamlets,[3] opening a space for the "inverted" or queer Hamlet and Shakespeare of Swinburne in the 1880s,[4] the same Shakespeare from which Browning's followers would try to distance their poet late in his career.

ELIOT, SHAKESPEARE, AND SYMPATHY

Eliot's conception of sympathy is closely related to what we now call empathy—an intense sympathetic identification with others. This impassioned sympathy, according to Elizabeth Ermarth, "involve[s] a difficult psychic negotiation between self and other" (Ermarth 1985, 23). Indeed, Eliot's close friend Charles Bray states that she always attempted to "show her friends off to the best advantage" (qtd. in Redinger 1975, 126), while J. W. Cross, her first biographer and husband, suggests that "it was this wide sympathy, this understanding of so many points of view," that gained her so many admirers from so many stations of society (Cross 1968, 3:344). Eliot's ability to see from many points of view—this "wide sympathy"— will be central to my argument that Deronda represents Eliot's feminized Hamlet, a Hamlet endowed with the sympathy that Eliot felt to be particularly feminine. As Deronda states, "I suppose our keen feeling for ourselves might end in giving us a keen feeling for others, if, when we are suffering acutely, we were to consider that others go through the same sharp experience" (Eliot 1988, 387).

George Eliot formulated her conception of sympathy by drawing from numerous sources, including Ludwig Feuerbach's *The Essence of Christianity*[5] and her culture's conception of sympathy, particularly Hazlitt's notion of Shakespearean sympathy. During this writing apprenticeship, Eliot was translating Feuerbach's philosophical treatise from German into English, and I believe this work provided Eliot with the philosophical framework for her conception of sympathy, as both "she and Feuerbach stress the therapeutic and liberating value of a double consciousness" (Ermarth 1985, 24).

For Eliot, "double consciousness" represents the ability to see not merely from a double viewpoint but from multiple viewpoints, sometimes concurrently; this kind of sympathy requires the psyche to be split, allowing for contradictory views to exist at the same time. Both Eliot and Feuerbach also sense a type of divinity in the sympathy I am defining and a nearly moral imperative to practice such identification with others.

In Feuerbach's philosophical formulation, mankind functions as an earthbound replacement for God, a humanistic substitution that Eliot also embraced. Indeed, writing to a friend, Eliot proclaimed, "With the ideas of Feuerbach I everywhere agree" (Eliot 1954–78, 2:153). Feuerbach contends that man *"has his highest being, his God, in himself;* not in himself as an individual, but in his essential nature, his species" (Feuerbach 1957, 281). Moreover, Feuerbach argues that feeling "makes God a man, but for the same reason it makes man a God" (281). This type of feeling is expressed, Feuerbach asserts, in sympathy, for "[f]eeling is sympathy" and "feeling arises only in the love of man to man" (283). Declaring that "[o]nly in sympathy does sensation rise into feeling," he concludes that "in feeling man is related to his fellow-man as to himself; he is alive to the sorrows, the joys of another as his own" (283). Eliot makes a similar assertion in her letters. Writing to Mrs. Henry Ponsonby in 1874, she argues that "the idea of God, so far as it has been a high spiritual influence, is the ideal of a goodness entirely human (i.e., an exaltation of the human)" (Eliot 1954–78, 6:98). It is this kind of sympathetic identification that informs Eliot's writings; this "activity of imagination on the behalf of others" also characterizes the point of view of her last protagonist, Daniel Deronda. Deronda, then, embodies the philosophical ideal for divine humanity that Feuerbach describes and Eliot both explores and appropriates in her writing.

While Feuerbach's work gave Eliot a philosophical foundation, Shakespeare provided an artistic ideal. Eliot's letters during this apprentice period indicate a growing interest in Shakespeare. Her first volume of letters—written between the ages of sixteen and thirty-two—is full of Shakespearean references. As early as October 1842, a friend of Eliot claimed that Eliot "could be content were she allowed no other book than Shakespeare"; and "in educating a child, this would be the first book" Eliot would give to her children (Cross 1968, 1:373). In an essay entitled "The Natural History of German Life," she proclaims, "The greatest benefit we owe to the artist, whether painter, poet, or novelist, is the extension of our sympathies" (Eliot 1963, 270). Eliot is strengthening the idea that literature cultivates sympathy by making a comparison between the beliefs of Shakespeare and Feuerbach. In an 1854 letter to Sara Hennell, both of her sources of sympathetic identification were clearly on her mind, as she mentions both

Feuerbach and Shakespeare in the same letter (14 July). For both philosopher and writer, therefore, sympathy is *the* defining characteristic of life and art.

The received ideas about Shakespearean sympathy that Eliot appropriates come from at least four related sources. The first is Coleridge's notion of Shakespeare as a "Proteus" who can transform himself into many forms, and the second is Keats's conception of Shakespeare as "camelion"-like. I would suggest, however, that even more important for Eliot are Hazlitt's ideas about Shakespeare's power of sympathy and lack of ego, and Anna Jameson's theory that Shakespeare "understood all truth" (Jameson 1889, 18).

Coleridge's ideas about Shakespearean characterization have been well documented: Emphasizing character over plot, for example, Coleridge asserts that the plays are always character-driven. He also claims that Shakespeare was a "nature humanized," possessing a "genial understanding directing self-consciously a power and an implicit wisdom deeper even than our consciousness" (qtd. in Bate 1992, 129). Moreover, Coleridge calls Shakespeare a "Proteus" who "passes into all forms of human character and passion" (Coleridge 1812, 179). This last point, I believe, is the most fundamental aspect for Eliot's understanding of Coleridge's concept: the "myriad-minded" Shakespeare of Coleridge, a Shakespeare who empathizes with and enters sympathetically into all types of human characters.

Although drawing from Hazlitt more than Coleridge, Keats makes similar assertions concerning Shakespeare but modifies Coleridge's image of Shakespeare as Proteus. For Keats, Shakespeare is the "camelion Poet" who "has no Identity" and is "continually . . . filling some other Body" (Keats 1958, 1:386–87). Eliot was to use this same image in a letter to her friends, the Brays, in 1849: "[M]y nature is so chameleon I shall lose all my identity unless you keep nourishing the old self with letters" (Eliot 1954–78, 1:302). (As Nina Auerbach points out, Eliot was somewhat chameleon-like herself, changing her name often, as she transformed herself from evangelical schoolgirl, to fallen woman, to Victorian sage [1985, 261–63]). Eliot, then, also seems to incorporate Keats's ideas into her developing critical approach to Shakespeare.

William Hazlitt, a writer whom the narrator in *Middlemarch* refers to as "the most brilliant critic of the day," meaning the early 1830s when the novel is set, was one of the major theatrical critics of his time. He assessed Shakespearean performances by Sarah Siddons as well as by Kemble and Edmund Kean. Of the four writers, Hazlitt seems most important in Eliot's understanding of Shakespeare's power of sympathy. Jonathan Bate, for example, claims that Hazlitt based his entire Shakespearean criticism on "the principle of sympathy," which Hazlitt "took to be the greatest quality of Shakespeare himself" (Bate 1992, 7). While Hazlitt borrowed from August Schlegel, he makes his Shakespeare a more sympathetic individual. As Bate puts it, "Where Schlegel theorizes, Hazlitt empathizes; where the German expounds the unifying structure of the play, the Englishman feels his way into it" (7). Hazlitt argues, for example, that Shakespeare was "the least of an egoist that it was possible to be. He was nothing in himself; but he was all that others were, or that they could become" (Hazlitt 1992, 181). Incorporating an image that G. H. Lewes later employed, Hazlitt also argues that Shakespeare, "[b]y an art like that of the ventriloquist . . . throws his imagination out of himself, and makes every word appear to proceed from the mouth of the person in whose name it is given" (184). Hazlitt concludes by returning to his key term for understanding Shakespeare, a term that will be central to Eliot's and Lewes's understanding of the playwright as well. The "objects of dramatic poetry," Hazlitt exclaims, "affect us by sympathy, by their nearness to ourselves, as they take us by surprise" (186).

Eliot, who had more of an interest in Shakespeare's female characters than these male critics, also read female writers on Shakespeare, particularly Anna Jameson's *Characteristics of Women*. Jameson provided Eliot with a model for abstracting characters from Shakespeare's plays and treating them as real people, another way to demonstrate sympathy. Alda, Jameson's persona in the introductory essay of *Characteristics*, maintains that Shakespeare's characters are "complete individuals, whose hearts and souls are laid open before us" (Jameson 1889, 13). Alda also states that Shakespeare's characters are "liked [and] disliked, as real human beings" (13). Finally, in "forming our opinions of them we are influenced by our own . . . habits of thought," Alda claims, "just as we are influenced with regard to our acquaintances and associates" in real life (13). Yet with Shakespeare's works "we can unfold the whole character before us" and then "take leisure to examine, to analyse, to correct our own impressions" (14), and therefore may sympathize more with our own friends. As Nina Auerbach suggests, Jameson's work releases Shakespeare's heroines "from the plays" and from "the demands of the plot" (Auerbach 1982, 211); I would add that Eliot also was able to free other characters from the constraints of Shakespeare's plots, particularly Hamlet, in her rewriting of his story in *Daniel Deronda*. As a woman writer, though, Jameson departs from her male critical forefathers. While Jameson borrows from the romantic notion "that Shakespeare enjoys a superior grasp of all human nature," she writes back against that tradition, "submit[ting] to male authority in order to supersede it" (Desmet 1990, 42). Jameson, like Eliot, struggled with the place of the female writer in nineteenth-century culture, part of the ongo-ing debate between ego and humility. Realizing that Shakespeare produced great art by denying the ego, Eliot begins appropriating Shakespearean sympathy as a way to mediate between her role as a woman in Victorian society and her strong desire to become a novelist.

Eliot, Lewes, and the Dramatic Art of the Novel

Another important influence on Eliot during this time was her relation-ship with G. H. Lewes, a relationship strengthened by a mutual admiration of Shakespeare. Lewes was particularly attracted to Eliot due to her intense sympathy for others, a sympathy both writers associated with Shakespeare. Most significantly for my argument, Lewes clearly contributed to Eliot's interpretation and subsequent appropriation of Shakespeare, a fact that is overlooked or relegated to a single paragraph or two by most critics. Part of the neglect can be traced to a fear of claiming that Lewes wrote (or even cowrote) Eliot's works; I propose no such thing. I believe, however, that this fear has caused critics to underestimate Lewes's influence.[6] Lewes was important to Eliot's development for three reasons. First, as a theatrical man he encouraged Eliot to view many of Shakespeare's plays and then discuss them with him. Second, Lewes and Eliot often read Shakespeare's plays aloud to one another. Finally, while Eliot recreates Shakespeare's Hamlet in *Daniel Deronda*, Lewes creates and secures Eliot's place in the Shakespearean tradition of sympathetic character identification, a tradition that can be traced from Shakespeare's dramas through Jane Austen's nov-els to George Eliot's art. A sympathetic portrayal of characters, in spite of follies, family, or station in life, distinguishes the most important works of all three authors.

Lewes was a man of many talents: a novelist, essayist, critic, actor, philosopher, scientist, playwright, journalist, and biographer. Indeed, a re-cent collection of Lewes's writings is entitled *Versatile Victorian*.[7] Although Lewes had diverse interests, his deepest roots lay in the theater. His grand-father was Lee Lewes, a professional actor well known for his comic roles in the eighteenth-century English theater. While there is less biographical information about Lewes's father, he also acted, and for a time managed the Theatre Royal in Liverpool. Lewes later claimed that most of his in-tense childhood moments were related to the theater. In 1875, at almost the same time as Eliot was finishing *Daniel Deronda*, Lewes published his book *On Actors and the Art of Acting*. In this work, Lewes claims that he was just "a little boy" when he first observed Edmund Kean in 1825. Yet writing half a century later, Lewes proclaims that his memory of Kean is "so vivid" that he can see "his looks and gestures and hear his thrilling voice" as if those "were sensations of yesterday" (Lewes 1878, 15). The acting of Kean should not be underestimated as another link between Shakespeare on the page and stage, as I agree with Bate that "Kean at his best made Hazlitt and other Romantic critics modify their skepticism about the possibility of doing justice to Shakespearean tragedy on stage" (Bate 1986, 165).

Lewes had a lifelong interest in the theater; attending the plays and commenting on them was not enough. Because of his energy (and lack of finances), Lewes worked in the theater as actor, producer, and playwright. In the 1840s and just prior to his relationship with Eliot, Lewes had his most notable stage experiences. At this time, Lewes had a brief fling with acting as an amateur in Charles Dickens's company (productions that we will consider in more detail in chapter 4), performing benefit shows in London and the provinces in 1847 and 1848, and raising funds for cultural causes such as the endowment of a curatorship for Shakespeare's house in Stratford-upon-Avon. Lewes acted in two of Shakespeare's plays, performing the role of Sir Hugh Evans in *The Merry Wives of Windsor* and the role of Shylock in *The Merchant of Venice*. Thus, according to Rosemary Ashton, we see Lewes "bidding for a career in the theater, an ambition which George Eliot said later only finally died down in 1853, that is, when he became intimate with her" (Ashton 1991, 81). I would suggest, however, that Lewes's new dramatic outlet was Eliot herself, as he scripted the role for her canonization as a novelist.

By the early 1850s, Lewes was a successful writer, literary critic, and amateur actor. At this time, however, two events occurred that would change the course of his personal and professional life. When his wife, Agnes, gave birth to a son in 1850, most of their friends realized that Thornton Hunt, Leigh Hunt's son, and not Lewes, was the father; one year later, he was introduced to Marian Evans by Herbert Spencer, and from the beginning, "their mutual intellectual interests stimulated a growing affection, and Lewes found himself turning to her for companionship and consolation when he had the greatest need for them" (Ashton 1992, 29). By the end of the 1850s, Eliot and Lewes "had read [Shakespeare's] plays to each other many times," and he and Eliot also saw Shakespeare "acted by Helena Martin, [Charles] Fechter, Rossi, Aldridge, and Salvini, to mention only those discussed in her letters" (Novy 1994, 49).[8] Moreover, perhaps due to Lewes's influence, Eliot came to believe that Shakespeare should be seen in performance as well as read in a text even if the performer is bad, because, as she noted in her letters, "Shakspeare moves one through the worst actor that can pronounce English" (Eliot 1954–78, 2:301, 24 February 1857). Two years later, Eliot wrote, "In opposition to most people who love to *read* Shakspeare I like to see his plays acted better than any others; his great tragedies thrill me, let them be acted how they may" (3:228). Recalling her evangelical upbringing she concluded: "I think it is something like what I used to experience in the old days in listening to uncultured preachers—the emotions lay hold of one too strongly for one to care about the medium" (3:228).

The central argument of three articles that Lewes wrote immediately before and continuing through the first decade of his relationship with George Eliot demonstrates two important concepts: that his perception of Shakespeare principally as a dramatist had a profound impact on Eliot's interpretation of Shakespeare, and that Lewes constructed a tradition of sympathy of character that links the plays of Shakespeare through the novels of Jane Austen to the art of George Eliot.[9]

For Lewes, drama and sympathy were intricately linked, the stirring of emotions related to the dramatic vehicle. Lewes makes this assertion in the *Edinburgh Review* in July 1849. In "Shakspeare's Critics: English and Foreign," Lewes defends Shakespeare's goal as a dramatist. Rhetorically asking what is "the first purpose of a dramatist—the very condition at least, under which he works?" Lewes answers, *"To interest and amuse an audience"* (Lewes 1849, 24). "For art," he claims, is "not *mere* amusement; but something which, *through* amusement, leads us into higher regions, and calls finer faculties into play" (24). One of the central purposes of the dramatist is to appeal "to that sympathy which man feels for man . . . and leave in us the abiding influence of great thoughts and noble aspirations" (24). The notion of sympathy is paramount in Lewes's understanding of Shakespeare's role as a poet as well as a dramatist, a notion to which Eliot also subscribed.

By viewing Shakespeare primarily as a dramatist, Lewes opposed those nineteenth-century critics, such as Charles Lamb and others, who felt that Shakespeare had haphazardly chosen the drama as his medium of expression. In other words, Lewes and Lamb are tacitly arguing over whether poetry, Shakespeare's medium, has to be read rather than heard. Writing in the *Westminster Review* in 1845, Lewes flatly declares that Shakespeare "did not regard his plays as poems" (Lewes 1845, 35). Although he "took great pains" with the plays, Lewes argues that Shakespeare "only wrote for theatrical success" (35). He contends that Shakespeare realized that the "demands of the stage, and the demands of the closet, were two different things," and "he did not write [the plays] for publication," because "he did not think them worthy of it" (35). In addition, Lewes takes exception to the standard argument of early-nineteenth-century critics that Shakespeare's plays were not intended for the stage. "It is in vain to object," Lewes states, that because "Shakspeare's plays manifest great literary excellencies," they "must have had a literary purpose" (36). Lewes claims this faulty opinion has "derived from modern usages" and from nineteenth-century dramatists, who are "obviously bent upon literary, no less than theatrical[,] success" (36). Lewes firmly concludes, however, that this "was not so with Shakspeare" (36).

Lewes makes a similar point four years later in the *Edinburgh Review*, arguing that it is ridiculous to "disregard the Stage in treating of the art of Shakspeare" (Lewes 1849, 24). This approach, for Lewes, is as silly as a man "point[ing] out the mechanism of a watch, without any reference to its powers of indicating time" (24). Citing critics such as Lamb, Goethe, and others who propose to "lay down rules" dating back to Aristotle, Lewes exclaims that the rules "cannot sway audiences," because "no audience ever wept academic tears" (24).

Lewes goes on to attack "such critics as Göthe [*sic*] and Charles Lamb," who have "gravely maintained that Shakspeare's very excellencies as a dramatic Poet prevented the success of his works on the stage" (Lewes 1849, 33). Lewes finds it ironic that these critics believe that "the excellencies were so great that they *failed* to produce the very effects for which they were employed!" (33). And while admitting that in the mid-Victorian period, the argument against "any stage representation . . . is very generally considered to be a mark of delicate and refined taste," Lewes counters that "Shakspeare would certainly have thought it but a sorry compliment" (33).

Using a standard that he would often invoke, Lewes asserts that only the most majestic of dramas pass the "double test" of enjoyment in both performance and text. Indeed, the two pleasures of reading and performance are "so far from being opposite and inconsistent, that neither of them will be ever experienced in the highest degree, except in the case of plays which are capable of standing the double test" (Lewes 1849, 34). Finally, Lewes is convinced that "the same persons who are most delighted in reading the plays at home [e.g., he and Eliot], will be those who are most delighted at seeing them well acted" (34). While Lewes disengages Shakespearean drama from the high art of poetry, he also links reading drama with viewing drama. In this way, Lewes establishes a connection between other literary genres intended for readers, such as the art of the novel.

Lewes pursues this same line of reasoning concerning the connection between the dramatist and the novelist in 1859, when he assesses Jane Austen's place in English letters. In this article for *Blackwood's* magazine, Lewes praises two points about Austen's fiction: her sympathy and her dramatic presentation. Lewes not only connects Shakespeare to Austen, but before concluding his argument, he also subtly invokes George Eliot as the heir to the Shakespeare/Austen tradition of sympathetic character portrayal. One of the first to argue that Austen "will doubtless be read as long as English novels find readers" (Lewes 1859, 99), Lewes quarrels with Hazlitt's omission of Austen from his canon of female writers: For Hazlitt, "Mrs Radcliff, Mrs Inchbald, Miss Opie . . . and Miss Edgeworth" constitute the best of the female comic writers. However, Lewes counters that while Austen's name "beyond the literary circle" is "most entirely unknown," this is a major omission (99). If one mentions Austen's name to a "cultivated reader," Lewes claims, a "sparkle in [the reader's] eye will at once flash forth sympathetic admiration" (99). The key word of *sympathy* is thus already entered into his argument. Using a method that he and Eliot also employ with Shakespeare, Lewes posits that reading aloud the novels of Austen "brings both merits and defects into stronger relief by forcing the mind to dwell on them" (101). After their fourth reading of Austen, he claims nothing but an "increase of admiration" (101).

Lewes suggests that realism, which he considers to be the hallmark of Austen's fiction, and sympathy, a quality associated with Shakespeare and the drama, can be fused. Making the first of many connections between Shakespeare and Austen, Lewes contends that Austen's art is "the representation of human nature in its familiar aspects, moving amid every-day scenes" (Lewes 1859, 102). And while it "is easy for the artist to choose a subject from every-day life . . . it is *not* easy for [the artist] so to represent the characters and their actions that they shall be at once lifelike and interesting" (102). However, "Miss Austen is like Shakespeare," because her characters are "inexhaustibly amusing, yet accurately real"; because of this feature, readers "never tire of her characters," since they "become equal to actual experiences" (102). Therefore, reading Austen's novels becomes similar to watching drama. Unlike the "larger than life" romantic protagonists in poetry or on stage, Austen's characters are drawn from real life, a definition that, according to Hazlitt, could also be applied to many of Shakespeare's characters: "His characters are real beings of flesh and blood; they speak like men, not like authors. One might suppose that he had stood by at the time, and overheard what passed" (Hazlitt 1992, 184).

Lewes goes on to reinforce this connection between page and stage when he asserts that it is Austen's character portrayal, her "delineation" of character that is "unsurpassed," and for this reason, "[s]he belongs to the great dramatists" (Lewes 1859, 103, 102). Assessing her gift, Lewes states:

"The secret is, Miss Austen was a thorough mistress in the knowledge of human character" (103). Unlike most writers, according to Lewes, who fail miserably at sympathetic character portrayal, Austen puts into her characters' "hearts and hopes, their motives, their struggles within themselves; and a sympathy is induced which, if extended to daily life and the world at large, would make the reader a more amiable person" (103). If readers read correctly and apply a degree of sympathetic understanding, they will come away with a "higher estimation of simple kindness and sincere good-will" (103–4). According to Lewes, therefore, readers benefit from Austen's fiction, because it has the power to transform them into better, "more amiable" human beings.

At this point in his argument, Lewes quietly slips in a reference to George Eliot's first work of fiction (although he may be foreshadowing the Eliot comparison earlier when he claims that most people, when hearing Austen's name would condescendingly reply, "Oh, yes; she translates from the German, doesn't she?" [Lewes 1859, 99]). Lewes argues that while in *Scenes of Clerical Life* Eliot "seems . . . inferior in the art of telling a story," the so-called "'economy of art,'" she is "equal in truthfulness, dramatic ventriloquism, and humour" to Austen (104). Employing a critical sleight of hand, Lewes then praises Eliot as "greatly superior [to Austen] in culture, reach of mind, and depth of emotional sensibility" and quotes three paragraphs from *Scenes* to support his point (104). Returning to Austen, he proclaims that she possesses the "rare and difficult art of *dramatic presentation:* instead of telling us what her characters are, and what they feel, she presents the people, and they reveal themselves" (105). In this respect, "she has never perhaps been surpassed, not even by Shakespeare himself" (105). Although at this point Lewes compares Eliot unfavorably to Austen, he attributes to Eliot a talent for "dramatic ventriloquism," which he then goes on to explain in terms of Austen's writing.

Echoing Hazlitt, but referring to Austen (and implicitly to Eliot and Shakespeare), Lewes praises Austen's "dramatic ventriloquism" and claims that, in characterization, "the best invention does not consist in finding *new* language for characters, but in finding the *true* language for them" (Lewes 1859, 105). Simply put, Austen, like Shakespeare, paints character portraits that are "many-sided and interesting" (105). Thus, it is the combination of drama and sympathy that links Eliot through Austen to Shakespeare. But even more significantly, by evoking the names of Eliot, Austen, and Shakespeare in the space of two pages, Lewes constructs a firm foundation for a critical tradition that remains in place even today.

ELIOT, *HAMLET*, AND *DANIEL DERONDA*

Eliot's interest in Shakespeare increased as she grew older and also as her relationship with Lewes intensified. Although Eliot often referred to Shakespeare's comedies such as *As You Like It* in her early letters, her references to *Hamlet* increased as she matured (Novy 1994, 118). Although Hamlet the character was important to most educated Victorians, he had a special meaning for Eliot. In her poem "A College Breakfast-Party," Eliot begins by telling us that the protagonist is "Young Hamlet, not the hesitating Dane, / But one named after him" (lines 1–2).[10] This Hamlet, however, strives "for honours" at Cambridge, "our English Wittenberg" (3). This lengthy poem presents a roundtable speculation about the proposed Religion of Man, but the fact that Eliot chooses to put the musings of these Cambridge students into the mouths of characters named after *Hamlet*'s dramatis personae (Laertes, Horatio, Rosencrantz and Guildenstern, and so forth) shows her ongoing concern with Shakespeare's tragedy. The poem, published in April 1874 while Eliot worked on her last novel, *Daniel Deronda*, indicates a growing interest in a protagonist whose constant "contemplative mood" has sprung from "roots of indecision" (Eliot 1988, 157). Novy correctly claims that the "blending of Hamlet characteristics with the Shakespeare characteristic most associated with 'female' values" allows Eliot to rewrite and revise Shakespeare from a female perspective in this novel (Novy 1994, 120). Yet, Eliot's perspective may also have been influenced by the nineteenth century's feminization of Hamlet, a feminization that contributed to Eliot's rewriting of *Hamlet* in her last novel, *Daniel Deronda*.

The theatrical and critical feminization of Hamlet has been traced most carefully by Lawrence Danson, who argues that in the late eighteenth century, "Hamlet's rougher, more murderous edges were smoothed away," while his delay, "no longer a matter of craft or madness, was softened by the pale cast of thought" (Danson 1993, 38). Paradoxically, in this introspective Hamlet, two seemingly conflicting nineteenth-century interpretations meet: "Hamlet the thinker is partly bred out of the stereotype of the Romantic hero, voyaging through strange seas of thought" (38), but "merely thinking on the event is passive, and passivity . . . was conventionally aligned with femininity, so that the Romantic Hamlet could also be seen as a womanly Hamlet" (38).

According to Danson, one of the first critical allusions to this feminized Hamlet appears in William Hazlitt's description of the prince in the early nineteenth century, when the romantic critic describes Hamlet's character as "made up of undulating lines; it has the yielding flexibility of a 'wave o' th' sea'" (Hazlitt 1818, 113). However, Danson relegates to a footnote an aspect of Hazlitt's criticism that may be even more significant. In the passage that follows this description of Hamlet, Hazlitt emphatically contends that even the two best *male* actors of his day cannot play the prince the way that Shakespeare imagined: "Mr. Kemble plays it like a man in armour, with a determined inveteracy of purpose, in one undeviating straight line." Kemble's interpretation, Hazlitt goes on to argue, is "as remote from the natural grace and refined susceptibility of the character, as the sharp angles and abrupt starts which Mr. Kean introduces into the part" (113). The phrases "natural grace" and "refined susceptibility" like the "wave o' th' sea," as quoted by Danson, suggest femininity, and this description contrasts sharply with the "lines" and "angles" of the male Hamlets. Hazlitt may, then, be arguing for some balance between the two—the "straight line" and the "sharp angles"—a balance that suggests a more curved image. Such a balance might be achieved by having a female play the role, a possibility that occurred at least twice in his own lifetime. Sarah Siddons first played the prince at Worcester in 1775 when she was twenty years old. She performed the role again in 1777, and again in Dublin in 1802. Mrs. Powell played Hamlet at Drury Lane in 1802. Closer to the time of *Deronda*'s publication, Alice Marriott played Hamlet at Marylebone Theatre in 1861. In 1863, Marriott assumed the management at Sadler's Wells, and she acted Hamlet there in 1864 (Grebanier 1975, 254–55). I believe this trend toward a feminine Hamlet was embraced by George Eliot, and she consciously incorporated the idea in her novel. By employing Jameson's model of abstracting a character from the constraints of Shakespeare's plays, Eliot rewrites Hamlet's story in *Daniel Deronda*. More importantly, her "Hamlet" possesses the sympathy necessary to function successfully as a human being.

In *Daniel Deronda*, Eliot appropriates this "feminized" Hamlet as a model for the construction of her protagonist. By examining George Eliot's interaction with Shakespeare and specifically *Hamlet*, I hope to prove that Eliot creates a protagonist who, like Eliot's version of Hamlet, possesses the ability to hold simultaneously many points of view, and who contains both masculine and feminine traits within one persona. To this end, I would like to focus on Daniel's relationship with women in the novel. His relationship with his absent mother, Alcharisi, parallels Hamlet's relationship with Gertrude, as both protagonists struggle with feelings of anger and resentment toward their mothers. Moreover, in Daniel's relationship with Mirah, Eliot rewrites Hamlet's relationship with Ophelia. Yet, Eliot's "Hamlet" fares much better than Hamlet does in his relations with others, particularly women, because he has the sympathy for others that Shakespeare's

Hamlet seemingly lacks.[11] In addition, Daniel's character possesses a love that disrupts and challenges the traditional definitions of gender. Indeed, in the novel, Daniel seems to participate in a double marriage, uniting with both Mirah and her brother, Mordecai. Ultimately, I suggest that Eliot's portrayal of Deronda as a feminized Hamlet may represent a pivotal point in nineteenth-century portrayals of the Prince of Denmark.

In her characterization of Deronda himself, Eliot emphasizes his "flexible sympathy" and his selfless identification with others, his "habit of seeing things as they probably appeared" to other people (Eliot 1988, 307). In fact, the initial presentation of Daniel highlights his ability to see from multiple perspectives. Later, Deronda can even empathize with Caliban, claiming "he had always felt a little" with the creature, and defend Caliban by arguing that he had "his own point of view and could sing a good song" (279). It seems that Eliot's central concern in this novel, like Shakespeare's, is with her hero's struggle to find his own perspective, and therefore, his own identity, an identity not bounded by traditional gender roles.

In *Daniel Deronda*, Eliot creates a protagonist who is like many nineteenth-century Hamlets in at least four respects: both are sensitively sympathetic, both question their manhood (as well as their origins), both possess feminine as well as masculine attributes, and, perhaps most important, both have intense relations with women. One of the first reviewers of the book made a specific connection between Hamlet and Deronda, referring to Deronda as "Hamlet without a grievance, without anything to avenge, or indeed necessarily anything to do in this world" (Review of *Daniel Deronda* 1876b, 459). The anonymous reviewer also claims that Daniel has "a vague yet lofty ambition, perpetually foiled by over-thought" and an "inability to make up his mind what to do or how to do it, [which] takes the place of that definite mission which the Prince of Denmark can never decide upon executing" (459).[12]

The "sensitivity" that binds Hamlet and Daniel is established primarily through verbal echoes in the language of both works. The narrator describes Daniel as a boy who has "read Shakespeare" (Eliot 1988, 141) and is characterized by his "reflective hesitation" (153). Hamlet, having just returned from Wittenberg for his father's funeral, ponders whether life is worth living, whether it is worth "suffer[ing] / The slings and arrows of outrageous fortune" (*Hamlet* 3.1.56–57).[13] Similarly, Daniel returns to England after his studying on the continent, "questioning whether it were worth while to take part in the battle of the world" (Eliot 1988, 157). Their thoughtfulness and sensitivity, of course, also link both with traditionally feminine characteristics.

Prior to Daniel's resolution, he, like Eliot's Hamlet, is preoccupied with his masculine identity. In Hamlet, then, Eliot chooses a model whose masculinity is called into question, not only by others but also by himself. In Knight's edition of the play, for example, Claudius calls Hamlet's grief "unmanly" (*Hamlet* 1.2.94), and Hamlet compares his powerlessness, expressed in his cursing, to that of a whore or drab (2.2.585–86). Moreover, he conjures up a symbol of meekness to describe his gentleness and hesitation: "But I am pigeon-liver'd and lack gall / to make oppression bitter" (2.2.577–78). The significance of the phrase "pigeon-liver'd" is explained by Harold Jenkins, who points out that the pigeon was a "symbol of meekness," and was "believed to have no gall, which was notoriously the source within the liver of bitter and rancorous feelings" (Jenkins 1982, 271). The narrator of Eliot's novel makes a similar case for Daniel's femininity: "He had not lived with other boys, and his mind showed the same blending of child's ignorance with surprising knowledge which is oftener seen in bright girls" (Eliot 1988, 141). He also possesses a "strong bent . . . towards a reverential tenderness" (543). Eliot's emphasis on Daniel's affectionate and tender nature is central to understanding the feminine side of Daniel's character.

Perhaps more importantly, both Hamlet and Daniel possess feminine characteristics that disrupt the binary opposition between masculine and feminine. Hamlet's "feminine side" has been explored by many critics, particularly David Leverenz, who, following Goethe, claims that Hamlet is "part woman" (Leverenz 1980, 111) and that the feminine "part" is repressed by a patriarchal tradition that makes women and weakness synonymous. As noted earlier, Hamlet himself exclaims that he "[m]ust, like a whore, unpack [his] heart with words, / And fall a cursing, like a very drab" (*Hamlet* 2.2.585–86). In addition, others see him as feminine; Claudius refers to his "unmanly grief," while Gertrude refers to him as a "female dove" whose temperament is as changeable as any woman's.[14] *Deronda's* narrator explicitly states that Daniel similarly transcends traditional gender expectations, and even a description of him as a child emphasizes his beauty: "He wore an embroidered holland blouse which set off the rich colouring of his head and throat, and the resistant gravity about his mouth and eyes . . . made their beauty the more impressive" (Eliot 1988, 143). Indeed, beauty is repeatedly associated with Daniel. When he and his mother are finally reunited, she exclaims to him, "You are a beautiful creature!" (535). More importantly, Daniel's physical comeliness seems to mirror his mother's beauty. This connection is made apparent when Daniel overhears Mr. and Mrs. Banks discussing his lineage. Mr. Banks, "with a wink and a cunning laugh," proclaims how Daniel "features the mother" (144). Likewise, the descriptions of Daniel as an adult reflect the softness and gentleness usually reserved for female representations. The narrator observes that with "his curls closely clipped, his mouth set with abundant soft waves of beard," he still bears a "disguised" resemblance to the "seraphic boy" of his youth (157). Perhaps most tellingly, whenever Daniel is overwrought, including during the reunion with his mother, he feels "himself changing colour like a girl" (535).

Further, the narrator points out that Daniel is "moved by an affectionate-ness such as we are apt to call feminine, disposing him to yield in ordinary details, while he had a certain inflexibility of judgment, an independence of opinion, held to be rightfully masculine" (Eliot 1988, 271). In his "temperament," Novy notes, "Daniel's viewpoint is close to what Eliot sees as a woman's" (Novy 1994, 129). Two of the most important relationships in the novel from a Shakespearean standpoint are his absent mother, Alcharisi, and his future wife, Mirah. Indeed, his reunion with his mother and its impact on Daniel's gender identification are significant aspects of Daniel's character. Interestingly, Daniel's mother is the "only woman in all George Eliot's fiction who finds a vocation and sticks to it" (Barrett 1989, 167); she is also a powerful woman, and, ironically, this woman who could actu-ally support a family has "rejected her family in order to pursue her voca-tion" (168).

Eliot highlights by structural means the similarities between Daniel's and Hamlet's ardent relationships with women: Hamlet with Ophelia and Gertrude, Daniel with Mirah and Alcharisi. There is, however, a striking reversal in Eliot's Hamlet-like character. Knight's Hamlet, obviously dis-gusted with his mother's actions, and by extension, all women, refers to them as "breeder[s] of sinners" (*Hamlet* 3.1.121), who "jig [and] amble" (3.1.147) and with painted faces make "marriage vows / As false as dicers' oaths" (3.4.52–53). In addition, he criticizes the brevity of women's love (1.2.140–60, 3.2.150) and chastises women's wantonness (3.1.146). Even in his most famous soliloquy, "the pangs of dispriz'd love" (3.1.77) fall fourth on the list of "heart-ach[es]" (3.1.67). Deronda, on the other hand, has always had an "interest in the fates of women" (Eliot 1988, 162). Ham-let, therefore, suffers from a self-imposed restriction that will not allow his sympathetic side to emerge; however, Daniel is comfortable with his femi-nine side, and he resolves his identity crisis in the long-delayed reunion with his absent mother.

Both Hamlet and Deronda confront feelings of anger towards their mothers, one the result of a psychological desertion, the other the result of a literal abandonment. Hamlet's anger manifests itself in the severity of his feelings toward his mother's remarriage. He contends that even a beast that lacks all reason would have grieved longer than his mother has for his father before her "o'erhasty marriage" (*Hamlet* 2.2.60; Knight's edition, which Eliot used, omits the dash in the adjective here). Indeed, as Rebecca Smith points out, in Hamlet's first soliloquy "twenty-three of the thirty-one lines express his anger and disgust at what he perceives to be Gertrude's weakness [and] insensitivity" (Smith 1983, 197). Unlike Hamlet's symbolic desertion, Daniel's desertion by his mother took place literally when he was "little more than two years old" (Eliot 1988, 544). All young Daniel can remember of this time is a "dim sense of having been kissed very much, and surrounded by thin, cloudy, scented drapery" (140). Yet the intensity of the separation is apparent in the very painful terms Daniel uses to conclude his description: "[H]is fingers caught in something hard, which hurt him, and he began to cry" (140). More significantly, the unconscious anxiety, a manifestation of the desertion, rears itself again when Daniel, at age thirteen, begins to question his lineage. After reading about popes with scores of illegitimate children, Daniel beings to wonder if he too might have been born out of wedlock. These burning secrets seem as ominous to Daniel as "falling flakes of fire" (142), and the "terrible sense of collision" between his questions and the dreaded answers finds relief only in a traditionally feminine form, in "big slow tears, which fell without restraint" (142).

After the confrontation in the closet scene of *Hamlet*, Gertrude admits that she must share in the guilt of which Hamlet has accused her. She confesses that Hamlet has turned her eyes "into [her] very soul," and there she sees "such black and grained spots, / As will not leave their tinct" (3.4.99, 100–101). Daniel's mother, trying to justify her desertion, argues that by giving him up to Sir Hugo's care, she "delivered [him] from the pelting contempt that pursues Jewish separateness" (Eliot 1988, 544). More daringly, she confesses that she "did not wish [him] to be born," adding that she "parted with [him] willingly" to pursue her acting career (543). She then connects the career and the boy in an interesting analogy: "A great singer and actress is a queen" (the "queen" at the end of the line reminding us of Gertrude), but, she exclaims, "she gives no royalty to her son," perhaps echoing Hamlet's dilemma as well (544). Finally, Alcharisi asserts that by giving Daniel to Sir Hugo, she was rejecting the patriarchal notion of her father, and by extension, Jewish society in general. She proclaims to Daniel, "But you were my son, and it was my turn to say what you should be. I said you should not know you were a Jew" (544). The desertion, then, creates a psychic disjunction that leads to Daniel's psychological anxiety about his birth, and, therefore, his identity.

In addition to their ardent relations with their mothers, Hamlet and Eliot's Deronda also have fervent relationships with the women who love them. Hamlet's passion takes the form of anger and resentment, while Daniel's powerful feelings are characterized by intense sympathy. Hamlet displaces his anger toward his mother's alleged desertion onto all women, and as the play progresses "his generalized outrage at women increases and spreads" (Smith 1983, 198), as he becomes convinced that "[l]ike whores, all women cannot be trusted" (Gohlke 1983, 153). At first, Daniel's relationships with women in the novel are equally problematic. Even his relationship with Gwendolen, although somewhat erotically charged, seems doomed to failure. The narrator notes that "the conception" that "she or any one else should think of him as her possible lover" was one "which never entered her mind; indeed it was equally out of the question with Mrs. Meyrick and the girls" (Eliot 1988, 165–66). Moreover, both Gwendolen's and Mirah's first encounter with Daniel involves a long mutual look, but neither woman blushes, a point the narrator carefully highlights. At the gaming tables, for instance, Gwendolen feels Daniel "examining her" with his gaze. The narrator, however, emphasizes that his look "did not bring the blood to her cheeks" (6) as a more pointed look might. Similarly, when Daniel first encounters Mirah, she also fails to redden. Indeed, although they are looking "straight at each other," it produces in Mirah "no blush, no special alarm" (159). Daniel's effect on these women, then, is clearly neither masculine nor sexually charged. At one point Gwendolen even asks Daniel, "But *can* you marry?" Deronda replies "Yes" in a "low voice," adding, "I am going to marry" (690).

Dorothea Barrett argues that his "unsurprised response" to what she calls "this bizarre and rather insulting question indicates that Daniel is aware of his asexuality" (Barrett 1989, 170). Although I agree with Barrett that the question is strange, I disagree that Daniel is aware of his "asexuality"; he seems to me instead to possess a very powerful love strong enough to disrupt and challenge the standard definitions of gender. Indeed, his love for Mirah's brother, Mordecai, constitutes a type of double marriage in the novel that dramatizes the conflict in Daniel's gender identity. All three characters—Mirah, Gwendolen, and Mordecai—are attracted to him because of an awareness on their part of Daniel's sympathetic sensitivity toward them, a priestlike compassion and understanding that is more powerful than any mere physical attraction.

The relationship between Mirah and Daniel also shows Shakespeare's influence as Eliot rewrites the affair between Hamlet and Ophelia that many nineteenth-century productions such as Edmund Kean's highlighted, suggesting that Ophelia and the Prince are romantically involved before the beginning of the play. We are made aware of this when Ophelia's father forces her to return Hamlet's love tokens and then forbids her to see him further. After Hamlet has accidentally killed her father, Ophelia becomes mad and drowns. Indeed, in some sense, Hamlet kills Ophelia, and he can only admit his love for her following her death.

Eliot rewrites the Hamlet/Ophelia relationship by endowing Daniel with a sympathetic understanding that allows him to overcome the single-mindedness of the protagonist of Shakespeare's tragedy. This rewriting is most evident in the chapter in which Daniel and his future wife Mirah first meet, a meeting that occurs when Daniel is out "rowing himself on the Thames," feeling that his "idleness" is beginning to "deepen [his] roots of indecision" (Eliot 1988, 157). Clearly, Eliot intends the reader to catch the verbal echoes to Shakespeare's protagonist as Daniel, like Hamlet, once again finds himself in "another . . . contemplative mood" facing the "labour of questioning" (157). In addition, Eliot reminds the reader of Daniel's anxiety about his lineage. He recalls how "[h]is own face . . . had during many years been associated for him with thoughts of some one whom he must be like—one about whose character and lot he continually wondered, and never dared to ask" (158).

As Daniel rows up the river singing aloud, his reverie is broken by the sight of a "girl hardly more than eighteen," one with a "slim figure" and a "most delicate little face" whose "eyes were fixed on the river with a look of immoveable, statue-like despair" (159), descriptions that echo those of Ophelia, the "young maid" (*Hamlet* 4.5.160) of Shakespeare's play. Interestingly, Mirah seems to sense immediately Daniel's presence: "[A]pparently his voice had entered her inner world without her having taken any note of whence it came, for when it suddenly ceased she changed her attitude slightly, and, looking round with a frightened glance, met Deronda's face" (Eliot 1988, 159). While her look resembles that of a frightened "fawn or [some] other gentle animal," a child only "half-conscious of her surroundings," under Daniel's gaze she feels "no special alarm" (159), and Daniel continues to row past her upstream. Like Jameson's Ophelia, Mirah is "far too soft, too good, too fair, to be cast among the briars of this working-day world, and fall and bleed upon the thorns of life" (Jameson 1889, 154). Although Ophelia and Mirah share an unworldly quality, in Eliot's hands this trait does not doom one to a tragic ending.

The "pale image of unhappy girlhood" (Eliot 1988, 159) that Mirah represents continues to haunt Daniel's imagination. And Daniel, who had "been occupied chiefly with uncertainties about his own course" in life (160), suddenly feels an "outleap of interest and compassion" (159). Indeed, the narrator points out that as Daniel was "forgetting everything else," his thoughts began to take the form of a "half-speculative, half-involuntary identification of himself with the objects he was looking at, thinking how far it might be possible habitually to shift his centre till his own personality would be no less outside him than the landscape" (160). I would suggest that for Eliot this shifting sense of perspective, this sympathetic identification, is closely identified with the feminine and, thus, with her Hamlet and her version of Shakespeare.

At this point Eliot carefully rewrites the scene of Ophelia's alleged suicide. On Daniel's return trip downstream, he again notices Mirah; this time she is moving on the "bank opposite him," a bank significantly "bordered by a line of willow-bushes" (Eliot 1988, 160), recalling Ophelia's brook, where "a willow grows aslant a brook" (*Hamlet* 4.7.155).[15] Mirah, thinking she is alone (like Ophelia), looks around her and, "gather[ing] security from the apparent solitude," hides her hat "among the willows" and quickly takes off her "woollen cloak" (Eliot 1988, 161). She then "deliberately dip[s] the cloak in the water," saturating it. Daniel feels "sure" that she means "to wrap the wet cloak around her as a drowning-shroud" (161), a shroud that resembles Ophelia's garments, a shroud that like Ophelia's is intended to drag "the poor wretch" down to her "muddy death" (*Hamlet* 4.7.171, 72).

In Eliot's version, however, the suicide is prevented as Daniel rows quickly to Mirah's side, sensing that her "mind was weakened by distress and hunger" (Eliot 1988, 161). Taking the heavy cloak from her "tired arms," Daniel exclaims, "I will die before I let any harm come to you" (161–62). Daniel then helps Mirah climb into the boat, wondering if "perhaps [his] mother was like this one" (162), thus linking the mother and lover together. Hamlet also worries that "perhaps his mother [Gertrude] was like this one [Ophelia]." The alleged duplicity of his mother can be seen in his projecting onto Ophelia the traits that he most fears. In the nunnery speech he exclaims, "[W]ise men know well enough what monsters you make of them" (*Hamlet* 3.1.141). Yet, the emotional outcomes are different. Hamlet remains disgusted by both women, while Deronda sympathizes with both mother and lover.

Daniel covers Mirah with his coat and she "begin[s] to feel the comfort of returning warmth and the prospect of life instead of death" (Eliot 1988, 163). Still, Daniel is troubled; he worries that Mirah's "mind might be disordered" and is certain that her actions were the "project of suicide" (163). Mirah admits as much when she begins sobbing, claiming, "If you had not come, I should have been dead now" (163). As in a later scene with his mother, Daniel intensely sympathizes with Mirah's ordeal, hoping that her "passionate weeping might relieve her excitement" (164). Exhausted from the ordeal, Mirah "submit[s] like a tired child" (165) as Daniel journeys with her to safety at the home of the Meyricks. Eliot thus removes Hamlet and Ophelia from the bonds of Shakespeare's plot. Indeed, her "Ophelia" seems to be drawn in part from Anna Jameson's interpretation of the character. Jameson describes Ophelia as full of "modesty, grace [and] tenderness" and argues that if "expanded under genial influences" Ophelia would become a "perfect and happy human creature" (Jameson 1889, 154). Embracing this possibility, Eliot endows her "Hamlet" with sympathetic identification; Deronda exerts his "genial influence" and Mirah/Ophelia becomes a "perfect and happy creature."

A second scene that Eliot rewrites is the reunion encounter with Deronda and his mother, a meeting that reconstructs, even while it revises, the closet scene in *Hamlet*. This intense confrontation combines two of the most important elements I have traced in Eliot's rewriting of Shakespeare: the sympathetic identification that Daniel possesses, a result of his feminization at the hands of Eliot and the theatrical tradition that she may have influenced, and the focus on the dramatic quality of a novelist, an idea shaped in part by Lewes's critical notions.

As Eliot restages this scene, she begins by alerting the reader to the dramatic quality of the encounter by stressing Alcharisi's vocation as actress. She was, we learn, a "great singer, and [she] acted as well as [she] sang" (Eliot 1988, 537). In fact, the narrator hints that a drama is unfolding when it is noted that Alcharisi's speeches—"the varied transitions of tone"—are delivered as "perfect[ly] as the most accomplished actress" (539) would deliver them. Alcharisi also possesses the capability to play many different roles both on and off the stage. Alcharisi claims that in her own life, following the failure of her career, she "made believe—[she] acted that part," in her marriage to a Russian prince (548). Even in her encounter with Daniel, she has the capacity to take on different roles: "[H]er face gave out a flash of admiration in which every worn line disappeared and seemed to leave a restored youth" (535). In Alcharisi, it seems, we witness perhaps another kind of Shakespeare—a female version—as the princess molds herself to fit the roles prescribed for her by the patriarchal society, projecting her genius into the parts she must play. Thus, her most telling line might be when she confesses to Daniel that she was "living a myriad [of] lives in one" (537), a line that Eliot might have borrowed from Coleridge's description of Shakespeare.

The conflicts in these two scenes—the closet scene and the reunion scene—are similar in that both sons are dealing with pent-up resentment toward their mothers. Hamlet feels that his mother has betrayed him, while Daniel demands to know why his mother has deserted him. Hamlet and

Gertrude's conflict remains dangerously unresolved. But Eliot restages Shakespeare in this dramatic encounter and once again reverses the tragic outcome.

Hamlet and Gertrude are represented as somewhat alienated from each other at the beginning of their encounter in the queen's chamber. In the Folio version, which Knight relies on primarily, Gertrude asks Hamlet, "Have you forgot me?" (*Hamlet* 3.4.16), to which Hamlet replies, "[B]y the rood, not so" (3.4.17). As he struggles with his feelings, however, Hamlet defines her first as someone other than his mother. "You are the queen," he exclaims, "your husband's brother's wife," concluding that "[y]ou are my mother" (3.4.18, 19). Hamlet, like Daniel, confronts his mother in an attempt to understand her motives.

Because Eliot seems to borrow so heavily from Shakespeare's dialogue, we should examine first the language of the confrontations. In Knight's *Hamlet,* the protagonist "wag[s his] tongue" in "noise so rude" (3.4.46–47) against the queen, while she questions him with what Hamlet calls her "idle tongue."[16] As Hamlet berates his mother for her alleged sins, Gertrude is overcome with emotion and begs him to "speak no more" (3.4.98). Yet Hamlet continues his verbal assault until she pleads again, "O, speak to me no more" (3.4.106). Gertrude then reverts to even more sexually charged language to characterize Hamlet's oral struggle. "These words," she exclaims, "like daggers, enter in my ears" (3.4.107).

For Daniel the case is similar, yet his struggle with language is more successful than Hamlet's, in part because of his sympathetic understanding of his mother's position, an understanding that will be reflected by his objective view of her before the end of the scene. Upon first seeing his mother, Daniel cannot "even conjecture in what language she [will] speak to him" (Eliot 1988, 535). Even as Daniel's voice "trembl[es] nervously," his mother calms herself, and after finding her own voice, replies "I am at ease now; I am able to talk" (536). Still, her voice sounds "harder . . . than before" (536), and suddenly language fails for Daniel. He feels "breathless" as he now perceives a "passionate self-defence in her tone" of address (537). She then reveals a slight movement in her closed lips that is "like the suppressed continuation of speech" (537), and at this juncture, Daniel rallies and cries out with a "deep-voiced energy," an outburst that causes his mother to "shrink a little backward" (537). He has a "veiled voice of passion" (537) as the mother's speech becomes almost violent, "firmly resistant in its finely-varied tones" (538). So, at least initially, both Deronda's language and Hamlet's language fail to achieve the communication necessary for an effective understanding of their mothers.

As a result of Daniel's sensitivity to his mother's feelings, however,

Daniel and his mother try to view "objectively" the confrontation as they both begin to speak of Alcharisi in the third person. When Alcharisi asks, "Shall you comprehend your mother—or only blame *her*," Daniel replies that "[t]here is not a fibre within me but makes me wish to comprehend *her*," adding "It is a bitter reversal of my longing to think of blaming *her*" (Eliot 1988, 540, italics mine). As Daniel reaches the climax of the struggle, however, language once again begins to fail him, as his mother's words raise "a crowd of remembrances which obstructed [his] speech" (542). The mother states, "I have nothing to give . . . . I did not wish you to be born. I parted with you willingly" (543). Yet Daniel can sympathetically identify with Alcharisi in a way that Hamlet cannot with Gertrude, as his "pity made a flood of forgiveness within him" (547). The immediate struggle is resolved, and the ability to communicate returns; Alcharisi's voice is now filled with "melodious melancholy," signifying resignation following the struggle (543). Daniel's speech patterns are also altered. Although Daniel speaks "entreatingly" to her, begging her to "take comfort," Alcharisi repels his affection, and Daniel is "painfully silenced" (547). Yet Daniel, now able to pity Alcharisi as a human being separate from his mother, realizes that her "outpourings" are genuine, and he is filled with the "anguish of compassion" (547). Daniel's sympathy, then, like his feelings toward Mirah, grant him the possibility of empathetic understanding.

Eliot also carefully stages the movement of the characters in chapter 51, producing her own version of the closet scene. Daniel and Hamlet initially move away from their mothers, but, upon feeling insecure, close the distance, trying to regain proximity, a movement symbolizing a psychological retreat to the comfort of the mother.

In many versions of *Hamlet*, at least according to Harold Jenkins, both mother and child are standing after Polonius's body is revealed.[17] Hamlet then entreats his mother to sit down so that he can more forcefully "wring [her] heart" (3.4.42). The proximity of the two is narrowed on stage as Hamlet produces miniature portraits—"counterfeit presentiment[s] of two brothers" (3.4.63)[18]—that he forces Gertrude to observe attentively. Before the struggle can be resolved, however, the ghost enters, and Hamlet quickly retreats to the other side of the room. Almost immediately, Hamlet leaves the bedchamber, still confused about his mother's actions and, in many interpretations, still angered by them. The psychic distance is signified by his concluding lines to the queen. Not only must he leave her side, but the physical distance is also extended, since Hamlet now "must to England" (3.4.219).

For Daniel, however, the struggle ends more positively. When Daniel first approaches his mother, he immediately tries to shorten the distance, as she is "at the other end of the large room" (Eliot 1988, 535). At this point they move to closer proximity on the sofa and the mother motions for Daniel to sit "near her" (536). Suddenly, they both rise with an impulsive movement, and Daniel struggles with the spatial distance, feeling overwhelmed, "clutching his coat-collar," as if he were "keeping himself above water by it . . ." (537). Now Daniel can only watch with "wonder, from the spiritual distance to which she had thrown him" (536). After explaining to Daniel the circumstances of the desertion, Alcharisi pauses, and Daniel moves away and throws himself sideways into a chair, "almost unconsciously" (538). Suddenly he draws his chair nearer to her and [gives] her his hand" (543). Although the mother kisses him "on the brow," she immediately adds that they "must part again soon" (543). She then rises quickly and walks to the other side of the room to reoccupy the space where she, and her role in the drama, began. Daniel also rises and stands as he removes himself a "little distance" from her (547).

The most important difference in the two protagonists is the sympathy that Daniel can call up, a sympathy that most Hamlets cannot summon towards their mothers. Hamlet's final words to Gertrude are less than sympathetic as he reminds her to avoid the king's wanton pinches as well as his "reechy kisses," and he seems to vow that harm will come to her if she reveals his secret (*Hamlet* 3.4.203)

At first Daniel, like Hamlet, is "shaken by a mixed anger which no reflection could come soon enough to check" (Eliot 1988, 537). Daniel is also "fired with an intolerance that seemed foreign to him" (538). At this precise moment, however, Daniel "tr[ies] hard to master himself and keep silence . . . lest he should say something too hard" (538). Daniel then "recover[s] his fuller self" and begins to sympathize with the "signs of suffering in [his mother's] frame" (538). At the conclusion of the reunion scene, Daniel's

> soul was absorbed in the anguish of compassion . . . . His pity made a flood of forgiveness within him. His single impulse was to kneel by her and take her hand gently between his palms, while he said in that exquisite voice of soothing which expresses oneness with the sufferer—"Mother, take comfort!" (547)

Although Daniel and Alcharisi kiss before parting, and even though they will briefly meet again, they are both painfully aware that this spiritual separation is final, and the mother exclaims to Daniel, "Leave me now" (548).

At the conclusion of the struggle, Daniel, unlike Hamlet, seems to re-cover his sense of identity, evincing both female and male traits, and finally, on the surface, becomes a being capable of marriage and fruitful inter-course. Shortly after his reunion with his mother, Daniel proposes to Mirah, and they are soon married. Eliot highlights his newfound role, ostensibly representing him as a typical Victorian husband and conventional patriar-chal protector, noting that the wedding itself "hid no doubtful tremors" (Eliot 1988, 693).

Yet, the most symbolic marriage in the novel may be the one that oc-curs between Daniel and Mordecai, with the wedding of Daniel and Mirah serving only as a substitute for the real union at the close of the novel. Here we may see Eliot's most emphatic evasion of the resolution of a conven-tional marriage plot. Gwendolen's desire for Daniel—the marriage that the first half of the novel seems moving towards—is defeated by the introduc-tion of Mirah. There is, however, a more subtle evasion of the marriage plot in the union between Daniel and Mirah, a union that reflects Eve Sedgwick's definition of male homosocial desire. According to Sedgwick, homosocial desire takes many forms: "male friendship, mentorship, en-titlement, rivalry, and hetero- and homosexuality" (Sedgwick 1985, 1). The "desire" she refers to is the "affective or social force, the glue . . . that shapes an important relationship" (2). Moreover, Sedgwick focuses on the notion of "triangulation," a way in which two men mediate their relation-ship through a woman. Indeed, the marriage of Daniel to Mirah seems to serve as a kind of conduit for the more spiritual marriage between Mordecai and Daniel. Sedgwick also contends that male bondings will "always be articulations and mechanisms of the enduring inequality of power between women and men" (5). Eliot's Hamlet/Deronda, however, seems to mitigate some of the "inequality of power" Sedgwick mentions, by relating to both Mirah and Mordecai, and both Daniel and Mirah join Mordecai in his vo-cational quest on behalf of the Jewish state.

Even the language describing the "union" of Daniel and Mordecai is sexualized. Deronda and Mordecai, for instance, possess "as intense a con-sciousness as if they had been two undeclared lovers" (Eliot 1988, 424). Further, Mordecai desires a "stronger . . . more-executive self" (406); Daniel responds to this stereotypical feminine need by claiming he will help Mordecai find "a better home" (676), stating, "I shall do as I like with you, being the stronger half" (676). Indeed, discussing Daniel's willingness to publish the older man's poems under Deronda's name, Mordecai makes the marriage metaphor explicit: "It has begun already—the marriage of our souls" (643). And he continues: "It waits but the passing away of this body, and then they who are betrothed shall unite in a stricter bond, and what is mine shall be thine" (643). Thus, the two will embark on a spiritual "marriage which melts soul into soul," resulting in a union of a "fuller soul" (643). I must agree with Joanne Long Demaria, who notes that compared to this marriage vow, "Deronda's proposal to Mirah is tepid indeed" (Demaria 1990, 413). And Demaria is also right to suggest that the relationship between the two men is informed by an "intellectual and emotional fusion, a fusion facilitated" by Deronda's and Mordecai's "appropriation of feminine values" (413–14).

Daniel, then, comes to represent Eliot's idealized being, a divine human. This notion can be traced to her translation of Feuerbach's discussion of the Trinity. Eliot's translation reads: "The Son is the mild, gentle, forgiving, conciliating being—the womanly sentiment of God" (Feuerbach 1957, 71). By analogy, on earth the "human son" is an "intermediate being between the masculine nature of the father, and the feminine nature of the mother," as he has not yet achieved the "rigorous consciousness" of the man and "feels himself drawn rather to the mother than to the father" (71). Thus, because he combines the features of the "masculine nature of the father and the feminine nature of the mother," he is, "as it were, still half a man, half a woman" (71). By applying Feuerbach's formulation to the most famous character in fiction, Eliot rewrites *Hamlet* from a particularly feminine point of view and endows Deronda with the sympathy Eliot associated not only with femininity but also with divinity. Indeed, Daniel's feminization and his spiritual marriage to Mordecai may represent a pivotal point in nineteenth-century representations of Hamlet: a space that allows intervention, creating a new genealogy for Hamlet. From Eliot's feminized Hamlet, it is only a short step to the actual female Hamlet of Edward Vining's book *The Mystery of Hamlet* (1881) and the "inversion" of Shakespeare by Samuel Butler and Oscar Wilde in the 1890s.

At this point Eliot's "Hamlet" takes on a life of its own.[19] In part because Eliot's own transcendental language falls short of explaining the gender dynamics of her novel, her text fails to constrain her creation within the bounds of the novel. Eliot's novel also demonstrates a more complex understanding of gender relations than her more theoretical prose—theological and critical—admits. And, therefore, the text of both Shakespeare and Eliot "commands and indeed permits, invents, all its misinterpretations and misreadings, which are functions of the text" (Said 1983, 199). Further, Lewes's writing of Eliot also may be considered a text and complements my implied argument that Eliot's influence may exceed even the role laid out for her by Lewes.

ELIOT'S INFLUENCE ON SHAKESPEARE

In one sense, then, Eliot influences Shakespeare; although this conten-tion may sound suspiciously like a statement from a David Lodge novel,[20] Eliot's creation clearly participates in a cultural movement that challenges traditional gender roles by feminizing Hamlet on both page and stage. As noted earlier, at least one contemporary review of the novel in October 1876 made the connection between Hamlet and Deronda, even going so far as to color Deronda with stereotypically feminine characteristics: Eliot's protagonist is a "kind of Hamlet," the critic argued, who possesses a "vague yet lofty ambition, perpetually foiled by over-thought" resulting in an "in-ability to make up his mind what to do or how to do it" (Review of *Daniel Deronda* 1876b, 159).[21] Although the reviewer does not directly state that Deronda is a feminized Hamlet, the implication seems clear and perhaps influenced others who took the feminization one step further.

The most curious of the post-*Deronda* Hamlets occurs five years later in Edward Vining's book *The Mystery of Hamlet* (1881). Vining claims that although when Shakespeare first "conceived and put the drama into shape" his hero was more masculine, there came "the gradual evolution of the feminine element in Hamlet's character" (Vining 1881, 59). He goes on to add that Hamlet is not only a "womanly man [but] might be in very deed a woman, desperately striving to fill a place for which she was by nature unfitted" (59). After a lengthy detailing of Hamlet's faults (jealousy, dis-traction, fear of bloodshed, and the like), Vining concludes, "[T]hat which before seemed at variance with all ordinary models of thinking now be-comes an exhibition of the deepest human feeling" (75). In other words, all the characteristics for which Hamlet has been criticized can now be praised if Hamlet is female. In Hamlet, therefore, Vining finds "an entire *inversion* of what should have been expected. [Hamlet's] admiration is expended upon men and masculine perfections alone" (55, italics mine). I believe it is significant, as Danson reminds us, that "inversion" was a key word for same-sex attraction at this time, and Danson is probably also correct when he argues that for Vining, it was easier to conclude that "a man who likes other men is by definition a woman," than to reach "the conclusion that [Hamlet] was gay" (Danson 1993, 42).

A similar destabilization of Hamlet's role also occurred on stage, at approximately the same time as the publication of *Daniel Deronda* and Vining's work. Citing an anonymous reviewer who had praised Henry Irving's performance—which included "outburst[s] hardly distinguishable from hysteria" (Vining 1881, 78)—Vining concludes that Irving's portrayal squares with his own thesis of Hamlet as woman. Shortly after, a number of women would play the role, culminating with Mrs. Bandmann-Palmer, who "gave over a thousand performances as Hamlet" (Grebanier 1975, 256); interestingly, she is mentioned in James Joyce's *Ulysses* as having played Hamlet "for the fourhundredandeighth time last night in Dublin" (Joyce 1961, 198), proving that the feminine Hamlet has escaped the bounds of Shakespeare's plot and taken on his/her own life in theater and fiction. Bandmann-Palmer was only one of the numerous female Hamlets of the fin de siècle. Even more significantly, while most female performances of Hamlet prior to the '80s had been panned, now there was an acceptance rather than a rejection of such possibilities.

Perhaps the most important critical point about Eliot's appropriation of Shakespeare overlooked by all critics is the dialectical function of her appropriation. While agreeing with those critics who highlight Eliot's use of Shakespeare, particularly *Hamlet*, I would add that it is important to remember that Eliot's work had potential for appropriation as well, this time by nineteenth-century actors and actresses assaying the role of Hamlet. This possibility seems even more likely when we remember that Eliot was composing her novel at a time when new constructions of masculinity were taking place. Michel Foucault points to Carl Westphal's article on "contrary sexual sensations" in 1870 as one important moment in the restructuring of masculinity (Foucault 1990, 43). In addition, J. A. Symonds, an early apologist for "homosexuality," published his *Studies of the Greek Poets* in 1873, one year before the first installment of Eliot's work appeared. His prose study, which advocated enlarging the boundaries of traditional ways of being masculine, was so important that he and Havelock Ellis decided to collaborate on a work that would later be titled *Sexual Inversion* (1897). Writers such as Eliot and Symonds were seizing a space of cultural rupture or discontinuity, the same space suggested by Foucault's analysis of sexuality in the nineteenth century, when challenges were made to older ways of being male, challenges that resulted in a "kind of interior androgyny, a hermaphrodism of the soul" (43). These reconstructions of masculinity, in part, enabled George Eliot to reconsider and rewrite *Hamlet* from a female point of view. Moreover, this same ideological ground was transferred to the stage, where performers such as Sarah Bernhardt were soon to produce not only feminized Hamlets but also *females* playing Hamlet. Significantly, perhaps, Eliot received the final page proofs for *Deronda* while in Paris in July 1876, and on the same day Lewes and Eliot went to the Théâtre Français (Eliot 1954–78, 9:179 n. 6). The next day they attended again and saw Bernhardt in *L'Etranger*, and Lewes wrote in his diary: "Very much interested both in piece and acting" (179 n. 6). Lewes would later make a comparison between the famous French actress, Rachel, and Bernhardt, praising Sarah's voice over Rachel's. Although there is no record of a meeting with the actress, it seems probable that Bernhardt would have known Lewes from his role as an important theater critic, and it is possible that she read his companion's new novel that portrayed a feminized Hamlet. While admitting that this particular point is merely speculative, what we do know for certain is that both Bernhardt and Eliot challenged gender stereotypes, and some twenty years later Bernhardt cast herself in that most famous of male Shakespearean roles.

Sarah Bernhardt's was the most influential of the female performances of Hamlet, and her five-hour production was praised in both Paris (May 1899) and London (June 1899). Prior to this cultural moment, however, female Hamlets had been rather "masculine" women. As Charles Shattuck points out, "The best of them, like Charlotte Cushman, Alice Marriott, and Emma Waller, were big-boned, big-voiced[,] rather mannish women" who had tired of playing strong female Shakespearean leads (Shattuck 1976, 136). More importantly, none of these actresses who attempted the role of Hamlet were "conspicuously successful" (136). Toward the close of the nineteenth century, however, male and female Hamlets began to express rather than repress their femininity. The first critics who observed Bernhardt's performances in Paris were particularly impressed. Theodore Stanton, writing in the *Critic*, exclaimed that Bernhardt's "Hamlet is unquestionably one of the great Hamlets" (Stanton 1899, 638). Indeed, he added, unlike the "masculine" Hamlets, Bernhardt's version portrayed "a certain delicacy and gentleness not at all out of keeping with a conception of Hamlet" (638). He concludes his review of the Paris opening by stating that the French critics "were all most unanimous in praise of her interpretation, and almost the same thing may be said of the English correspondents in Paris" (640). Although the reviews in London were mixed, the critic for the *Times* (13 June 1899) proclaimed it an "interesting tour de force," a production "worked out with care and intelligence and with a consistent grip upon the character" (7). In her book *The Art of the Theatre*, which she wrote a quarter of a century later, Bernhardt defended her decision to play Hamlet in a chapter entitled "Why I Have Played Male Roles." Confessing that "it is not male parts, but male brains that I prefer" (Bernhardt 1924, 137), she concluded that "male parts are more intellectual than female parts"; but, she hastened to add, only women can play them, because women are "able to preserve their character of unsexed beings, and their perfume of mystery" (139). The very rhetoric of "unsexed beings" who enchant with a "perfume of mystery" recalls Foucault's image of an "interior androgyny," "hermaphrodism of the soul," and even the notion of sexual inversion.

This movement toward what Marvin Rosenberg terms the "sweet Hamlets" also affected actors performing the role (Rosenberg 1992, 115). Indeed, many male Hamlets began to emphasize the feminine side of their interpretations. For instance, the American Edwin Booth, who had read Vining, believed that the "feminine" side of his portrayal was essential to his performances. In a letter to the critic William Winter, Booth claimed, "I have always endeavoured to make prominent the femininity of Hamlet's character and therein lies the secret of my success" (qtd. in Rosenberg 1992, 109). And he added, "I doubt if ever a robust and masculine treatment of the character . . . will be accepted so generally as the more womanly and refined interpretation" (109). Even "England's master-Hamlet of the late nineteenth century," Henry Irving, emphasized the feminine in his portrayals at the close of the century (Rosenberg 1992, 114). Besides noting the "hysterical" outbursts mentioned earlier by Vining, many reviewers praised Irving for his "exquisite expression of refinement" (Scott 1874, 69), while others referred to him as "womanish," "gentle," "dreamy," "feminine," and "endearing" (Rosenberg 1992, 114). Indeed, reviewers such as Clement Scott highlighted Irving's "infinite love and tenderness" (Scott 1874, 67), words used often by Eliot in describing Daniel Deronda.

In this chapter, I have traced two phenomena: the dialectical relation of Eliot's writing of Shakespeare and Lewes's writing of Eliot. Lewes puts Eliot in a literary genealogy based on the concept of sympathy (Shakespeare as father, Austen as mother), and other critics followed his lead by often comparing her to the playwright.[22] Yet Eliot's demonstration of how her own identification or sympathy with Shakespeare works in Daniel Deronda disrupts traditional systems of gender more radically than Lewes's literary genealogy and even Eliot's own critical and theoretical language would allow: While Lewes constructs a standard, heterosexual genealogy for Eliot with a male "father" and a female "mother," Eliot constructs a literary genealogy for Hamlet that is less traditional—as the sympathy she senses in the playwright allows Shakespeare to become both mother and father, possessing perhaps the "interior androgyny" mentioned by Foucault—and more prophetic of future literary and theatrical developments.

Finally, the "inversion" that Danson refers to in Vining's work on Hamlet (which was published only five years after Eliot's novel) becomes, in the '80s and '90s, a code word for same-sex attraction. More importantly, the term "inversion," as well as "perversion," will be applied to a small group of Shakespearean critics such as A. C. Swinburne.

2

Characterizing Shakespeare:
A Study of Algernon Charles Swinburne

In a chapter in *The Sacred Wood*, tellingly entitled "Imperfect Critics," T. S. Eliot disparagingly refers to Algernon Charles Swinburne as "an appreciator and not a critic" of Shakespeare (Eliot 1950, 19). Condemning Swinburne's "faults of style" (17), Eliot concludes that readers of Swinburne will become "fatigued by a hubbub that does not march" (21). Other critics, following Eliot's lead, also censored Swinburne, so that thirty years later, Kenneth Muir felt comfortable denouncing Swinburne's Shakespearean criticism as "unpalatable" (Muir 1961–64, 2:283). What I propose, however, is that it is not so much Swinburne's "unpalatable" style as what his criticism advocates that bothers these critics. I will show that the brilliance of Swinburne's rhetoric blinds critics to its subversive potential. Swinburne's *A Study of Shakespeare* (1880) demonstrates most clearly how one critic appropriates Shakespeare to promote a radical agenda in politics, religion, and sexuality.

As a Shakespearean critic instead of an appropriating novelist or poet, Swinburne's use of Shakespeare is both public and personal. Swinburne's appropriation is also more overtly political than George Eliot's, as he attempts directly to intervene in the reading of Shakespeare. Confronting other Shakespearean critics with whom he disagrees, Swinburne shapes his version of a Victorian Shakespeare. Interestingly, his criticism proceeds in two directions, alternating back and forth between public and private, sometimes simultaneously. His focus on gender is also more explicit than Eliot's, and he tends to read Shakespeare's characters by sometimes blurring gender lines. Therefore, his private complexity, expressed in a public forum, reflects his own struggle with notions of sexual identity. Like Eliot, he also sympathizes and identifies with Shakespeare's characters, but his promotion of his beliefs is much more strident than hers.

In his criticism on *Hamlet*, Swinburne challenges critics such as Thomas Carlyle, who argued for the inseparability of morality and art. Moreover, Swinburne's careful attention to textual matters in *Hamlet* allows him to displace moral issues with textual ones. Swinburne also disputes Carlyle's notion that Shakespeare's plays such as *Hamlet* were divinely inspired. In his critique of *King Lear*, Swinburne valorizes Hellenic aestheticism over Christian morality, and argues that this play proves Shakespeare's sympathy with radical political causes. Indeed, Swinburne's rhetoric in *Lear* inverts traditional readings of the play by promoting agnosticism over Christianity, aestheticism over morality. Swinburne appropriates Shakespeare, therefore, to further his own radical agenda, which promoted liberal politics, agnostic religion, and Hellenic aestheticism.

In Swinburne's critique of *1 Henry IV*, we witness Swinburne's swerve away from the two central tragedies of *Hamlet* and *Lear* to focus on the character of Falstaff. Specifically, Swinburne defends Falstaff and his actions against conservative critics, such as Samuel Johnson, who condemned Falstaff for his alleged immorality. By raising this topic dialogically, Swinburne participates in a movement that defends Falstaff's alleged immorality. Moreover, by proposing a potentially homoerotic relationship between Hal and Falstaff, Swinburne opens up a space for critical discussion of love between men in the play, as well as in mid-Victorian society. Swinburne's critical approach allows him to speak to dual audiences simultaneously. While one audience is made up of Victorian "gentlemen," who would read his writing as traditional Shakespearean criticism, a second audience would "hear" Swinburne advocate an aesthetic, potentially radical reading of Shakespeare's plays. Specifically in his criticism on *1 Henry IV*, Swinburne's championing of aestheticism in the 1860s foreshadows the refashioning of masculinity in the late Victorian period. This refashioning, which took the form of extending the boundaries of Victorian masculinity, was an ongoing concern at the time of the publication of Swinburne's *A Study of Shakespeare*.[1]

Swinburne's first published reviews of poetry some twenty years earlier provide a basis for understanding his later work on Shakespeare. Thaïs Morgan argues that in his criticism of the 1860s, Swinburne employs a rhetorical strategy she calls an "aesthetic minoritizing discourse" (Morgan 1993, 316). Morgan posits that this dual-voiced language is addressed to a smaller audience within the larger audience (317). I agree with Morgan that Swinburne's criticism was intended for two sets of readers: the larger audience who heard it simply as a championing of a new avant-garde movement in literature, and the minority group who heard, as we shall see, allusions to homoerotic desire. Yet Morgan never applies her compelling analysis to Swinburne's most important critical work, *A Study of Shakespeare.*

Building on Morgan's analysis and borrowing from Mikhail Bakhtin, I will argue that Swinburne's Shakespearean criticism also speaks with a "double-voice," one that "serves two speakers at the same time and expresses simultaneously two different intentions" (Bakhtin 1981, 324). "In such discourse," Bakhtin argues, "there are two voices, two meanings and two expressions" (324). As many critics have pointed out, Walter Pater's essays in the last half of the nineteenth century (from 1868 on) represent "the emergence of a gay or homosexual discourse," one that "destabilize[s] early Victorian formations of manhood and of the masculine in literature and art" (Sussman 1995, 1). I want to term Swinburne's Shakespearean criticism "alternative-voiced discourse." By employing this term, as opposed to Morgan's use of "minority," I hope to avoid any negative connotations or suggestions of size or number. By the 1880s, when Swinburne published his Shakespeare criticism, and because of the influence of Pater and others, the dual audiences were probably closer in size than they were during the earlier criticism of the 1860s that Morgan analyzes. "Alternative-voiced discourse" also presents a much more accurate description of Swinburne's project on Shakespeare. Definitions of "alternative" suggest a proposition or situation offering a "choice" between two or more options; with this choice comes an opportunity for a reader to "decide" between the two courses or propositions. No word, according to Bakhtin, "exist[s] in a neutral and impersonal language . . . but rather it exists in other people's mouths, in other people's contexts, serving other people's intentions: it is from there that one must take the word, and make it one's own" (Bakhtin 1981, 294). Many words, he adds, do not "submit equally easily to this appropriation" (294). Words that are contextually charged, however, could be seized by Swinburne and his intended audience. After Swinburne appropriates such words as "masculine," "androgyny," "languid," and "Greek" into his criticism, there is the strong possibility that a portion of the readers seeing the words in their own homosocial or homosexual context would understand Swinburne's message. For the more traditional reader, on the other hand, the words would "remain alien, sound foreign," because "they cannot be assimilated into [the reader's] context" (294). Most significantly, these "shifting planes of intention permit an exhilaratingly chaotic freedom of expression" (Richter 1989, 725), a freedom no monologic discourse would ever allow. In addition, the definition of the word "alternate" denotes a movement back and forth between two things, and Swinburne's Shakespearean criticism does just that, alternating between a traditional voice and a subversive one. Swinburne's criticism, then, offers an "alterna-tive" view of received criticism that creates a disjunction in his work, a gap between conservative readings and subversive interpretations of Shake-speare's plays. At this site of rupture, space is opened for new discourses on Shakespeare, discourses that challenge conservative, elitist readings of the playwright.

POLITICS, RELIGION, AND MORALITY

Before narrowing our attention to Swinburne's alternative-voiced criti-cism of specific plays, we can witness the radical nature of Swinburne's interpretations by comparing his reading of Shakespeare to a representa-tively conservative nineteenth-century critic, Thomas Carlyle, whose view of Shakespeare seems particularly elitist. In his essay on "The Hero as Poet," Carlyle claims that Shakespeare possesses "a true English heart" that "breathes, calm and strong, through the whole business" (Carlyle 1966, 110). Not only is Shakespeare a true patriot, but he is even more royal than "an English King," because, Carlyle exclaims, "no time or chance, Parlia-ment or combination of Parliaments, can dethrone [him]!" (114). "This King Shakespeare . . . shine[s] in crowned sovereignty, over us all, as the noblest, gentlest, yet strongest of rallying-signs; *in*destructible," he contin-ues by analogy (114). So Shakespeare, like a "radiant aloft," will shine over all the "Nations of Englishmen, a thousand years hence" (114). For Carlyle, then, Shakespeare functions as a noble rallying site for the English nation. Expanding this theme and folding together Shakespeare and Impe-rialism, Carlyle adds that even though England lost the colonies in America, Shakespeare is a "real, marketable, tangibly-useful possession"; Shakespeare displays his "marketability" in his power to unite the English-speaking world as "virtually one Nation" (Carlyle 1966, 113). Carlyle's choice of words, such as "possession" and "marketable," not only reflects the lan-guage of the new industrial marketplace, but also signals his obsession with the cultural currency that Shakespeare represents. Carlyle also asks whether, if an Englishman had to choose, he would "give-up [his] Indian Empire or [his] Shakspeare" (113). He answers that Shakespeare is a more important possession than India, as the "Indian Empire will go . . . some day; but this Shakspeare does not go, he lasts for ever with us; we cannot give-up our Shakspeare" (113). "No," he reiterates, "Indian Empire, or no Indian Empire; we cannot do without Shakspeare!" (113).

By contrast, Swinburne, an avowed republican throughout most of his life, sees Shakespeare as less royal and less nationalistic. It should be remembered that Swinburne's early political leanings were rather radical, and he was dedicated to many patriots of nationalistic causes, particularly Giuseppe Mazzini, the founder of the Young European Movement. Mazzini had not only been Swinburne's idol for decades, but the poet had hung the patriot's portrait in his room at Balliol. Swinburne even inscribed his second collection of poems to Mazzini, and in the dedication to *Songs before Sunrise*, Swinburne called his poems, "sword[s] of songs" that shall "cry the republican cry" (Swinburne 1896, lines 19, 36). The content of these poems, advocating the overthrow of repressive regimes, attests to Swinburne's championing of radical causes. Indeed, when Swinburne died in 1907, Mazzini's portrait, along with those of William Morris and Landor and other champions of liberty, still hung above his bed. Significantly, Swinburne appropriates Shakespeare, taking the cultural currency granted by conservative critics such as Carlyle and leveraging it against the traditional patriotic understanding of the playwright. Swinburne argues, for instance, that the "godlike equity of Shakespeare's judgment" was "too deeply ingrained in the very core of his genius to be perverted by any provincial or pseudo-patriotic prepossessions" (Swinburne 1895, 113). Because of this equity, all of Shakespeare's heroes and villains are judged fairly, as Shakespeare has "not two weights and two measures for friend and foe" (115). In *Julius Caesar*, specifically, Swinburne declares, "Shakespeare has made full amends, if not to all modern democrats, yet assuredly to all historical republicans, for any possible or apparent preference of royal to popular traditions" (159). "Whatever manner of man may have been the actual Roman," he adds, "our Shakespearean Brutus is undoubtedly the very noblest figure of a typical and ideal republican in all the literature of the world" (159). The curious thing here is that Carlyle, born of peasant stock, elevates Shakespeare to a royalist position, while Swinburne, of noble stock, sees Shakespeare more as a democrat.

Carlyle's traditional interpretation of Shakespeare's religion also raises Swinburne's ire. For example, Carlyle calls Shakespeare the "melodious Priest" of the "'Universal Church' of the Future and of all times" (Carlyle 1966, 111). Proclaiming that he "cannot call this Shakspeare a 'Sceptic,' as some do," Carlyle explains that Shakespeare's "indifference to the creeds and theological quarrels of his time mislead[s]" those critics who portray Shakespeare as a nonbeliever (111). Carlyle argues, therefore, that Shakespeare is no "sceptic, though he says little about his Faith" (111). For Carlyle, Shakespeare represents divinity, a gift from above: "For myself," Carlyle confesses, "I feel that there is actually a kind of sacredness in the fact of such a man being sent into this Earth" (111). Swinburne, on the other hand, was an outspoken critic of most religions. Even at the end of his life, he demanded that the Church of England burial service should never be read at his funeral. In addition, his poetry constantly challenged traditional Christianity in such poems as "Hymn to Proserpine," where Swinburne argues for a relativity that shall cause even Jesus, the "pale Galilean," to be "dethroned and deceased . . . wiped out in a day!" (Swinburne 1970, lines 35, 13). It should come as no surprise, then, to see Swinburne construct Shakespeare in a similarly non-traditional manner. In an important reading of Hamlet's "To be or not to be" soliloquy, Swinburne challenges Carlyle's reading, concluding that in this speech, one finds solid evidence of Shakespeare's unorthodox thought: "That Shakespeare was in the genuine sense—that is, in the best and highest and widest meaning of the term—a free thinker, this otherwise practically and avowedly superfluous effusion of all inmost thought appears to me to supply full and sufficient evidence" (Swinburne 1895, 165–66). The pondering of suicide, which offended some auditors in the nineteenth century, proved to Swinburne, at least, that Shakespeare was no traditional Christian.

On Shakespeare's morality, the two also differ. Carlyle argues that morality and intellect are indivisible. Carlyle states, "[W]e hear of a man's 'intellectual nature,' and of his 'moral nature,' as if these again were divisible, and existed apart" (Carlyle 1966, 106). He posits that "without morality, intellect were impossible for [Shakespeare]; a thoroughly immoral *man* could not know anything at all! To know a thing . . . a man must first *love* the thing, sympathise with it: that is, be *virtuously* related to it" (107). Carlyle concedes, however, that Shakespeare was unaware of this virtue, adding that in Shakespeare's "unconscious intellect" there is "more virtue . . . than he himself is aware" (107). Swinburne argued throughout his lifetime against the connection between morality and art. In an essay written in 1862 defending Charles Baudelaire, for instance, Swinburne states that the "poet's business" is "to write good verses, and by no means to redeem the age and remould society" (Swinburne 1925a, 13:417). In a critique penned six years later on William Blake, Swinburne exclaimed, "Let us hear no more of the moral mission of earnest art; let us no longer be pestered with the frantic and flatulent assumptions of quasi-secular clericalism" (1925e, 16:139). Finally, just eight years before *Study*, Swinburne makes a clear distinction between morality and art:

> The rule of art is not the rule of morals; in morals the action is judged by the intention, the doer is applauded, excused, or condemned, according to the motive which induced his deed; in art, the one question is not what you

mean but what you do. . . . [T]he one primary requisite of art is artistic worth; "art for art's sake first, and then all things shall be added to her." (Swinburne 1972b, 147)

We clearly see, then, Swinburne's challenge to conservative, elitist readings of the connection between mortality and art such as those of Thomas Carlyle. By evoking the name of Shakespeare, Swinburne is granted the cultural currency to promote his own radical agenda.

HAMLET: ART AND ARTIFICE

In matters of art, Swinburne challenges not only Carlyle's interpretation of Shakespeare's creation of *Hamlet*, but also the interpretation of other critics such as Alexander Pope. Both older critics argue that Shakespeare's art, like his morality, is almost unconscious. Swinburne, on the other hand, perceives *Hamlet* to be the result of a hardworking reviser; he transforms Shakespeare from divine messenger to laborious playwright, and undercuts the overromanticized notions of Shakespeare that dominated the nineteenth century and that still appear in recent works such as Harold Bloom's *Shakespeare: The Invention of the Human* (1998).[2] By redefining Shakespeare's creative process, Swinburne also redefines Hamlet's character in aesthetic terms. Indeed, Hamlet's lack of consistency becomes for Swinburne a textual issue rather than a moral one. By opening up new, less idealized ways of judging and interpreting Shakespeare's works, he helps to remove the blinders of earlier Shakespearean criticism.

Swinburne particularly takes issue with Carlyle and Pope over Shakespeare's creative process. According to Carlyle, Shakespeare's art, like his morality, was almost unconscious. Proclaiming that "Shakspeare's Art is not Artifice," Carlyle adds that "the noblest worth of it is not there by plan or precontrivance. It grows-up from the deeps of Nature, through this noble sincere soul, who is a voice of Nature" (Carlyle 1966, 108). Shakespeare's plays are like nature's houses: "The built house seems all so fit,—everyway as it should be, as if it came there by its own law and the nature of things," and he concludes, "The very perfection of the house, as if Nature herself had made it, hides the builder's merit" (103). We see in Carlyle's interpretation the notion that Shakespeare's art is organic and divinely inspired, as if Shakespeare had no choice but to become the voice of Nature. Pope strikes a similar note about Shakespeare's "Nature": "The Poetry of Shakespear was Inspiration indeed: he is not so much an Imitator, as an Instrument, of Nature; and 'tis not so just to say that he speaks from her, as that she speaks thro' him" (Pope [1743–44] 1969, viii). Swinburne could not abide such readings. He particularly questions Carlyle's and Pope's assertions that Shakespeare's plays such as *Hamlet* came fully-formed into the world:

> Of all vulgar errors the most wanton, the most wilful, and the most reso-lutely tenacious of life, is that belief bequeathed from the days of Pope, in which it was pardonable, to the days of Mr. Carlyle, in which it is not excusable, to the effect that Shakespeare threw off *Hamlet* as an eagle may moult a feather or a fool may break a jest; that he dropped his work as a bird may drop an egg or a sophist a fallacy. (Swinburne 1895, 162–63)

To underscore his point, Swinburne contends that "scene by scene, line for line, stroke upon stroke and touch after touch, [Shakespeare] went over all the old laboured ground again" (163). (In the manuscript of Swinburne's work located in the Folger Shakespeare Library, Swinburne does exactly the same thing. The original lines in his manuscript read: "scene by scene, line by line, stroke by stroke, he went over all the laboured ground again" [Swinburne 1875]). To those like Pope, who viewed Shakespeare's cre-ations as written for "'gain, not glory,'" he adds, "Not one single alteration in the whole play can possibly have been made with a view to stage effect or to present popularity and profit" (164). We see, then, Swinburne echo-ing Charles Lamb and others, particularly when he adds, "Every change in the text of *Hamlet* has impaired its fitness for the stage and increased its value for the closet in exact and perfect proportion" (164). Swinburne also argues that Shakespeare labored over his revisions not to "fill his pockets with contemporary pence" but to make his play "worthy of himself and his future students" (164). By dismantling the divinity of Shakespeare as an infallible genius, Swinburne redefines the playwright as a textual crafts-man, making him more a poet than a dramatist.

Referring to *Hamlet* as the "bridge between the middle and the final period of Shakespeare" (Swinburne 1895, 160–61), Swinburne leaves be-hind his conversation with other critics and goes on to demonstrate his superior knowledge of Shakespeare's textual matters, specifically the de-bate concerning the First and Second Quartos of *Hamlet*. The subversive nature of his argument, furthermore, is also apparent here as he replaces simple moral issues with textual complexity. Contending that the two ver-sions are almost different plays, Swinburne claims that the First Quarto is

> more accurately definable as the first play of *Hamlet* than as the first edi-tion of the play. And this first *Hamlet*, on the whole, belongs altogether to

the middle period. The deeper complexities of the subject are merely indi-
cated. Simple and trenchant outlines of character are yet to be supplanted
by features of a subtler suggestion and infinite interfusion. (Swinburne 1895,
161)

Moreover, Swinburne adds, the "Queen, whose finished figure is now something of a riddle, stands out simply enough in the first sketch as confidant
of Horatio if not as accomplice of Hamlet" (161).[3] Once again, we see
Swinburne replacing a moral issue with a textual one. Instead of debating
the queen's alleged licentiousness, Swinburne turns our attention to important textual issues, sidestepping nineteenth-century concerns with her morality. Hence, Swinburne's insistence on aesthetic details over moral ones
in art may alert some readers to a potential counterdiscourse.

When he turns his attention to Hamlet himself, we see less theoretical
argument and more personal agenda by Swinburne. "[I]t should be plain to
any reader that the signal characteristic of Hamlet's inmost nature is by no
means irresolution or hesitation or any form of weakness," Swinburne
claims, "but rather the strong conflux of contending forces" (Swinburne
1895, 166). Swinburne himself was often accused of moral "weakness,"
and I believe Swinburne was using an alternative-voiced discourse to defend himself against such charges by suggesting that the "weakness" of
any profound thinker may be a result of "strong . . . contending forces."
The powerful rhetorical signal here suggests that possessing contradictory
impulses in one's nature, whether sexual or otherwise, is not necessarily
immoral. Reversing Coleridge's emphasis, Swinburne sees a "smack of
himself" in Hamlet. Hamlet's so-called irresolution, according to Swinburne,
was due to the fact that "Hamlet had somewhat more of [a] mind than
another man to make up, and might properly want somewhat more time than
might another man to do it in" (166–67). A person, therefore, like
Hamlet (or Swinburne) might be permitted more time to make up his mind,
because he had more of a mind to make up.

It is also clear to Swinburne that Shakespeare wanted us to view Hamlet as an active rather than a passive character—someone not weak-willed
or indecisive. The "superfluous episode" (Swinburne 1895, 167) of the
voyage to England Swinburne sees as the best example of Hamlet's active-
ness:

[Hamlet's] discovery by the way of the plot laid against his life, his inter-
ception of the King's letter and his forgery of a substitute for it . . . , the
ensuing adventure of the sea-fight, with Hamlet's daring act of hot-headed
personal intrepidity, his capture and subsequent release . . . serves no pur-

pose whatever but that of exhibiting the instant and almost unscrupulous resolution of Hamlet's character in time of practical need. (167–68)

Finally, the very fact Hamlet sometimes has a "suspicion as to his own *character*, tells much rather in disfavour than in favour of its truth" (168, italics mine). That is to say, a "man whose natural temptation was to swerve, whose inborn inclination was to shrink and skulk aside from duty and from action, would hardly be the first and last person to suspect his own weakness" (168). In this quote I also detect Swinburne's defense of himself in a double-voice; by defending Hamlet, he defends himself. Swinburne was continually accused of moral weakness, and his own character came constantly under attack.

The problem for most critics stemmed from their inability to separate Swinburne's personal actions from his works, and many of their diatribes denounced Swinburne's "character," as two representative examples attacking his personal life and his public work will show. First, John Morley, writing in the *Saturday Review* of 4 August 1866, claimed, "If the *character* of his genius drives him pretty exclusively in the direction of libidinous song, we may be very sorry, but it is of no use to advise him and to preach to him" (Morley 1866, 145, italics mine). Morley goes on to argue that Swinburne is "so firmly and avowedly fixed in an attitude of revolt against the current notions of decency and dignity and social duty that to beg of him to become a little more decent, to fly a little less persistently and gleefully to the animal side of human nature, is simply to beg him to be something different from Mr. Swinburne" (145). Second, Robert Buchanan, the infamous author of "The Fleshly School" attack, characterized Swinburne as the "Absalom of modern bards,—long-ringleted, flippant-lipped, down-cheeked, amorous-lidded" (Buchanan 1866, 137), a man whose verse is filled with "impure thought," and in whose work "sensuality [is] paraded as the end of life" (138). In fact, Buchanan hopes that Swinburne will reform his character, but asserts that in order to do so, Swinburne must "cast [his] evil advisers aside" and "humble himself" by "think[ing] seriously on life and art" (138). Because Swinburne refused to adhere to the prevailing critical ideology, his work and his personal character were severely attacked. I agree with Thaïs Morgan who offers this explanation for the critical assaults: "Swinburne's work hit a very tender spot in the Victorian conscience: a consciousness of the gap between sexual practice and moral discourse which still lingers in the minds of those modern critics who refuse to acknowledge the intelligence of Swinburne's sexual politics" (Morgan 1984, 176). Yet, wrapped in the cultural shroud of Shakespeare studies,

Swinburne covertly responds to his own critics by comparing himself to Hamlet, the nineteenth-century Everyman.

Swinburne concludes that "Hamlet will too surely remain to the majority of students, not less than to all actors and all editors and all critics, the standing type and embodied emblem of irresolution, half-heartedness, and doubt" (Swinburne 1895, 168), but he denies Hamlet's alleged "weakness" by suggesting that Hamlet is active, and therefore, positive. As Robert Peters suggests, Swinburne's reading of the play was "particularly far-sighted," not only in textual matters but also because he disputed the "prevalent critical practice of exaggerating [the character] Hamlet to the neglect of the play's total design," an emphasis that would become a concern of early-twentieth-century critics such as G. Wilson Knight (Peters 1965, 112). More importantly, however, by carefully examining the textual issues of the play, Swinburne elides the moral issues in *Hamlet* and puts forth an aesthetic reading of the play that squares with his own beliefs about the nature of art and life.

KING LEAR: HELLENISM, RELIGION, AND POLITICS

We see in Swinburne's criticism of *King Lear* three of the more subversive aspects of his criticism. In addition to his unorthodox religion and radical politics, Swinburne promotes Hellenic aestheticism, and by doing so, he replaces the play's moral issues with aesthetic ones. Swinburne's alternative-voiced discourse allows him to speak to dual audiences simultaneously—to the more traditional critics of Shakespeare and the classics, on the one hand, and to other readers seeking to extend the boundaries of Victorian masculinity, on the other. By comparing Shakespeare to Aeschylus, Swinburne signals a disjunction in the text, opening up a space for a radical reading of *Lear*. Moreover, Swinburne challenges critics who read the play in orthodox religious terms by focusing on the redemption of Lear by the saint-like Cordelia. Interestingly, however, Swinburne's rhetoric reverts back to a more traditional reading, and, hence, his interpretation begins a dialogue with itself.

Swinburne argues that of all Shakespeare's plays, *King Lear*, this "most elemental and primeval" play, is unquestionably Hellenic in its scope. "It is by far," he proclaims, "the most Aeschylean" of Shakespeare's works due to its "oceanic and Titanic" form (Swinburne 1895, 171). That is, it is the play where Shakespeare "has come nearest to the height and to the likeness of the one tragic poet . . . greater than himself" (170). However,

Swinburne continues, *Lear* is unlike Aeschylus's plays in that its "fatalism is of a darker and harder nature" (171). By positing that Shakespeare's work is even bleaker than Aeschylus's work, Swinburne implies that Shakespeare's work surpasses that of the Greeks in its darkness. This rhetorical strategy tends to align Shakespeare with Swinburne's own agnostic, pre-Christian sympathies.

Swinburne's emphasis on the Greek playwright also raises another important issue in his criticism, an issue that was being constantly debated by advocates of mid-Victorian aestheticism. The very notion of Hellenism would raise suspicions about the content of the Shakespearean critique. In his first volume of verse, *Poems and Ballads*, Swinburne drew much of his subject matter from classical works. He was harshly criticized, as we shall see, for his "Hellenistic" influences, a term sometimes employed in the middle-to-late Victorian period for "unnatural" sexual behaviors (this is the same Hellenism embraced by Walter Pater and Matthew Arnold, although Arnold "bleach[es]" the term "free of sexual connotations" [Dellamora 1990, 69]). The cultural battle over what constituted true "Hellenism" was ongoing in mid-Victorian discussions of culture as well as sexuality. According to Jeffrey Weeks, "from the 1860s on," a number of people, such as J. A. Symonds, mentioned earlier, were "attempting to grapple with the new theories of inversion which were appearing in Europe" (Weeks 1989, 111). Later, Symonds would codify such ideas in his work entitled *A Problem in Greek Ethics*, "privately printed," which "examined homosexuality as a valid lifestyle in Ancient Greece" (111). The role of Victorian Hellenism in legitimizing "homosexuality" is also addressed by Linda Dowling, who argues that the term "derives ultimately from its promise, so powerfully expressed by advocates as Mill, Arnold . . . and Jowett, to restore and reinvigorate a nation fractured by laissez-faire capitalism and enervated by the approach of mass democracy" (Dowling 1994, 31). This movement by leading university reformers such as Benjamin Jowett, Swinburne's tutor and friend, attempted to establish Hellenism as an alternative cultural and religious system. By substituting Greek culture for traditional Christian values, less rigid sexual mores were also promoted. While some tried to separate Greek homosexuality from this cultural movement, it required a special pleading that, in most cases, quite failed. A review of the Hellenistic aspect of Swinburne's art will bring into clearer focus both Swinburne's Shakespearean criticism and its potential for an alternative-voiced discourse.

Swinburne's first volume of poetry (1866) included a number of sexually charged poems, and one poem that seemed particularly to outrage critics was entitled "Anactoria." The poem, which attempts to recreate the

Greek poet Sappho's "Ode to a Beloved," also incorporates a great deal of sadomasochism by way of the Marquis de Sade, whom Swinburne had read in 1862.

In the opening lines of Swinburne's work, Sappho passionately addresses a complaint of love to a young woman named Anactoria:

> My life is bitter with thy love; thine eyes
> Blind me, thy tresses burn me, thy sharp sighs
> Divide my flesh and spirit with soft sound.
>   (Swinburne 1970, lines 1–3)

Sappho admits her love, but also reveals her contradictory feelings of attraction and revulsion: "Yea, all thy beauty sickens me with love" (56), and she pleads, "Would I not hurt thee perfectly?" (134). Of course, such graphic sentiments caused a critical outcry in the somewhat decorous mid-Victorian period. By focusing on lesbian relationships, however, Swinburne was granted a greater freedom of expression about all forms of sexuality, including male homoeroticism. As Richard Dellamora convincingly suggests, the use of lesbian love affairs allowed male writers to "express dissatisfaction with conventional male gender norms" (Dellamora 1990, 69), a possibility we shall consider in Swinburne's discussion of Falstaff and Prince Hal. Moreover, other poems in Swinburne's collection portray symbolic representations of male-male desire, including references to sodomy in "Hermaphroditus" and fellatio in "Fragoletta." While critics also attacked poems on other grounds —such as "Laus Veneris" for explicitly praising the pleasures of the goddess of love and "Hymn to Proserpine" for pointing out the relativity of truth as well as religion and morals—the sexuality of the poems was the most frequently cited and most often censured aspect of the collection. The rebelliousness of the entire volume and its devoted Hellenism influenced later writers, such as Walter Pater, who also challenged the prevailing Victorian ideology.

The intensity of the debate over true Hellenism can be seen in critiques of Swinburne's work, as many critics tried to distance Swinburne's poetic Hellenism from that of the ancients. John Morley, for instance, claimed that *Poems and Ballads* displayed "how far removed Mr. Swinburne's tone of mind is from that of the Greek poets" (Morley 1866, 146). Morley went on to make a distinction between an "attempt to revivify . . . the grand old pagan conceptions of Joy" and "an attempt to glorify all the bestial delights that the subtleness of Greek depravity was able to contrive," a depravity that he felt Swinburne embraced (145). Morley concluded that there "are not twenty stanzas in [Swinburne's] whole book which have the faintest tincture of soberness" (146). Another aspect of Swinburne's Hellenism that Morley censors is the many references to acts that are "nameless shameless abominations" (145). This reference to "nameless" acts, of course, refers to lesbianism and to the "perversion" that many readers found in Swinburne's poems as well as in his personal life.

Significantly, Shakespeare becomes one site for the cultural battle being waged over the Hellenic influence of Swinburne's verse. A second anonymous critic writing in the *London Review* also chastised Swinburne, arguing that Swinburne had "deliberately select[ed] the most depraved stories of the ancient world, and the most feculent corruptions of modern civilization" (Review of *Poems and Ballads* 1866, 130). This critic goes on to cite Shakespeare as the type of writer Swinburne should aspire to be, a criticism that Swinburne might be answering in his own Shakespearean critiques. In other words, while Swinburne might not write *like* Shakespeare, he gains the cultural currency associated with the playwright by writing *about* Shakespeare. The anonymous critic wonders "[i]f Mr. Swinburne has any ambition of earning for himself a permanent place in English literature," because if so, "he is doing his best to destroy all chance of ever realizing such a dream" (130). The author concludes his attack by invoking the name of Shakespeare—not once, but twice. He states that if Swinburne does not reconsider his subject matter (as well as his personal behavior), he could become like "the contemporary dramatists of Shakespeare [who] have perished . . . in consequence of the strange fascination they found in forbidden subjects" (130). One might assume here that the reviewer was referring to either the incest of some early modern writers, or more likely, to Christopher Marlowe's alleged homosexuality. (As Thomas Dabbs points out, it was during the nineteenth century that a "major problem" for Marlowe scholars was how to "approach an author whose reported depravity made it unseemly for a critic to approve of his works" [Dabbs 1991, 31].) The anonymous critic concludes by "beg[ging] of Mr. Swinburne to reconsider his course. The region to which we would have him confine himself is no contracted domain. It sufficed for Homer and for Shakespeare, and might surely content him" (131). The critic warns, however, that if Swinburne continues on his present path, "his bright commencement will set in tumult and disgrace" (131).

We see that this critic has set rigid boundaries for what is "culturally" correct, boundaries he believes to be defined by Shakespeare and Homer—boundaries that, at least according to this critic, Swinburne constantly crosses or at least challenges. By turning his critical attention to Shakespeare, however, Swinburne answers such criticism. He writes within the traditional boundaries, but he then extends the boundaries by subverting traditional readings, so that his criticism becomes a "transgressive authority" (Riede 1993).[4] More specifically, Swinburne's aesthetic agenda becomes more authoritative by being mapped onto a traditional subject matter such as Shakespeare. Conversely, if moral standards no longer apply to literature, they certainly lose some importance as measurements in personal matters.

What Swinburne accomplishes in his criticism is to displace one cultural standard, the morality of Christianity, by arguing for a better cultural example in the aestheticism of Greeks, signifying more relaxed standards in relation to sexuality and morality. We see in Swinburne's critique of *Lear* his refusal to believe that Shakespeare could be defined as a traditional Christian. In this tragedy, Swinburne declares, Shakespeare portrays "no subtleties as in *Hamlet*," no "problem half insoluble" (Swinburne 1895, 171). In *Lear*, darkness covers all: "[W]e look upward and downward, and in vain, into the deepest things of nature, into the highest things of providence; to the roots of life, and to the stars; from the roots that no God waters to the stars which give no man light; over a world full of death and life without resting-place or guidance" (171). Swinburne suggests that Shakespeare, like himself, believed in a godless universe. More importantly, Swinburne's rhetorical strategy undermines any attempt to read the play in Christian terms and subverts any insistence on the moral nature of the play or Shakespeare. In his interpretation, I also detect Swinburne's personal animosity toward orthodox religion, feelings so violent that there was never any "question of his being buried in Westminster Abbey" (Johnson 1979, 144). Swinburne points out that while there is some hope of redemption in Aeschylus's work, "on the horizon of Shakespeare's tragic fatalism we see no such twilight of atonement," and words such as "redemption, amends, . . . pity and mercy" are void of "meaning here" (Swinburne 1895, 171–72). In a dark world such as this, there is no hope for salvation, Christian or otherwise. "We have heard," he continues, "much and often from theologians of the light of revelation: and some such thing indeed we find in Aeschylus: but the darkness of revelation is here" (172). Referring to *Lear* as the "most terrible work of human genius," he states that in this play the "veil of the temple of our humanity is rent in twain" (172). By rhetorically rending in his review this "veil of the temple" of Christian faith, Swinburne, in effect, destroys Shakespeare's alleged Christianity in this play as well. One might also argue that in the space created, Swinburne situates Shakespeare as the high priest of the new religion of aestheticism.

Swinburne's interpretation of the female characters in *Lear* also challenges traditional Christian readings of the play. Many critics saw Goneril and Regan as demi-devils set in opposition to the saintly Cordelia. Unlike critics such as Coleridge, who had called Goneril and Regan the only characters in Shakespeare whose wickedness is supernatural, he claims that these women are representatively human. While Swinburne admits that the sisters are "hot and hard, cold and cunning, savage and subtle as a beast of the field or the wilderness or the jungle," he contends that these characteristics are what makes them human: "But such dangerous and vicious animals are not more exceptional than the very noblest and purest of their kind" (Swinburne 1925c, 11:234). Stating that in Regan it is "impossible to find a touch or trace of anything less vile than it was devilish," Swinburne suggests that to create her "Shakespeare has gone down perforce among the blackest and the basest things of nature to find anything so equally exceptional in evil." However, she is still human, just as the "depth of human hell is so foul and unfathomable" (Swinburne 1895, 173–74). Once more, Swinburne implies that these devils are human, not some cast-off devils of an omnipotent god. Even Cordelia is not without faults, as she portrays "one passing touch of intolerance" toward her father that "redeems her from the charge of perfection" (173). Thus she is a mere mortal; although she may be "Godlike," her "very godhead is human and feminine" (174). He adds, "We love her . . . with a love that at once tempers and heightens our worship, for the rough and abrupt repetition of her nobly unmerciful reply" to her father's demands (Swinburne 1925c, 11:233). And this one response, "[a]lmost cruel and assuredly severe," ignites the "spark which kindles into eternal life the most tragic of all tragedies in the world" (233). Challenging the interpretations of Cordelia as saintly and the sisters as pure devils, Swinburne posits instead that they are complex renderings of the highest and lowest examples of human behavior, respectively.

Human behavior is also a central element in Swinburne's discussion of the meaning of "Nature" in the play. In an important line in relation to sexuality, Swinburne claims that in this play "Nature herself . . . is revealed—and revealed as unnatural" (Swinburne 1895, 172). Once again, Swinburne's double-voice may be defending himself against his critics, as he was often accused of "deviant" and "unnatural" behavior in his private life. As Wendell Stacy Johnson points out, Swinburne "became for his contemporaries the very embodiment of debauchery, [and] of sin" (Johnson 1979, 128). He was, in addition to being an atheist, a "masochist who loved to be whipped by women, by men, by anyone" and, "as he presented himself in his verse, he was also "involved in or fascinated by various sexual deviations—lesbianism and male homosexuality, necrophilia, pederasty, and sadism" (128). In language that echoes charges against his own sexual behavior, Swinburne adds "[o]nly the supreme self-command of this one poet could so mould and handle such types as to restrain and prevent their passing from the abnormal into the monstrous" (Swinburne 1895, 173). Once more, "abnormal" and "monstrous" were common terms for "deviant" sexuality in the mid-Victorian period. Could it be that Swinburne was also drawn to this play because he could empathize with those charged as "abnormal" and "monstrous"?

Swinburne's political reading of *Lear* is nearly as radical as his religious and sexual interpretation. He argues that *Lear* demonstrates two points of Shakespeare's beliefs—first, his sympathy for the masses, and second, his revolutionary ardor. "It should be a truism," Swinburne declares, "upon the evidence given in *King Lear* of a sympathy with the mass of social misery more wide and deep and direct and bitter and tender than Shakespeare has shown elsewhere" (Swinburne 1895, 174–75). Swinburne concludes that the "author of *King Lear* [has] avowed himself in the only good and rational sense of the words a spiritual if not a political democrat and socialist" (175). In a separate essay entitled "Four Plays," Swinburne elaborates on Shakespeare's politics in *King Lear*. The central point of the play, according to Swinburne, is "the fiery protest against the social iniquities and the legal atrocities of civilised mankind, which none before . . . had ever dreamed of daring to utter in song or set upon the stage" (Swinburne 1925c, 11:237–38). This radical reading points out that *Lear* represents "the first great utterance of a cry from the heights and the depths of the human spirit on behalf of the outcasts of the world—on behalf of the social sufferer, clean or unclean, innocent or criminal, thrall or free" (238). Thus, according to Swinburne, Shakespeare is advocating "a change [that] must come upon the social scheme of things which shall make an end" of the great divide between "the judge and the cutpurse, the beadle and the prostitute, the beggar and the king" (238). What *Lear* proposes, claims Swinburne, is "[n]ot political reform, but social revolution . . . the key-note of the creed and the watchword of the gospel according to Shakespeare" (239).

At this point, however, Swinburne's alternative-voiced discourse reverts back to a more traditional reading, one that sounds quite nationalistic if not outright jingoistic, and suddenly his rhetoric begins a dialogue with itself:

> The rule of Elizabeth and her successor may have been more arbitrary than we can now understand how the commonwealth of England could accept and could endure; but how far it was from a monarchy, from a government really deserving of that odious and ignominious name, we may judge by the fact that this play could be acted and published. (Swinburne 1925c, 11:238)

These very indictments, he proclaims, "could be thundered from the English stage at the dawn of the seventeenth century" (238). Yet, he adds, if it were "within the power of omnipotence to create a German or Russian Shakespeare" and this sort of play, "could anything," he asks, "of the sort be whispered or muttered or hinted or suggested from the boards of a Russian or German theatre at the dawn of the twentieth?" (238–39). When someone like "Tolstoi . . . can do it with impunity in success, it will be allowed that his country is not more than three centuries behind England in civilisation and freedom" (239). These arguments would please traditional readers who recently celebrated Victoria's accession to the rank of "Empress of India" in 1877 and who would soon be preparing for her Diamond Jubilee in 1897. By doubling back on itself, Swinburne's rhetoric creates an alternative-voiced discourse that would appeal to readers of various political leanings by promoting "social revolution" but still championing English society.

When discussing *Lear*, Swinburne addresses two audiences simultaneously: traditional critics of Shakespeare and other readers interested in extending the boundaries of Victorian aestheticism. What Swinburne ultimately accomplishes in his interpretation is something akin to *critical* inversion: promoting darkness over light, atheism over orthodoxy, rebellion over the status quo, and humanity over divinity. The end result is a much bleaker reading of the world of *King Lear* and the characters who reside there.

1 HENRY IV: SEXUALITY AND AESTHETICS

We see Swinburne's most prominent use of alternative-voiced discourse in his criticism of *1 Henry IV*. By turning his attention away from the central plays of *Hamlet* and *King Lear*, Swinburne participates in the allegedly disreputable side industry of Shakespearean criticism—according to Samuel Johnson and others—that defended Falstaff's character. Yet if Hamlet may be said to represent the intellectual Everyman and Lear to represent the bad Victorian father, one might argue that Falstaff combines the two characters, possessing the intelligence of Hamlet, combined with the paternalism of Lear. Indeed, many critics have grudgingly admitted to his intellect. Even William Richardson, who chastised Falstaff's morality in the eighteenth century, praised Falstaff's "intellectual endowments" (Richardson 1818, 27). More recently, Harold Bloom has argued that Falstaff engages us because he is a "teacher of wisdom" who has a "cognitive strength" that surprises us (Bloom 1982, 2). Falstaff also signifies the site of the physical body, an important aspect for Swinburne's agenda. It is in this complex character that Swinburne sees most clearly a "smack" of himself. On the one hand, Swinburne addresses traditional readers of Shakespeare by engaging with other critics who wrote on Falstaff—Samuel Johnson, William Richardson, and Maurice Morgann—but then Swinburne's essay goes on to position him as a vocal advocate of Falstaff, an "immoral" Shakespearean character. Swinburne's critique, I will conclude, opens up a space for subversive readings of Falstaff, specifically for interpretations that focus on the potentially homoerotic relationship between Falstaff and Prince Hal.

We find the earliest example of Swinburne's use of alternative-voiced discourse in his criticism of Charles Baudelaire in 1862. First published in the *Spectator* on 6 September 1862, Swinburne's essay defends *Fleurs du Mal*, by employing critical aesthetic standards and refusing to judge the poems that English and French critics called "obscene" and "immoral." In part, the charges stemmed from Baudelaire's portrayal of various sexual "perversities": lesbianism, masochism, necrophilia, and prostitution. We also hear in this review Swinburne articulating the necessary separation of art from morality, what a younger generation would champion as "Art for Art's Sake."

Swinburne strengthens the connection between poet and poems by arguing that the style of the verses combines masculinity with femininity, creating an androgynous verse form. He claims that "the sound of [Baudelaire's] metres suggests colour and perfume," while the style is "sensuous and weighty" (Swinburne 1925a, 13:419). The words "perfume" and "sensuous" may suggest a feminine style of writing, while "weighty" conjures notions of manliness and strength. By the end of the essay, however, Swinburne alternates back to a more conservative discourse, attempting to defend Baudelaire's morality. In fact, while Baudelaire expressed his appreciation for the review, he argued that Swinburne overstated the defense on moral grounds. Comparing Baudelaire to Poe, Swinburne suggests that while Poe "has written poems without any moral meaning at all," for Baudelaire, "there is not one poem of the *Fleurs du Mal* which has not a distinct and vivid background of morality to it" (423). Swinburne seems to be addressing two audiences here, both of which would both be interested in the new literary movement developing in France. Yet, by valorizing aesthetic values over moral values, especially those regarding sexual preference, Swinburne hints at the possibility of new mores of masculinity.

In his discussion of *1 Henry IV*, Swinburne focuses on the character of Falstaff, a character who also challenges standard measures of masculinity, and one with whom Swinburne closely identifies. While siding with

critics such as Maurice Morgann who defend Falstaff, Swinburne then challenges those such as Samuel Johnson who dismiss Falstaff as dangerous
and "malignant" (Morgann 1972, 315). His critical stance on Falstaff, in
fact, anticipates those of contemporary critics such as Jonathan Goldberg.

A brief examination of Shakespearean character criticism vis-à-vis
Falstaff will provide us with a background against which to highlight
Swinburne's identification and critique. This character, who has elicited
nearly as much critical comment as Hamlet, seems to take on a life of his
own, unrestrained by critics or morality. In the late eighteenth century,
Falstaff, despite his paradoxical nature, became a favorite topic for critics.
As Christy Desmet explains, "Falstaff's resistance to allegorical readings
. . . only made the early character critics redouble their efforts to explain
him" (Desmet 1992, 43). Although critics had considered character as somewhat important prior to this time, "[w]hat is new in the last quarter of the
eighteenth century is that essays and whole books are devoted to individual
characters, and those alone" (Vickers 1981, 11). Instead of subordinating
character to plot, critics began to look upon characters as autonomous creations, sometimes in control of their own destiny unrelated to constraints
of the plot.

The debate over Falstaff intensified in the latter half of the eighteenth
century beginning with Samuel Johnson's critique (1768), with which
Swinburne would quarrel in his own essay. Taking a moral approach,
Johnson claims that "*Falstaff* is a character loaded with faults." Specifically, Johnson argues that Falstaff is "a thief, and a glutton, a coward, and
a boaster, always ready to cheat the weak, and prey upon the poor" (Johnson
1952, 315). Johnson also dismisses Falstaff as both "corrupt" and "despicable" (315), and his conclusion makes it perfectly clear that Falstaff represents an exemplum intended to teach a moral lesson: "The moral to be
drawn from this representation is, that no man is more dangerous than he
that with a will to corrupt, hath the power to please; and that neither wit nor
honesty ought to think themselves safe with such a companion when they
see *Henry* seduced by *Falstaff*" (316). The crucial aspect of this essay is
that Johnson reduces Shakespeare to a writer of morally instructive plays,
with Falstaff serving as an example of corruption. Moreover, Johnson's
critique treats Falstaff as merely allegorical. Most importantly, the very
language Johnson uses—the notion of Falstaff "seducing" Hal—will play
an important role in the ongoing debate over Falstaff's character.[5]

The controversy concerning Falstaff continued the following year, when
Elizabeth Montagu (1769) defended not so much Falstaff's character, as
Shakespeare's creation of him. Arguing that "we must certainly admire"
the character of Falstaff, and "own it to be perfectly original" (Montagu

1769, 106), her essay begins a trend attempting to reconcile Falstaff's appeal with his dubious moral character, a movement that accepts his contradictory nature. Even though "gluttony, corpulency, and cowardice, are the peculiarities of Falstaff's composition," Montagu argues, there is still an "air of jest and festivity about him" (106). Her contribution, reminding us of Falstaff's carnivalesque aspects, anticipates those of twentieth-century critics who focus on Falstaff's physical presence in the play.

William Richardson (1789), following Johnson more than Montagu, treats Falstaff as an agent of vice, one whose example teaches a moral lesson. He characterizes Falstaff as a "mean sensualist, incapable of honorable and worthy thoughts, [who] is irretrievably lost; totally, and for ever depraved" (Richardson 1818, 55). Most importantly, like Johnson, Richardson emphasizes that Falstaff's actions create "an important and awful lesson" from which the reader should learn and take heed (55).

Maurice Morgann's essay on Falstaff (1777) deserves particular notice, as Swinburne engages with Morgann's discussion, calling it an "able essay" and commending Morgann for a job "well done" (Swinburne 1895, 111). Part of Morgann's project, which Swinburne continued, was to defend Falstaff from attacks like those by Samuel Johnson. Morgann initially sets out to dispute the prevailing notion that Falstaff is a coward: "I do not," he proclaims, "clearly discern that Sir *John Falstaff* deserves to bear the character so generally given him of an absolute Coward" (Morgann 1972, 145). Instead, he declares, "the Courage of *Falstaff* is my theme" (155). According to Daniel Fineman, editor of Morgann's work, Morgann's argument was "heresy absolute and unmitigated," because "it flouted the seemingly self-evident fact, unanimously reported by a round score of commentators from 1625 to 1777, that cowardice is a basic and inalienable ingredient in Falstaff's composition" (12). Addressing these very critics, Morgann adds that Falstaff "has met with as little justice or mercy from his final judges the critics, as from his companions of the Drama" (153). Morgann then positions himself as a champion of Falstaff, and he finds numerous ways to defend him, mostly by creating nontextual suppositions. For example, he argues that because Falstaff was descended from nobility, and because Shakespeare's audience related nobility to courage, it follows that Falstaff also possessed courage. Moreover, Morgann posits that Sir John at the very least kept up "a certain *state* and *dignity* of appearance; retaining no less than four, if not five, followers or men servants in his train" (165). Further, Morgann posits that Falstaff had not only a house in the country but also one in London (165). Thus, by the end of the essay, Morgann assigns Falstaff dignity, "*reputation*, at least, if not *fame*, noble connection, birth, attendants, title," and so forth (173). In (re)writing Falstaff's life,

Morgann creates a pseudobiography for Falstaff, the critic fighting with the author for textual control. As Desmet posits, "Morgann's interest" in Shakespeare's text "makes him conscious of the critic's role in forming and deforming Falstaff" (Desmet 1992, 56). Swinburne's character criticism of Falstaff will address such "forming and deforming," as well as "reforming."

Swinburne's essay on *1 Henry IV* also positions him as a defender of Falstaff, yet Swinburne's agenda differs significantly from Morgann's. Indeed, the eight pages devoted to this play focus almost completely on Falstaff's character. Unfortunately, Swinburne's Shakespearean criticism on Falstaff has received little attention. When it is anthologized, some of the most important lines are omitted. In Harold Bloom's anthology on Falstaff, for example, he includes the middle portion of Swinburne's essay on *1 Henry IV*, yet Bloom cuts the lines that I believe hold the key to Swinburne's identification with Falstaff, lines we will consider shortly. Moreover, Bloom completely omits Swinburne's dialogue with other critics. Specifically, I will argue that Swinburne identified with Falstaff's dissolute ways, as well as with Falstaff's alleged attempts to reform. As Hélène Cixous posits, in a not completely approving manner, a character is "offered up to interpretation, with the prospect . . . that seeks its satisfaction at the level of a potential identification with such and such a 'personage'" (Cixous 1975, 385). The auditor then proceeds, according to Cixous, to enter "into commerce with the [work] on condition that he be assured of getting paid back, that is, recompensed by another who is sufficiently similar to or different from him—such that the reader is upheld, by comparison or in combination with a personage, in the representation that he wishes to have of himself" (385). By defending Falstaff, Swinburne, in effect, defends himself.

During the ten years he was composing *A Study*, and whether partly as a response to the critical hostility or not, Swinburne also began a decade of dissipation. During these years, he significantly increased his consumption of brandy, an indulgence that confined him to his bed suffering from "influenza" for days at a time. In addition, Swinburne began to frequent brothels in London, becoming a regular client at one referred to as the "Grove of the Evangelist" or the "Grove of the Beloved Disciple," a veiled reference to the Apostle John's allegedly homoerotic relationship with Jesus (Henderson 1974, 127). The combination of Swinburne's drinking and the public exposure of his sexual escapades prompted his friends to convene to decide on a course of action.

Initially, a doctor was summoned to restore Swinburne's health, but to no avail. In a letter to George Powell, Swinburne relates that finally his friends "wrote to Holmwood [the family estate] that I was very unwell and my poor dear father came up to see me, old as he is, and take me out of town again, and it was very wretched altogether" (Swinburne 1959–62, 2:155). In the same letter, dated 24 August 1871, Swinburne writes, "I am up here in the Highlands with Jowett, after staying a fortnight or so at Holmwood to recruit, being decidedly the worse for wear, malgré [despite] our friend Dr. Crosse" (2:154). The excesses prompted Swinburne to reconsider his behavior, and he continues his letter by promising reform: "I must 'purge and live cleanly' [1 Henry IV 5.4.68–69] like Falstaff," he states, "or the devil will have me before his time" (154–55). This reformation can take place, he believes, only if he removes himself from his previous surroundings. He shall "live cleanly," he adds, if he can secure "some durable and endurable pied-à-terre [temporary lodging] in London," where he "shall not be dependent on the tender mercies of landladies or hotel-keepers" (155). It is a distinct possibility that the "landladies" and "hotel-keepers" to whom he refers were the hostesses of the brothels he visited, who had also summoned his father with the message that he was "unwell." The whole scenario—hard drinking, fast living, and sexual license—reminds one of Falstaff's favorite tavern, the Boar's Head, in Eastcheap. The connection, it seems, was not lost on Swinburne either. We see in this letter, then, one example of Swinburne's identification with Falstaff. Essentially, Swinburne is rewriting, or in Desmet's terms, "forming and deforming," Falstaff from a very singular perspective.

While Swinburne's excessive behavior diminished as he finished his research on Shakespeare, his interest in Falstaff never waned. In a letter dated 20 July 1879, written to his friend (and later "caretaker") Theodore Watts, Swinburne inquires, "Can you tell me the exact title, date, and author's name of the Essay on the Character of Falstaff by one Mr. (? Maurice) Morgan [sic] published in the latter years of the reign of Dr. Johnson[?]" (Swinburne 1959–62, 4:75). Even Swinburne's rhetoric reveals his resistance to critics such as Johnson who "reigned" over other critics, imposing their own "morality" on Shakespeare's characters, while championing the traditional view of Falstaff. Swinburne adds that Johnson made Morgann's essay "the subject of a good joke which was also (as usual) bad criticism" (4:75). Swinburne refers to a jest cited in Boswell's *Life of Johnson:* being asked his opinion of Morgann's essay, Johnson responded: "Why, Sir, we shall have the man come forth again; and as he has proved Falstaff to be no coward, he may prove Iago to be a very good character" (Boswell 1887, 4:192 n. 1). At the close of the letter, Swinburne advises Watts that he is "just now elaborately completing [his] own study on that great subject," and he concludes that "all true lovers of Sir John owe a debt of honour to

Mr. Morgan which I for one will not leave unpaid" (Swinburne 1959–62, 4:75). Swinburne repays the debt by restating part of Morgann's argument in *A Study of Shakespeare*, which was published the following year in 1880. He also appropriates Morgann's formation of character to shape his own version of Falstaff, one that anticipates some current views of Falstaff and Prince Hal.

Referring to Maurice Morgann's essay, Swinburne confesses that "[i]t is needless to do over again the work which was done, and well done, a hundred years since" by a critic who wrote an "able essay in vindication and exposition of the genuine character of Falstaff" (Swinburne 1895, 111). Claiming that Morgann's "argument is too thoroughly carried out to require" much addition, Swinburne adds, "[T]he attempt to *appropriate* any share of the lasting credit which is his due would be nothing less than a disingenuous impertinence" (111, italics mine).

Aligning himself with Morgann against Johnson, Swinburne believed that Falstaff had suffered enough from undue critical attack. And while he denies any "attempt to appropriate" Morgann's view, he does just that, reshaping Falstaff like Morgann, but remolding the character to suit his own agenda. While admitting that Falstaff possesses "actual lust and gluttony," Swinburne posits that "the imaginary cowardice of Falstaff" has been "gravely and sharply rebuked by critical morality" (Swinburne 1895, 110). In fact, Swinburne accomplishes a double appropriation, borrowing Morgann's borrowing of Shakespeare. Swinburne believes that the very first scene where Falstaff is mentioned is a key to the question of Falstaff's cowardice: "[H]is creator has put into the mouth of a witness no friendlier or more candid than Ned Poins" (111) that the real distinction about Falstaff is that Falstaff "will fight no longer than he sees reason" (112). He concludes: "In this nutshell lies the whole kernel of the matter; the sweet, sound, ripe, toothsome, wholesome kernel of Falstaff's character and humour" (112). While adjectives such as "sweet," "sound," and "wholesome" may seem outlandish when applied to Falstaff, they indicate clearly Swinburne's opinion of the character. By adding that the knight "will fight as well as his princely patron, and, like the prince, as long as he sees reason" (112), Swinburne aligns Falstaff with Hal; morally the knight is no better or worse than his patron.

Swinburne also challenges Victor Hugo's more recent attack on Falstaff. This response was much more difficult for Swinburne, as he greatly respected Hugo, referring to him as the "Shakespeare of France" (Swinburne 1895, 106). Swinburne exclaims it is "as grievous as it is inexplicable" that Hugo could have misunderstood Falstaff's nature (106). Because he admired Hugo, he is humbled by having to disagree, and actually apologizes for doing so; the strength of his protest signals Swinburne's passionate feelings about Hugo's "misjudgment" of Falstaff. Swinburne proclaims, "[A]gainst his classification of Falstaff . . . I must and do with all my soul and strength protest" (107). In particular, Swinburne disputes Hugo's reference to Falstaff as "'swine-centaur,'" a phrase Hugo uses to connect Falstaff with Rabelais's Panurge. "The admirable phrase of 'swine-centaur' *(centaure du porc)* is as inapplicable to Falstaff as it is appropriate to Panurge," Swinburne argues (107). (Interestingly, one of the epithets *Punch* used to attack Swinburne was "Swine-born.") Adding that "the gradation from Panurge to Falstaff is not downward but upward" (108), Swinburne turns to Falstaff's alleged "immorality," claiming that as "[s]ingular as may seem the collocation of the epithet 'moral' with the name 'Falstaff,' I venture to maintain my thesis; that in point of feeling, and therefore of possible moral elevation, Falstaff is as undeniably the superior of Sancho as Sancho is unquestionably the superior of Panurge" (108). Swinburne distinguishes the types of love that the three characters possess: Panurge is capable only of self-love, while Sancho is a "creature capable of love—but not of such love as kills or helps to kill, such love as may end or even as may seem to end in anything like heartbreak" (109). Swinburne believes, therefore, that Shakespeare created a very different portrait than the other authors, a man with fleshly desires, yes, but also one with a boundless spirit and a genuinely passionate and complex love for Prince Hal.

At about the same time as Swinburne was composing *Study*, critics continued to attack him, not on morality per se, but on his lack of masculinity. Alfred Austin, for example, charged that Swinburne sang loudly in "falsetto notes," resulting in an "emasculated poetical voice" (Austin 1970, 109). And even poets such as Robert Browning began to fault Swinburne's "feminine" impulse. In a letter to Isa Blagden in 1870, Browning wrote, "As to Swinburne's verses, I agree with you—they are 'florid impotence'" (Browning 1951, 332–33). The challenge to Swinburne's masculinity, was, of course, an attack on his personal behavior, but it came at a time when questions about masculinity were ongoing concerns in society at large, and Swinburne's Shakespearean criticism and the assaults on his own character reflected these issues.

For example, Swinburne goes on to lament that Hugo could miss the "deep tenderness" in the relationship between Falstaff and Prince Hal (Swinburne 1895, 106). Swinburne argues that the Hostess's line "The King has killed his heart" in *Henry V* (2.1.79)[6] is one of the most tender and overlooked passages in Shakespeare. In addition, he contends that the line is a result of Shakespeare's revision process: "It should . . . be noted that the finest touch in the comic scenes, if not the finest in the whole portrait of

Falstaff, is apparently an afterthought, a touch added on revision of the original design" (Swinburne 1895, 106).[7] That Shakespeare would so carefully add this line convinces Swinburne that it was a central element in Falstaff's design.

In the above line (*Henry V* 2.1.79), according to Swinburne, we see the key aspect of Falstaff's tender relationship with Hal, a "point in Falstaff's nature so strangely overlooked" by critics such as Hugo (Swinburne 1895, 106). When we recall Swinburne's description of the love between Hal and Falstaff—"such love as kills or helps to kill," such love that cannot "end in anything" but heartache (109)—one might conclude that Swinburne was alluding to masculine desire, specifically the love between men. This type of love, forbidden by the "morality" of the Victorian period, was referred to as the "love that could not speak its name," a love that could not "end in anything" but heartache or frustrated desire. Swinburne concludes his essay by challenging both critics and the prevailing morality, blaming "critical morality" for the numerous misconceptions concerning Falstaff (110).

One hundred years after Swinburne's comments, the debate over the relationship between Hal and Falstaff continues. Contemporary readings of Falstaff argue for his being a "literary fat woman," or, more recently, a pregnant woman described in Bakhtinian terms. These arguments make sense, as Falstaff's body extends across the boundaries of gender, and often he is associated with females. For example, he plays the role of Dame Mortimer in the trial scene with Henry; he refers to himself as a sow that has overwhelmed her piglets; he claims at one point that his "womb" has undone him; and he is "transformed" into the fat woman of Brainford in *The Merry Wives of Windsor*. More recent arguments, however—ones that Swinburne would likely have applauded—suggest that these feminized readings of Falstaff are a defensive tactic by critics "in order not to have to think about his sexual relations with men" (Goldberg 1992, 173). In other words, these critics attempt a "heterosexualizing of homosexuality" in their discourse (173). Reviewing these current critical stances demonstrates that Swinburne's criticism ushers in a new way of thinking about Falstaff's relationship with Hal.[8]

Swinburne's criticism seems to champion the homoerotic view of Falstaff, one that most critics ignore, and a critique that could only speak its name one hundred years after the publication of *A Study of Shakespeare*. In a chapter entitled "Desiring Hal," in his book *Sodometries*, Jonathan Goldberg examines the relationship between Falstaff and Hal from a distinctly homosexual viewpoint. While admitting that "modern regimes of sexuality are only imperfectly, incipiently to be found in the text" (Goldberg 1992, 148), Goldberg goes on to point out particular instances that intimate such a reading. Goldberg particularly challenges critics who identify with Hal's coming-of-age story, arguing that "the celebration of Hal's maturity" suggests a "complicity between criticism and the reinforcement of a misogynist heterosexuality always in danger of homophobia" (148). Goldberg argues that numerous critics, from J. Dover Wilson through C. L. Barber, in their "imaginary identification" with Hal, are blinded to the brilliant display of Hal's overtly theatrical performance.[9] Goldberg's arguments, I will suggest, square with Swinburne's reading of the relationship between Hal and Falstaff.

In the very first scene introducing Falstaff and Hal in *1 Henry IV*, the old knight queries the prince: "Now, Hal, what time of day is it, lad?" (1.2.1). Goldberg asks, if Falstaff "is just waking up, what is Hal doing?" (Goldberg 1992, 163). If the notion of "bedfellows" seems absurd, we must remind ourselves that in *Henry V*, the newly crowned king is infuriated because one of his closest allies, his "bedfellow" Scroop, is revealed to be a traitor. (Shakespeare borrowed the term "bedfellow" from Holinshed, who writes that Lord Scroop "was in such favor with the king that he admitted him sometime to be his bedfellow," because in his "fidelitie the king reposed such trust" [Bullough 1957–73, 4:384].) As Goldberg argues, Scroop's "crime is not what he did in bed," but his treasonous act. Goldberg concludes: "Thus, while Hal is forever casting off his companions, it is not bedfellows per se that are called into question. Hence there is no reason not to suppose that Hal and Falstaff were bedfellows too" (163). Further, Hal's response to Falstaff's question about time conjures up a cross-dressed version of himself. Hal replies that time would be of interest to his fat companion only if the "blessed sun himself" were to appear like a "fair hot wench in flame-coloured taffeta" (1.2.8–9).[10]

Swinburne's critique of *1 Henry IV* is complex, and his attachment to Falstaff is particularly challenging. While other mid-Victorian champions of a male-male aesthetic, such as Walter Pater, were valorizing the classical Greek model of masculinity canonized in Western art (and subversively codified in the late Victorian period as homoerotic), Swinburne's identification is with Falstaff, the unfinished, unctuous, grotesque body. Perhaps part of Swinburne's identification is due to Falstaff's "consumptive" behavior, a behavior sometimes associated with the "sodomite."[11]

We see in Swinburne's reading of *1 Henry IV* a complicated interpretation of Falstaff's character and that character's relation to Prince Hal, and it is possible that Morgan is partly correct when she states that "Swinburne is not at all committed to the project of legitimizing homosexuality, but rather to the project of aestheticising all kinds of sexualities" (Morgan 1993, 330). Still, to open up a space for such a discourse aligns Swinburne with those challenging the status quo. But in contrast to Morgan, I believe that Swinburne's discourse also betrays his publicly expressed reservations about homoeroticism and sodomy. For example, one contemporary of Swinburne's, Arthur J. Munby, recalls meeting with Swinburne at a dinner party. When Swinburne began to attack Christianity loudly, Munby turned Swinburne's attention to Shakespeare's sonnets as an evasive tactic. According to Munby, however, this next topic "led to worse talk" (qtd. in Hudson 1972, 283). Although Swinburne asserted an admiration for lesbianism, he "expressed a horror of sodomy," according to Munby, but "*would* go on talking about it" (283). And although he claimed that he abhorred sodomy, Swinburne's written discourse, as well as his public speech, "goes on talking about it."[12] It appears then that Swinburne's words sometimes belie their meaning. Perhaps, as Morgan points out, Swinburne might have "recoil[ed] in horror at the idea of homosexuality itself" while "identify[ing] with the minority group of homoerotically inclined male readers which he addressed" in his criticism (Morgan 1993, 329). Perhaps we will never know for certain, but Swinburne's alternative-voiced discourse speaks for itself, and it sounds suspiciously like a voice that has only recently dared to speak its name.[13]

RECEPTION OF *A STUDY OF SHAKESPEARE*

It is important to remember that until later in his life, Swinburne scarcely altered his agenda on aesthetics, politics, sexuality, or religion. What he did learn, however, was accommodation in the form of subject matter. By turning his attention to Shakespeare, Swinburne promoted a radical agenda through a traditional source. Focusing on three major aspects of the book, the critics all noted the elaborate style, the critical acumen, and the appendix in which Swinburne parodies the New Shakspere Society. In addition, there are one or two veiled comments on Swinburne's morality. At least two reviews also mention the same argument that I have been proposing throughout this chapter—that in this book we learn as much about Swinburne as we do about Shakespeare. His appropriation of Shakespeare through his alternative-voiced discourse was a striking success, as we shall see in the contemporary reviews of *A Study of Shakespeare*.[14]

While each reviewer considers the style of Swinburne's critique, the comments here are somewhat mixed, some complaining about the often exaggerated tone, but many praising a certain energy, enthusiasm, and eloquence. The *Examiner*, for instance, argues that the book sometimes "sins by over-volubility," but adds that the book "more than compensates for these faults of manner by furnishing us with examples of ornate English which no other living writer is competent to supply" (Review of *A Study of Shakespeare* 1880a, 49). Damning Swinburne with faint praise, the *Saturday Review* compares the work to his other writings, claiming that the book is "much more sober and dignified in style, and much less overweighted with ornament, than anything we have received from his pen of late" (Review of *A Study of Shakespeare* 1880c, 159). The critic seizes this reformation as an opportunity for an even greater "improvement in manner" (159). I believe the rhetoric of these reviews suggests that Swinburne's morality is still an important issue. That is, the critics suggest that while Swinburne may still "sin" stylistically on occasion, his more "sober" and "dignified" writing signifies a critical refinement. But the critics also intimate that Swinburne's "conversion" process has yet to be completed, as there is still room for advancement in his "style." The *Spectator* also comments on the style of the review, granting that there is a "glow of feeling" and a "magniloquence of language," but wondering if a tribute to Shakespeare might not be "better paid in calmer and quieter language" (Review of *A Study of Shakespeare* 1880d, 850–51). The reviewer concludes that Swinburne's "mode of writing requires a corresponding enthusiasm—we had almost said fanaticism—on the part of the poetical student" (851). Once more, words like "wholesome" and "fanaticism" may be subtle glances back to Swinburne's radical past, and although Swinburne's distinctive style clearly bothered his critics, many were caught up in the energy of his assessments.

Although the reviews seem hesitant about the style, they unanimously praise Swinburne's critical insight. The *Examiner* proclaims that "its intrinsic excellences as criticism are not only great in degree but excellent in kind," adding that "Mr. Swinburne is eminently possessed of that critical qualification which Macaulay thought so rare that he singled it out for special commendation in Leigh Hunt" (Review of *A Study of Shakespeare* 1880a, 49). To the question of whether or not a "new study of Shakespeare was wanted," the reviewer answers "unhesitatingly" in the affirmative regarding Swinburne's book (49). After the influence of the "Foreign critics," he continues, it is "of no small importance that someone of recognised literary position should take up the task of Dryden and Coleridge and Hazlitt and Lamb" (50). The nationalistic nature of this quote seems paradoxically to position Swinburne against the very "foreign critics" and writers he had recently been championing; it also, however, begins to secure Swinburne's place in a celebrated line of English critics. Swinburne's critique, the reviewer concludes, considers "Shakespeare's own work from the standpoint of individual culture and intelligence and express[es] the results in choice language"; therefore, Swinburne's "work is a contribution," because on the whole it "contains [an] abundance of excellent criticism" (50). Now that Swinburne possesses both "culture" and "intelligence," although of a characteristically "individual" manner, his work may be deemed "excellent criticism," and he may now be admitted to the ranks of the most revered nineteenth-century critics.

The *Saturday Review* is equally orthodox in its praise, offering up a rhetoric that would please traditional critics of Shakespeare. Claiming that Swinburne "has something fresh and bright to tell us," the critic adds, "[I]t is refreshing to read the sensible and conservative criticism of a poet whose insight teaches him to revere the old traditions and venerable canons of Shakspearian faith," as he "proceeds on the same lines as Dryden and Coleridge before him" (Review of *A Study of Shakespeare* 1880c, 159). By invoking these names, Swinburne's position becomes even more established in a line of "conservative" criticism. What these critics hear, of course, is only one half of Swinburne's alternative-voiced discourse, the voice that appeals to traditional critics of Shakespeare who reject any radical or progressive readings of the plays. The *Spectator*, a journal Swinburne did not want to review his work, also displays begrudging praise. "The purport" of the book, the reviewer states, is "altogether just and praiseworthy" (Review of *A Study of Shakespeare* 1880d, 851). Striking a similar note to the *Saturday Review*, it claims that despite Swinburne's "impulse and overflowing enthusiasm, the author is a conservative critic. We imagine that between his judgment and that of Coleridge there would be no startling difference" (851). Once more, Swinburne's criticism has won for him a conventional audience of traditional Shakespearean scholars. Adding that he "find[s] little to dissent from" in Swinburne's comments, the critic for the *Spectator* even praises Swinburne's originality, a characteristic constantly derided in his other work: "[I]f occasionally, as in his view of Hamlet's character, he may be said to break new ground, he gives ample reasons for his faith" (851). Swinburne must have sensed a delicious irony in his new "conservative" mantle.

Notes and Queries also gives Swinburne exceedingly high marks. "No one," the reviewer argues, "who takes up this book will throw it down again unread or half read; it is too full of piercing insight, choice illumination, [and] amusing invective" (Review of *A Study of Shakespeare* 1880b, 368). "Mr. Swinburne's *A Study of Shakespeare*," he continues, "exhibits in numberless instances the highest critical faculty. It is one of the most suggestive and readable books in this branch of literature issued for a long time" (368). The reviewer also declares that the book "has the high merit of being usually in the right where the question is of differences of opinion, the higher merit of being able to expound the right and carry conviction, and the highest merit of being based wholly on poetic intuition or perception as opposed to mechanical analysis" (368). The writer concludes that "it is the most Shakspearian book on Shakspeare which has been published for a great while" (368). What seems obvious in all these remarks, therefore, is that Swinburne's work presented compelling criticism on Shakespeare for his own time, a significant contribution that has been neglected from the mid-twentieth century on.

The "mechanical analysis" mentioned in the final review refers to the methods of the New Shakspere Society, a group whose "objects can stand as the very model of Victorian scientism," according to Terence Hawkes, and whose "central project was nothing less than Darwinian." By tracing the growth and evolution of Shakespeare's works, the Society hoped to "get his life and times straight, his plays accurately edited and classified, to align the one exactly with the other, to fix the shape of both irretrievably, and to weld them together for ever as a single, comprehensible and coherent unity" (Hawkes 2002, 118–19). Swinburne, who had been publicly quarreling with the group, continually championed aestheticism over mechanical analyses, and his book dealt one of the most fatal blows to this type of criticism by satirizing the group in an appendix to *A Study of Shakespeare*.

In his parody entitled REPORT OF THE PROCEEDINGS ON THE FIRST ANNIVERSARY SESSION OF THE NEWEST SHAKESPEARE SOCIETY, Swinburne begins by noting that Mr. A. had delivered a paper "on the disputed authorship of *A Midsummer Night's Dream*" in which Mr. A. had argued that he was "decidedly of the opinion that this play was to be ascribed to George Chapman" an opinion based "principally on the ground of style" (Swinburne 1895, 276). Mr. A. admitted, however, that "[f]rom its similarity of subject he had at first been disposed to assign it to Cyril Tourneur . . . and he had drawn up in support of this theory a series of parallel passages extracted from the speeches" of the major characters (276). Another member, a Mr. B., challenged the idea, however, proclaiming he

> could prove by a tabulated statement that the words "to" and "from" occurred on an average from seven to nine times in every play of Chapman; whereas in the play under consideration the word "to" occurred exactly twelve times and the word "from" precisely ten. He was therefore of opinion that the authorship should in all probability be assigned to Anthony Munday [an Elizabethan hack writer]. (277)

Swinburne's wicked parody helped to crush such absurd conjecturing, and the journals lined up to continue the assault. The *Examiner*, for example, argued that Swinburne's book would help to end the "absurd antics in which

Shakesperian criticism has for some time been indulging" (Review of *A Study of Shakespeare* 1880a, 49), so much so that most of the public believes that the "average Shakesperian commentator is *ipso facto* an ass" (49). Certainly,

> a person who counts the number of times of occurrence of a certain word in a certain poem or play, is a harmless but pressingly deserving candidate for Bedlam, and that a whole society of gentlemen who spend their time in allotting to their own satisfaction separate scenes and acts of Shakespeare to different authors among his contemporaries, must be candidates of the same class. (49–50)

These critics also suggest that it "would be a very sensible thing if the New Shakespeare [*sic*] Society were to buy up [Swinburne's] edition and distribute it among their members" both "to show them what they should for the future avoid, and what they should in the future imitate" (50). Even the *Spectator* sides with Swinburne, claiming that his work will strike "hard blows at the metre-measurers, and also at the too prevalent mode of solving difficulties by the easy method of double authorship" (Review of *A Study of Shakespeare* 1880d, 851). The *Saturday Review* makes particular mention of the appendix, calling it "a parody of the funniest description, which is yet quite within the limits of good taste" (Review of *A Study of Shakespeare* 1880c, 159). With his two-pronged approach—promoting his aesthetic agenda, and sinisterly satirizing the "metre-mongers," Swinburne's book obviously helped to topple other more technically minded critics engaged in nineteenth-century Shakespeare scholarship.

Suggesting that his Shakespearean appropriation had not completely cleansed Swinburne from the "stain" of his past, the sacrilegious nature of Swinburne's work is also mentioned in one review, the *Spectator* claiming that a certain "characteristic of the volume will offend many readers" (Review of *A Study of Shakespeare* 1880d, 851). The reviewer argues that "it has been ever Mr. Swinburne's wont to apply the most sacred words of scripture—words which, for Christians, possess a divine and unique meaning—in order to emphasise his judgment of poets and their verses" (851). This application, he continues, "strikes us as execrable" (851). The same reviewer also believes that Swinburne's reference to Carlyle is hypocritical. Swinburne had written that Carlyle "holds," over the "'Eternal Cesspools' . . . for ever an everlasting nose,—or rather, in one sense, does not hold, but expand[s] it for the fuller inhalation of their too congenial fumes" (Swinburne 1895, 195). This slur on Carlyle's taste was too much for the

Spectator, and the reviewer complains that "the rebuke, considering the source from whence it comes, strikes us as in the highest degree comical" (Review of *A Study of Shakespeare* 1880d, 851). It is obvious that in some ways, many of these reviews are addressing Swinburne's morality metaphorically by condemning the "sins" and "overindulgences" of his style. And, in this last instance, the real import of the critic breaks through the surface rhetoric to condemn openly Swinburne's morality in his language. Yet to be called "conservative" by so many members of the critical establishment must have given Swinburne subversive delight.

Swinburne's *A Study of Shakespeare* champions a number of radical causes by employing an alternative-voiced discourse. While his interpretations of *Hamlet* and *Lear* are revolutionary, Swinburne's critique of *1 Henry IV* represents his most personal and powerful contribution to Shakespearean criticism by focusing on a reimagined masculinity. I have argued that Swinburne's championing of Hellenism and aestheticism helped to reshape the ideas about male sexual identity in mid-Victorian England. Indeed, in the decades following the 1860s when Swinburne first began to write, "Greek studies operated as a 'homosexual' code" (Dowling 1994, xiii). This is the same Hellenism that Pater and Wilde would later develop as a "homosexual" counterdiscourse able to justify male love in ideal or transcendent terms (xiii). Swinburne, among others, seizes this space of cultural rupture or discontinuity. And prefiguring Wilde, Swinburne maps his radical agenda onto a traditional subject, that of Shakespeare studies. In this manner, Swinburne's alternative-voiced discourse works as a subversive agent in overthrowing elitist ideas about Shakespeare and politics, Shakespeare and religion, and, perhaps most notably, Shakespeare and sexuality.

The 1870s, when Swinburne was composing *A Study of Shakespeare*, produced a number of counterdiscourses to the traditional way of seeing Greek history. As I have suggested, Swinburne's Shakespearean criticism represents one of the powerful, yet often overlooked, counterdiscourses. J. A. Symonds, a prominent Victorian homosexual apologist, published in 1873 his *Studies of the Greek Poets*. This work examined the Greek *paiderastia*, and articulates his hopes for male erotic "communities" (Symonds 1983, 1). Swinburne, it must be remembered, enthusiastically endorsed Symond's work while composing *A Study of Shakespeare*.[15] I would add that another counterdiscourse can be seen in Swinburne's alternative-voiced discourse on Shakespeare; its voice functions so successfully during this cultural moment because of the challenges to traditional sexual roles. As Foucault argues:

There is no question that the appearance in nineteenth-century psychiatry, jurisprudence, and literature of a whole series of discourses on the species and subspecies of homosexuality, inversion, pederasty, and "physic hermaphrodism" made possible a strong advance of social controls into this area of "perversity"; but it also made possible the formation of a "reverse" discourse. (Foucault 1990, 101)

I would count Swinburne's criticism as one of the most powerful "reverse" discourses. The critics who chastised Swinburne were simply lagging behind his advanced thoughts on aesthetics, politics, and sexuality. Today, Swinburne's Shakespearean criticism—open to the possibilities of radical politics, agnostic beliefs, and reimagined masculinity—represents an important voice in nineteenth-century Shakespearean appropriation.

Perhaps most importantly, Swinburne's employment of Shakespeare to promote his own personal (and marginalized) agenda anticipates contemporary Shakespearean appropriation. Disputing Carlyle's reading of Shakespeare as a Tory, Swinburne sees Shakespeare as a liberal instead of a conservative, an agnostic instead of an orthodox Christian, and he presents an early example of Shakespeare's ability to give expression to nontraditional groups. Today, when Shakespeare provides voice for numerous marginalized persons—Maya Angelou's claim that "Shakespeare was a black woman" is one recent example (Angelou 1985)—it is apparent that Swinburne was a nineteenth-century pioneer in Shakespearean appropriation.

When T. S. Eliot called Swinburne an "imperfect critic," his comments pushed Swinburne's work to the margins of Shakespearean criticism. In a revealing passage, however, Eliot repeats the same mistakes as the mid-Victorian critics who confused Swinburne's personal "immorality" with his "immoral" style of writing. Eliot denigrates Swinburne's criticism, characterizing it as full of "undisciplined sentences," which are "the index to the impatience" and "perhaps laziness of a disorderly mind" (Eliot 1930, 17). Eliot also refers to Swinburne's "infirmities" as a thinker, adding that Swinburne's criticism is faulty because it is never "consciously directed to any purpose" (22, 20). I would argue instead that Eliot overlooked or merely ignored Swinburne's "purpose," troubled by the alternative-voiced discourse that promoted a radical agenda in sexuality and politics. Considering Eliot's personal politics, it is apparent that what offended him was not Swinburne's criticism, but Swinburne's personal beliefs, beliefs that Eliot would have found untidy at best, sordid at worst. Displaying his ambivalence once more, Eliot concludes the essay with a positive appraisal of Swinburne, allowing that "[i]n the whole range of literature covered [i.e., Tudor-Stuart drama],

Swinburne makes hardly more than two judgments which can be reversed or even questioned" (19). Finally, Eliot concedes that Swinburne was "sufficiently interested in his subject-matter and knew quite enough about it," adding that "this is a rare combination in English criticism" (24). He concludes that Swinburne has secured a "very respectable place as a critic" (24). Perhaps even Eliot was unaware of just how damaging his assessment of Swinburne was. All the post-Eliot criticism of Swinburne highlights his difficult prose style; what recent critics refuse to add, however, is the importance of Swinburne's critical insight on Shakespeare.

Interestingly, the contemporary reviews of *A Study of Shakespeare* intimate the argument I have developed in this chapter—that Swinburne appropriates Shakespeare to promote his own radical agenda. Claiming that the "book conveys on every page a vivid sense of the author's personality," the *Spectator* posited that "[i]t will repel, and it will attract; it will arouse the combativeness of critics, and stimulate readers fond of literary warfare" (Review of *A Study of Shakespeare* 1880d, 852). The *Saturday Review* adds, it is "not surprising that Mr. Swinburne draws from the study of Shakspeare those brilliant qualities which pervade his own best lyrical writing" (Review of *A Study of Shakespeare* 1880c, 159), and "[w]e see in it perhaps more clearly than anywhere else" what Swinburne "really values and delights in, and what figures he would depict, what virtues he would celebrate, if his genius were more fully under his own control" (159). They conclude with words that anticipate my own thesis: "It is almost more as a study of Swinburne than as a study of Shakspeare that this book will attract posterity" (159).

3

The Shakespeareanization
of Robert Browning:
The Objective and Subjective Poet

Summoned as a witness in a libel suit, Robert Browning appeared in court in June 1879. A freelance editor, who was suing the *Athenaeum* for damages, charged that the magazine had committed slander by referring to him as a "literary vampire" for his republication of Elizabeth Barrett Browning's poetry without her family's permission. As Browning stepped into the witness box, the defense counsel, a Mr. Parry, decided to forgo the custom of asking the witness to identify himself. Instead, Parry loudly announced, "I need not ask who you are; I would as soon ask William Shakespeare." According to the *Daily Telegraph* (16 June 1879), Browning ceremoniously "bowed" and confessed, "I have been before the public for some years" (2).

For at least twenty years prior to this court appearance, Robert Browning had carefully manipulated his public image in order to borrow Shakespeare's cultural authority for his works. His "Essay on Shelley" (1852) represents Browning's first successful attempt in this enterprise, and his poem "House" (1876) signals one of the last. In the years between the publication of these two works, many critics of the mid-Victorian era began to speak of Browning's work in Shakespearean terms. While most critics have assumed that Browning's movement toward Shakespeare was a direct result of the scathing critique of *Pauline*, John Woolford suggests that Shakespeare, or at least one prominent actor playing Shakespeare, may have also influenced Browning during the composition of the poem.[1]

Browning's first poem, *Pauline* (1833), was panned by many critics for its confessional mode based on the romantic notion of subjectivity, particularly Shelleyan subjectivism—introverted, personal, prophetic. The most famous example is the never-published review by John Stuart Mill. Mill was preparing a rather negative critique for *Tait's Edinburgh Magazine* when another review appeared first; consequently, Mill returned his copy of *Pauline* to Browning with withering comments scribbled in the borders of the work.[2] What we shall see is that when Browning claimed in the margins of the poem that he conceived of his scheme of poetical ambition while watching Edmund Kean playing Richard III, the poet was not only responding to Mill's critique but also revising his own critical history and subsequent Shakespearean appropriation.

Browning's use of Shakespeare proceeds differently from either George Eliot's or A. C. Swinburne's. Browning employs Shakespeare to lend cultural currency to his poetic attempts in a much more self-conscious way than George Eliot. Partly because he had no G. H. Lewes to construct his image, Browning had to Shakespeareanize himself. And unlike Swinburne, Browning appropriates Shakespeare to gain rather than subvert more traditional critical authority. In a sense, Browning's appropriation combines elements of both Eliot's and Swinburne's methods. As a critic, Browning tries to shape a reader's understanding of Shakespeare. Therefore, his public pronouncements, like Swinburne's, speak directly to a large audience of readers interested in Shakespeare. Yet in his poetic appropriations, Browning proceeds more subtly, transforming Shakespeare's characters as Eliot does, sometimes endowing them with a sympathy that is not seen in Shakespeare's original creations. Browning also reproduces Shakespeare in a more decidedly "masculine" manner, and some critics even began to advocate Browning as an antidote to the "feminine" French influence promoted by those such as Swinburne.

By combining reception study with cultural criticism, I will show how one poet defined himself in relation to Shakespeare. Browning distanced himself from the romantics and their particularly subjective poetry by creating a new form in the dramatic monologue, a genre that calls to mind the "objectivity" of Shakespearean drama. Moreover, Browning insisted on a distinction between the private lives of poets and the public works they create. A second level of appropriation also occurred in the 1880s when the Browning Society promoted Browning himself as a Victorian Bard, more masculine and more religious than Shakespeare—in short, a more wholesome national poet.

ROBERT BROWNING AND EDMUND KEAN

During the writing of *Pauline*, the models of Shelley and Shakespeare fought for control of Browning's muse, and the Shelleyan influence in

Pauline is undeniable.[3] Clearly the twenty-year-old Browning wrote *Pauline* with Shelley as one of his principal models, and only after Mill's criticism does Browning seem to have found himself increasingly drawn to the objectivism of Shakespeare's dramatic characters. Early on, he heard about Shakespeare from his father, and it is probable that his father also read Shakespeare to him from his private library, which contained over six thousand volumes. Browning's Uncle Reuben read and discussed Shakespeare with him as well.

Not only had Browning read Shakespeare's plays, but he also had seen them performed as early as his eighteenth year. In a letter addressed to W. C. Macready, for instance, Browning talks of seeing *Hamlet* on 21 October 1830. The most telling detail of the influence of Shakespearean performance, however, can be seen in Browning's subscript to *Pauline*. It reads simply:

RICHMOND,
October 22, 1832.

In Mill's notes on his copy of the poem (which was subsequently returned to Browning), Mill complained not only about the self-indulgence of the poem but also about the abruptness of the transition from addressing Pauline to the recounting of a specific place and a contemporary date. Browning responded to Mill's criticism in the margin of the returned copy of the poem:

> Kean was acting there: I saw him in Richard III that night, and conceived the childish scheme already mentioned: there is an allusion to Kean, page 47. I don't know whether I had not made up my mind to *act*, as well as to make verses, music, and God knows what.— que de châteaux en Espagne [castles in the air]! (qtd. in Woolford 1989, 23)

The "childish scheme" mentioned by Browning was his plan not only to produce a number of works, including *Pauline*, a novel, and an opera, but also to attach a different pseudonym to each one, therefore casting himself in different roles. Obviously, Browning was increasingly intrigued by the possibilities of dramatic performance as well as dramatic poetry, an idea hinted at in the postscript of the poem.

Browning had been affected by Edmund Kean's acting in Shakespeare's tragedies, but more importantly, Kean's portrayal of Shakespeare may have provided Browning with one way out of the dilemma of how to decide between the subjectivism of Shelley and the objectivism of Shakespeare.

On the afternoon of 10 October, Browning and his sister Sarianna traveled on foot the ten miles from their house in Camberwell to the King's Theatre in Richmond to see Kean perform the starring role in *Richard III*. What Browning would have witnessed in 1832, however, was a Kean who was far removed from his glory days as the single most influential actor of the romantic stage. Although the fiery Kean had been celebrated by nearly every drama critic of the early nineteenth century, his life off the stage was as flamboyant as his life on the stage, and he burned out early; he would die only six months after Browning witnessed the production alluded to in Browning's marginalia. Browning, however, began to filter the subjectivity he had inherited from Shelley (and to a lesser extent from Byron) through the influence of actors like Kean performing Shakespearean roles.

While Browning wrote that he witnessed Kean's performance prior to writing *Pauline*, John Maynard and others dispute this notion. Citing evidence in unpublished correspondence in the British Museum, Maynard claims that Sarianna "recalled quite explicitly that it was while he was finishing the poem, not—as he implies—while he was conceiving it, that he was seeing Kean. In her remembrance, he composed the end of the poem in his head on one of several trips he made to Richmond around 1832" (Maynard 1977, 222). Interestingly, Sarianna's account suggests that Browning probably witnessed Kean in other Shakespearean roles during the same theatrical season. In the Harvard Theater Collection there is a playbill for *Othello* for 29 October 1832, and the season ended 9 November. In addition to *Richard III*, *King Lear* and *Macbeth* had also been acted on 26 September and 3 October (Maynard 1977, 436 n. 73). It seems apparent, then, that Browning observed with interest Kean's donning of a number of dramatic masks, a central feature of Browning's later and more successful poems.

Kean's personal history also influenced Browning, as he witnessed this more earthy and less ethereal actor. In *Pauline*, the direct allusion to Kean mentioned by Browning reads:

> I will be gifted with a wond'rous soul,
> Yet sunk by error to men's sympathy,
> And in the wane of life; yet only so
> As to call up their fears, and there shall come
> A time requiring youth's best energies;
> And strait I fling age, sorrow, sickness off,
> And I rise triumphing over my decay.
>
> (*Pauline,* lines 669–75)[4]

So ill at this point in his career that he lived in the house adjoining the theater to save his strength for his performances, Kean's brandy-bolstered energy was the one thing that kept him going on many nights. The allusion to Kean, then, becomes clearer when we consider the Kean that Browning witnessed. Although enervated and dissipated from tuberculosis and alcohol, Kean was still able to summon the energy to startle an audience with his outbursts of sudden energy.[5] As Browning's speaker exclaims, by casting off "age, sorrow, [and] sickness," Kean "Triumphs over decay." Part of Kean's appeal was the fact that through sheer willpower, Kean could force himself to continue his majestic performances on stage. Browning clarified this point later by changing the last line to read, "And rise triumphant *through* decay" (675, italics mine); in other words, the decay itself seems central to both Kean's triumph and Browning's admiration.

Kean also appealed to Browning because of the actor's ability to play numerous Shakespearean roles while maintaining his own identity. As William Hazlitt observed of Kean:

> Our highest conception of an actor is, that he shall assume the character once for all, and be it throughout, and trust to this conscious sympathy for the effect produced. Mr. KEAN's manner of acting is, on the contrary, rather a perpetual assumption of his part, always brilliant and successful, almost always true and natural, but yet always a distinct effort in every new situation, *so that the actor does not seem entirely to forget himself, or to be identified with the character.* (Hazlitt 1930, 5:184, italics mine)

Kean's example offered one way to combine the subjective and objective, by playing roles but also by maintaining one's own distinct persona. In other words, through Kean, according to John Woolford, Browning began to realize that "the writer differs from the speaker in the same way that an actor differs from his part" (Woolford 1989, 28). Further, Browning accepted the idea that writing, like acting, can be both a performance and a revelation of one's own persona. We see this idea in many reviews of Kean's performances as well.

In the wooing scene in *Richard III*, for instance, Kean acts the part of Richard, but retains elements of his own persona, and Hazlitt praised Kean's ability to play multiple parts while also playing himself. Pronouncing the wooing scene "an admirable exhibition of smooth and smiling villainy," Hazlitt concluded that Kean was successful because he played him as an actor: "Richard should woo, not as a lover, but as an actor" (Hazlitt 1930, 5:182). This same notion is evident in *Pauline*, in which the speaker seems to be trying on a number of roles. This stage of Browning's development, then, marks a transition to the more mature writer who can successfully portray numerous characters, all projected from his own distinct persona.

Another feature of Kean's Shakespearean performances that affected Browning concerns the aspect of sympathy, the sympathy the audience would feel even for a villain like Richard III. Even though Richard is quite simply a true villain, Kean stressed instead his power and ambition, portraying him as an overreacher of the first magnitude.[6] Hazlitt not only also praised Kean's ability to fill "every part of the stage" but also his ability to portray Richard's "mental superiority, and power to make others the playthings of his will" (Hazlitt 1930, 5:182). This same ability to endow despicable characters with such triumphant willpower can be seen later in Browning's speakers of dramatic monologues such as the Duke in "My Last Duchess."

Kean's Shakespearean performances offered Browning a new way of considering the poet's role. Witnessing the earthiness of Kean following his flights of fancy with Shelley returned Browning to firmer ground on which to make his poetical stand. Hence, Kean's performances of Shakespeare helped to usher Browning from his imitation of Shelley to a new dramatic realism that he incorporated into his dramatic monologues; it represented a turn away from the introverted confessional mode, and a swerve toward the impersonal yet identifiable nature he related to Kean's performances. This change would enable Browning later to wear masks that would both reveal and conceal. For the time being, Browning was smitten with the notion of dramatic portrayal, an aspect of his art on which he would begin to focus all his energies.

BROWNING AND THE STAGE

During the mid-1830s, Browning would move further from the personal mode of writing and more toward dramatic portrayal. Spending a great deal of the next six years of his life trying to reproduce the success of Shakespeare's dramatic art on the Victorian stage, Browning never quite succeeded in this pursuit. Yet, the practice served as an essential apprenticeship, a time in which Browning profitably struggled with the problems of dramatic character portrayal.

Browning's opportunity to immerse himself in the world of Victorian drama came rather suddenly. After reading Browning's *Paracelsus* (1835), Macready decided that Browning might be the savior of nineteenth-century drama, and he arranged a meeting with the twenty-four-year-old Browning. Two days after the meeting, Browning wrote to Macready accepting a challenge to write for the stage: "I will give you my whole heart and soul to the writing of a Tragedy . . . to be ready by the first of November" (Browning 1950, 12). Browning's ambition is also apparent in the closing lines of the letter: "[S]hould I succeed, my way of life will be very certain, and my name pronounced along with yours" (12). It seems Macready was not the only one to see Browning as a savior for nineteenth-century drama, as Browning also felt that he could somehow redeem the English stage. His move from Shelley to Shakespeare had now begun in earnest.

While Browning's attempts at drama are generally overlooked, it is important for us to consider them, not only because they represent Browning's attempts to reproduce Shakespeare in the playwright's most popular medium, but also because they serve as early exercises in Shakespearean appropriation. Browning's first attempt at drama was *Strafford* (1837), and the play, a psychological drama in which the action seems only loosely related to the plot of the play, was first produced in May 1837. In the preface, Browning set out his intentions, as he continued to grapple with the relation of character to action: "[I] am not without apprehension that my eagerness to freshen a jaded mind by diverting it to the healthy natures of a grand epoch, may have operated unfavorably on the represented play, which is one of Action in Character rather than Character in Action" (Browning 1969–, 2:9). After reading the preface, one would expect Browning's typical psychological portrait of "Action" within "Character." But it appears that Browning was so obsessed with succeeding on the stage that he tended to neglect the poetic elements in the drama. As William Irvine and Park Honan argue, Browning "understood the private drama of passions and ideas occurring in the mind, but not the public drama of men acting and conflicting in the great world of politics and business" (Irvine and Honan 1974, 71). The play seemed, however, to fail on both dramatic and poetic terms.

According to reviews and attendance figures, Browning was no Shakespeare, at least at this point. Produced five times before diminishing attendance and cast disputes caused Macready to withdraw it from production, the play was performed one final time on 30 May. Following the play's failure, Browning blamed the actors, the condition of the theater, Macready's interference—everything but the script of the play. Part of the problem was Browning's failure to fuse the lyrical and the dramatic, and also a failure to understand the audience. By serving an "overwhelming imaginative purpose," according to Sarah Wood, Browning's dramas "could not at the same time make happy contact with Macready's familiar London audience" (Wood 2001, 60). Thinking in dramatic terms, however, did have a favorable impact later on Browning's poetry. While the play was a failure, the

Shakespearean apprenticeship—the struggle with dramatic portrayal—was not.

The Return of the Druses (1843), Browning's next dramatic attempt, was also criticized despite its echoes of *Othello*. Once again, Browning tried to elicit from Macready a favorable response. In the first two plays Browning had tried to convince Macready of the value of psychological drama, but in the *Druses* he tried to please Macready by focusing on the actor/director's notions of good drama, including elaborate spectacle, abundant action, and a central love plot. Yet the play concerned a tribe that no one had ever heard of, and the central character, Djabal, written for Macready, proved strikingly unsympathetic. There are, however, some interesting *Othello*-like details. Djabal, who is described as having a "swarthy brow," inadvertently kills his betrothed; full of remorse, he addresses her dead body, concluding the speech and the play by violently stabbing himself in the heart. Even with the minor Shakespearean borrowings, however, the play failed to convince. On 3 August, Macready wrote in his diary, "Read Browning's play, and with the deepest concern I yield to the belief that he will *never write again*—to any purpose. I fear his intellect is not quite clear" (Macready 1912, 2:72). The charge of "obscurity" would haunt Browning throughout his dramatic and poetic career,[7] but paradoxically, as we shall see, Browning's supporters employed the same term as a way to link the poet with Shakespeare.

In his next drama, *A Blot in the 'Scutcheon* (1843), Browning began to rely more heavily on Shakespeare's model for dramatic portrayal, incorporating overt Shakespearean echoes throughout the play. There is, for example, a balcony scene that recalls *Romeo and Juliet* and a scene of vengeance reminiscent of *Othello*. Mildred, the sister of the jealous and "haughty" Lord Tresham, is being sought in marriage by Earl Mertoun. Tresham agrees to the match, but later that evening he is told by a servant that Mildred has been covertly entertaining a nightly lover in her chamber. Although Tresham confronts Mildred with the accusation, she refuses to reveal her lover's name, so Tresham sets a trap and catches the clandestine lover, who turns out to be Mertoun. Whether from a displaced attraction to his sister, such as in *The Duchess of Malfi*, or merely from his sister losing her virginity before marriage, this discovery incites Tresham's anger, and the enraged Tresham slays Mertoun on the lawn below Mildred's window. When Tresham tells Mildred of the slaying, she blesses her brother before dying of a broken heart. Filled with remorse for his hasty actions, Tresham swallows poison and kills himself.

The most obvious Shakespearean echoes are of *Romeo and Juliet:* like Romeo, Mertoun is described as "young," "[h]andsome," and possessing the "utmost bravery" (*A Blot in the 'Scutcheon* 1.1.10–13),[8] and also like Romeo, Mertoun is secretly involved with the daughter of a noble and proud family. Moreover, both girls have premonitions of impending doom. "Like a death-knell," Mildred's "soul" hears the words, "this will not be!" (1.3.100–103), while Juliet makes a similar pronouncement, when she proclaims, "Oh God, I have an ill-divining soul!" (3.5.54). The balcony scene is also similar as Mertoun follows Romeo's lead by calling on his mistress under "night's cloak" (*Romeo and Juliet* 2.1.117).[9] Like Romeo, he woos his lover from below the balcony, singing her praises, and complimenting "her voice's music" (*A Blot in the 'Scutcheon* 1.3.86), echoing Romeo's claim that Juliet's voice sounded like the "softest music to attending ears" (2.1.211). Regrettably, Browning's poetry fails to match Shakespeare's. Below Mildred's balcony, for instance, Mertoun sings: *"There's a woman like a dew-drop, she's so purer than the purest; / And her noble heart's the noblest, yes, and her sure faith's the surest"* (1.3.81–82). If the childish rhyme (which, unfortunately, can be sung to "The Yellow Rose of Texas")[10] is not offensive enough, the sentiment of the line surely is.

In addition to *Romeo and Juliet*, *Othello* and *Much Ado about Nothing* are also referenced in *Blot*. Tresham's pride in his image and his extreme jealousy over his sister's sexual liaison are two distinctly Othello-like features, while the subplot contains a pair of battling lovers such as Benedick and Beatrice from *Much Ado about Nothing*. Moreover, the Beatrice-like character stands by Mildred in a manner similar to Beatrice standing by Hero. None of the Shakespearean appropriation helped, however, and the play closed after three nights at Drury Lane.

The stinging critical responses were not unlike the reviews of Browning's earlier dramas. The *Times* stated that "though [Browning] went to work with a good fundamental idea," he has "produced one of the most faulty dramas we ever beheld" (Review of *A Blot in the 'Scutcheon* 1843c, 5). Charging that "[i]f to pain and perplex were the end and aim of tragedy," then Browning's drama "would be worthy of admiration," the *Athenaeum* went on to dismiss the play as "a very puzzling and unpleasant piece of business" (Review of *A Blot in the 'Scutcheon.* 1843a, 166). The *Spectator*, echoing the description of the play-within-a-play in *A Midsummer Night's Dream*, stated the play is "brief, yet tedious: shocking, but unimpressive; and melodramatic, without being effective" (Review of *A Blot in the 'Scutcheon* 1843b, 159). Although the attempted Shakespearean appropriation was noticed by the critics, they sarcastically used a similar ploy of appropriating Shakespeare's words to chastise Browning's attempt.

Perhaps to spite Macready, Browning wrote his next drama, a new romance entitled *Colombe's Birthday* (1844), for Macready's rival, Charles

Kean. The play, a love story, is based on the standard fairy-tale in which the beautiful princess falls in love with a working-class citizen. Yet the play was not produced until nine years later, when Kean took over the management of the Haymarket Theatre. While the critics posted decent reviews, the play was removed from production after just seven performances. Although Browning later composed two closet dramas, he would never again write for the Victorian stage. While all the plays failed to achieve any stage success, the effect of thinking in dramatic terms would give Browning the impetus to move toward his greatest achievement, the dramatic monologue.

OBJECTIVE AND SUBJECTIVE POETRY

At the beginning of the 1850s, Browning began to distinguish even more carefully between the art of Shelley and that of Shakespeare. While residing in Paris during the winter of 1851, Browning was asked to write an introduction for a new collection of what were believed to be Shelley's letters. Although the letters were later discovered to be spurious, the "Essay on Shelley," as it has come to be known, represents one of the few pieces of literary theory ever written by Browning. In the "Essay," Browning carefully outlines the distinctions he sees between an "objective" poet such as Shakespeare and a "subjective" poet such as Shelley. In so doing, Browning works out his own role as a poet.

Browning defines the objective poet as a person "whose endeavor has been to reproduce things external (whether the phenomena of the scenic universe, or the manifested action of the human heart and brain) with an immediate reference, in every case, to the common eye and apprehension of his fellow men" (Browning 1997, 574). The objective poet explains the world in terms understood by many, because he sees "external objects more clearly, widely, and deeply, than is possible to the average mind" (574). Being "in sympathy" with the "narrower" conception of the object under consideration and "careful to supply it with no other materials than it can combine into an intelligible whole" (574), the objective poet such as Shakespeare is attracted to the drama as a medium. His works are intelligible in part because his characters are both complete and concrete. Thus, while the abstract notion of "intellectual paralysis" may seem remote and incomprehensible, when viewing a character such as Hamlet, we understand the concept, because the character seems complete. Browning calls the objective poet a "fashioner" (574): "[T]he thing fashioned, his poetry, will of necessity be substantive, projected from himself and distinct" (574–

75). For this reason, poetry has nothing to do with the biography of the poet; though biographies may be "fraught with instruction and interest," they are ultimately dispensable, because the "man passes, the work remains" (575). In the "Essay on Shelley," Browning even refuses to name Shake-speare; in the single reference he makes, Browning calls him, instead, the "inventor of 'Othello'" (575).

While the objective poet deals with "humanity in action," the subjective poet struggles with "the primal elements of humanity" (Browning 1997, 576). The subjective poet, then, is a "seer," a prophet rather than a "fash-ioner," and what he "produces will be less a work than an effluence" (576). His biography, unlike the objective poet's life story, is important because "[t]hat effluence cannot be easily considered in abstraction from his per-sonality,—being indeed the very radiance and aroma of his personality, projected from it but not separated" (576). Therefore, a knowledge of the personality of the subjective poet is essential: "[I]n apprehending it we apprehend him, and certainly we cannot love it without loving him" (576).[11]

Browning, however, remained troubled over which kind of poetic model was best, concluding in the "Essay" that there is no way to judge which of these poetic gifts is the greater, as there is a need for both types of poetry and poets. While it might seem that the subjective poet is "the ultimate requirement of every age," Browning regards the objective poet as equally important, "[f]or it is with this world . . . that we shall always have to concern ourselves: the world is not to be learned and thrown aside, but reverted to and relearned" (Browning 1997, 577). Browning, therefore, suggests a cyclical view of poetic history: After the lofty insight of seers and prophets, there will come an "imperative call for the appearance of another sort of poet, who shall at once replace this intellectual rumination of food swallowed long ago, by a supply of the fresh and living swathe" (578). It seems in these lines that Browning defends his own attempts to create new, "fresh" ways of looking at the world, to distinguish himself from the dominating influence of Shelley and other romantic predecessors and to associate himself with Shakespeare. The poetic result is Browning's dramatic monologue.

While a single definition of the dramatic monologue is impossible, the form usually contains a speaker who unconsciously reveals more about himself than he intends.[12] Unlike many of the romantics, who purportedly drew their inspiration from solitude and isolation, Browning writes about "men among men," combining the perspective of the subjective, philo-sophical speculator with dramatic action concerning people of this world. Joseph Milsand, a contemporary and friend of the poet, suggests that Brown-ing sought "to reconcile and combine" the subjective and the objective, "in order to find a way of being, not in turn but simultaneously, lyric and dramatic, subjective and pictorial" (1856, 545). In *Men and Women* and *Dramatis Personae*, Browning attempts this fusion with the dramatic monologue.

Performing Appropriation

Browning's effort to blend objective with subjective perspectives manifests itself in two poems that appropriate Shakespeare: "Childe Roland to the Dark Tower Came," which was composed (January 1852) soon after the "Essay on Shelley" and based on *King Lear;* and the later poem "Caliban upon Setebos" (published 1864), which rewrites Shakespeare's *The Tempest*. In these two poems, we see Browning struggling with his role as poet; in "Childe Roland," he aligns himself firmly with the goals of objective poetry, yet in the later poem, Browning seems to return to the agonistic stance of the romantic or subjective poet, competing with Shakespeare even as he empathizes with Shakespeare's maligned character.

"Childe Roland to the Dark Tower Came" focuses on a young knight, a "Childe," on a quest to find the mysterious "Dark Tower." At the beginning of the poem, the quester watches as a "hoary cripple, with malicious eye" (line 2) points him in the direction of what may or may not be the "ominous tract" leading to the Dark Tower (line 14). At the conclusion of the poem, Roland "[b]urningly" realizes, "all at once," that he has reached his goal (line 175). In front of him lies the "Tower itself / The round squat turret, blind as the fool's heart" (lines 181–82). At this point, Roland recalls the names "[o]f all the lost adventurers," his "peers" who have struggled to reach the same place (line 195). As their images surround him, Roland puts his trumpet to his lips and blows *"Childe Roland to the Dark Tower Came"* (line 204).

The most obvious intertextual relation between *King Lear* and the poem is Edgar's song, which Browning appropriates for the epigraph of "Childe Roland."[13] By telling the reader to "See Edgar's song in 'LEAR,'" Browning overtly seeks the cultural authority that this Shakespearean reference can grant to his poetry. After the storm scene on the heath, Edgar, still in disguise, speaks these lines as the party heads toward Gloucester's castle:

> Childe Rowland to the dark tower came,
> His word was still—fie, foh, and fum,
> I smell the blood of a British man.
>
> *(King Lear* 3.4.170–73)[14]

In his correspondence, Browning also suggested that *Lear* was a primary influence on the poem. Responding to Irene Hardy's questions about the work, Browning wrote: "My own performance was wholly suggested by the line from 'Lear' in connection with a tower I happened to see among some hills near Carrara in Italy" (Hardy 1913, 54). The word "performance" is significant here, for even if Browning was not always clear in response to letter writers, his insistence on the connection to the play signals his move to a more Shakespearean mode and also a personal quest toward Shakespearean objectivity. More importantly, the word "performance" signifies not only the dramatic quality of the poem but also the role of the poet as performer.

One of the most important points of intersection between "Childe Roland" and *King Lear* is the subjective nature of both landscapes. King Lear, for instance, projects his emotions onto the landscape, specifically in the storm scene. The howling wind "crack[s]" its own "cheeks" in rage, and the storm "rumble[s its] bellyful" (*King Lear* 3.2.1, 13). Perhaps Lear even refers to his own reproductive capability when he exclaims, "[A]ll germens spill at once, / That make ingrateful man!" (lines 8–9) or, one might add, ungrateful daughters. Unconsciously personifying nature, Lear refers to the "wrathful skies" (line 41) and the "groans of roaring wind and rain" (line 45). Roland similarly casts his feelings onto the landscape. When he suspects that the cripple is lying, his doubt should suggest to the reader that Roland's perceptions may not always be trusted. Agreeing that the poem is a quest for understanding, Eugene Kintgen claims that Roland must have an "attribution of malicious intent" toward the landscape (Kintgen 1966, 253). What he means is that Roland, like all people, has what he terms a "perversity of the mind—that opposes the pursuit of a goal" by blaming external factors (254). This attitude sounds similar to the type of predisposition Edmund so carefully describes in *Lear:*

> This is the excellent foppery of the world, that, when we are sick in for-
> tune, often the surfeit of our own behavior, we make guilty of our disasters
> the sun, the moon, and the stars; . . . An admirable evasion of whore-master
> man, to lay his goatish disposition to the charge of a star! (1.2.109–12,
> 116–17)

Roland and Lear, then, both unwittingly shape the setting to reflect their own inner consciousness.

The landscape in both works also functions as a locale for a rite of passage, an initiation for both Roland and Lear as they learn to go beyond themselves "by acts of sympathetic imagination" to a sense of "the intrinsic nature of inanimate objects" (Shaw 1968, 129). On this route, Lear's empathy shifts from the inert landscape to various animals, and then, finally, to other human beings. The king sees in the storm another person who resembles himself or one of his family. Yet Lear sympathizes with and forgives the storm's fury, because he never "gave [it] kingdom" nor "called [it] children" (*King Lear* 3.2.16). Therefore, the storm "owe[s]" Lear "no subscription" as daughters do (line 17). Indeed, Lear's daughters seem even less worthy than beasts, as Lear at least feels some identification with animals. He states, for instance, that "[m]an's life's as cheap as beast's" (2.4.262), and compares "unaccommodated man" to a "poor, bare, forked animal" (3.4.98–100). Eventually, when Lear totters toward insanity, he himself becomes, in essence, like "a beast, that wants discourse of reason" (*Hamlet* 1.2.150) and wanders madly on the heath. Finally, Lear learns to sympathize with others, including Kent and the Fool. In the hovel scene, for instance, Lear invites others to go in first. "Prithee, go in thyself," he says to Kent, "seek thine own ease" (*King Lear* 3.4.24). Lear then turns to the Fool, asserting, "In, boy. . . . You houseless poverty— / Nay get thee in" (lines 27–28). As the two precede him into the shelter, Lear remains alone on the heath, prayerfully proclaiming the words that signify his epiphany: "O, I have ta'en / Too little care of" others less fortunate (lines 33–34).

Roland goes through a similar progress toward selfless empathy, an initiation signaled in part by the title of "Childe," bestowed on a young warrior awaiting knighthood. His journey also begins through an identification with inanimate objects, which he endows with human characteristics: the "[d]esperate" earth ("Childe Roland," line 147), the "blotches" of soil that look like "boils" (lines 151, 153), which might recall Lear's descriptions of his daughters as "boil[s], and "embossed carbuncle[s]" (*King Lear* 2.4.218–19). Even the "willows" growing by the "wrath[ful] . . . black eddy" on Roland's path seem to fling themselves, like a "suicidal throng," downward "in a fit / Of mute despair" ("Childe Roland," lines 117, 113–14, 117–18). Roland's empathy at this point grows so strong that even the animals take on human qualities. The "water-rat['s]" cry (line 125) sounds "like a baby's shriek" (line 126), while the "stiff blind horse" is full of "grotesqueness" and "woe" (lines 76, 82). By the end of the journey, Roland himself feels hunted like an animal, caught as "when a trap shuts [and] you're inside the den!" (line 174). Roland achieves a level of sympathy comparable to that of Lear when he recalls other humans, addressing them with understanding in spite of their failures and dishonor. Roland recalls "all the lost adventurers my peers," and remembers "[h]ow such a one was strong, and such was bold" (lines 195–96). Like Lear, Roland sympathizes with the precarious nature of the human condition.

On the most literal level, the "dark tower" in Edgar's song probably represents Gloucester's castle, where evil lurks after Lear's banishment to the heath. The lines may also suggest Edgar's fear of death, if he, as Gloucester's "child," returns home. In addition, the lines foreshadow the bloody blinding of Gloucester by Cornwall and Regan two scenes later. As Cornwall plucks out the "vile jelly" of Gloucester's eyes, the blind man becomes a "dark and comfortless" tower who is expelled from his own castle, condemned to "smell / His way to Dover" (*King Lear* 3.7.88, 96–97). Certainly Edgar's lines express the potential for numerous dangers on the path to enlightenment. The dark tower, which is at once (in Shakespeare) the father Gloucester and (in Browning) the goal of Roland's quest, may symbolize the conflation of inanimate and human. In reaching the tower, Childe Roland reaches the state of complete empathy that both Lear and Edgar have achieved before him.

Roland also shares other important characteristics with Edgar. Both are solitary figures, who feel betrayed by those they trusted, but continue on in spite of this difficulty. In Edgar's case, his "foolish honesty" allows his half-brother Edmund's deceitful "practices" to "ride" casily upon him (*King Lear* 1.2.165–66). Roland feels betrayed by former members of his band: Cuthbert, whose "one night's disgrace" leads to his ruin, and Giles, a "traitor, spit upon and curst!" ("Childe Roland," lines 95, 102). And this duplicity, in turn, makes them feel like outcasts, both literally and symbolically. Edgar has been sentenced to death for his alleged attempts on his father's life, and he disguises himself as a bedlam beggar, feeling like one of the "lowest and most dejected thing[s] of fortune" (*King Lear* 4.1.3). Roland also finds himself alone, like a "sick man very near to death," who feels alienated from and unable to communicate with his former friends ("Childe Roland," line 25).Yet, both endure to the end of the quest in spite of the solitary nature of their respective journeys. As Edgar proclaims at the end of *Lear*, "[m]en must endure / Their going hence, even as their coming hither" (5.2.9–10), and Roland, despite the "starved ignoble nature" ("Childe Roland," line 56) of the setting and his pursuit, eventually finds the Dark Tower. Even Browning seems to have endorsed this idea, for he agreed with another correspondent who suggested that the theme of the poem was "he that endureth to the end shall be saved."[15]

Browning appropriates from Shakespeare one final element often neglected in discussions of both *Lear* and "Childe Roland," that of dark humor. As C. C. Clarke contends, in both works nature "is both fool and fooler" (Clarke 1962, 327). When in Browning's work, for instance, the "hoary cripple" breaks into a "skull-like laugh," the poet warns the reader of impending comic potential ("Childe Roland," lines 2, 10). Throughout the poem, Roland's hyperbolic descriptions border on the grotesquely comic, as he emphatically declares, "[N]othing throve: / For flowers—as well expect a cedar grove!" (lines 56–57). In a wasteland such as this, he continues, a "burr had been a treasure-trove" (line 60). The reliance on exaggeration pushes the descriptions to the limits of reality and tragic seriousness. There is even something slightly comic in the description of the "drenched willows," in unison flinging themselves "headlong in a fit / Of mute despair" (lines 117–18). As he nears the end of the journey, Roland realizes that some mischievous prankster, or "some trick of mischief," has pulled an elaborate practical joke on him, when he hears the "click" of the "trap" and feels caught "inside the den" (line 174). Two stanzas later, we bear witness to the object of the journey, the "Tower itself / . . . blind as the fool's heart" (lines 181–82), presided over by the "tempest's mocking elf" (line 184). In these last lines, one can see Browning's signpost back to the humor in *Lear*, specifically that of the Fool. The collocation of the terms "blind" and "fool" reminds us of Lear's inability to see and the complete contrast with the Fool's clear sight.

The conclusion of Browning's poem returns us to the title and the beginning of his journey. As Roland reaches the "Dark Tower," he hears "toll[ing] / . . . like a bell" the "[n]ames in [his] ears / Of all the lost adventurers [his] peers" (lines 193–95), and in this "one moment knelled the woe of years" (line 198). As the images of his former companions are "ranged along the hill-sides," creating a "living frame," Roland declares, "I saw them and I knew them all" (lines 199, 202). Roland describes the Tower as "blind as the fool's heart" (line 182) echoing, perhaps, the biblical passage the "fool hath said in his heart, / 'There is no God'" (Ps. 14:1–2). Anne Williams's characterization of Roland as "the archetypal 'wise fool' who is wiser than he knows" (Williams 1983, 40) leads us once more back to *King Lear* and the wise Fool in the play who knows much more than the "blind" Lear or Gloucester. The impossibility of a single interpretation may be suggested by Roland's lines preceding the conclusion, when the speaker seems to challenge the reader: "[S]olve it, you!" ("Childe Roland," line 167). Still, the blowing of Roland's horn recalls the scene in act 5 of *Lear* in which Edgar appears on the "third sound of the trumpet" (5.3.113) to reclaim his real identity and to triumph over his evil brother Edmund in battle. Further, Roland's lines "I saw them and I knew them all" ("Childe Roland," line 202), coming as they do in the last stanza, signal a new perspective, whether it be the recognition of death or the emergence of a new empathy with mankind, or both. In "Childe Roland" Browning achieves a dramatic vision of an objective Shakespeare that he helped to construct.

Although Browning's assertion that "Childe Roland came upon me as a kind of dream" sounds suspiciously like other poets' claims, such as Coleridge's assertion about the impetus for *Kubla Khan,* the second part of Browning's quote is even more revealing. He proclaims that he "had to write it, then and there," and "finished it the same day" (qtd. in DeVane 1955, 229). The description of his own quest to finish the poem deliberately echoes Shakespeare's line from *The Tempest* (a play from which he will substantially borrow soon), which describes life as "such stuff / As dreams are made on, and our little life / Is rounded with a sleep" (4.1.156–58). Not only literary composition but also life may be no more than a mere dream, or in Childe Roland's case, a disturbing nightmare. In focusing on Childe Roland's replication of Lear's journey from blindness to self-knowledge, Browning's poem concentrates on the drama of "men among men," prefiguring a strain of humanist criticism that focuses on the heroic journey toward enlightenment of Shakespeare's "great" tragic heroes.[16] Only a hint of the unconscious, the nightmare recognition of life's insubstantial status, disturbs the careful and complete delineation of Roland's quest and growing awareness of the human condition. The relation between the objective poet's subordination to the world and the subjective poet's assertion of self coheres less smoothly, ironically enough, in the later poem "Caliban."

A second way to evoke Shakespearean authority and still ward off charges of influence is to write what today would be called a prequel. Long before materialist and post-colonialist critics attended to his situation, "Caliban upon Setebos" portrays the Caliban of Shakespeare's *The Tempest* in the moments before the play begins. Therefore, Browning inverts the idea of literary authority by turning Shakespeare into Browning's literary heir. The intertextual struggle between poem and play not only concerns the "evolutionary creature" Caliban but also demonstrates the evolution of Robert Browning as a poet. As Harold Bloom argued in his earlier theoretical phase, a poet "'completes' his precursor" by borrowing from the "parent-poem," but then altering or extending the meaning "as though the precursor had failed to go far enough" (Bloom 1973, 14). Hence, Browning ups the ante by "completing" Caliban, transforming the creature to reflect the poet's own ideas.

When Browning selected Caliban as the protagonist for his prequel in the late 1850s, Shakespeare's character had recently undergone a significant transformation in literary criticism as well as stage portrayals. Until the 1830s, Caliban was almost always performed as a nasty, rather brutish monster, with few or no redeeming qualities. Some romantic critics, however, began to soften the creature's rough edges. Hazlitt claimed, for instance, that Caliban was "one of the wildest and most abstracted of all Shakespear's characters, whose deformity whether of body or mind is redeemed by the power and truth of the imagination displayed in it" (Hazlitt 1818, 118). Moreover, according to Hazlitt, Shakespeare "makes the strange monster amiable" by creating this "savage with the simplicity of a child" (120). And measured against Stephano and Trinculo, Caliban even "acquires a classical dignity in the comparison" (117). One year later, Hazlitt went even further in a lecture, taking a "more political view of Caliban, arguing that he, not Prospero, was the legitimate ruler of the island" (Vaughan and Vaughan 1991, 104). Hazlitt's analysis, then, begins a process that questions Prospero's right to hold an indigenous island creature in bondage. Indeed, Jonathan Bate argues that Hazlitt was "the first to read *The Tempest* in terms of imperialism," since he was one of the leading critics to challenge Prospero's dominance over Caliban and the island itself (Bate 1989, 144).

William Macready's 1838 production of *The Tempest* also followed the lead of the romantics by characterizing Caliban as primitive but dignified. Patrick MacDonnell, who reviewed the play, wrote that this new portrayal of Caliban "arouses our sympathies," because it clearly depicts Caliban as an oppressed victim. Caliban, MacDonnell continues, represents "a creature in his nature possessing all the rude elements of the savage, yet maintaining in his mind, a strong resistance to that tyranny," so much so that in Macready's production, Caliban elicits our "pity more than our detestation" (MacDonnell 1840, 16–19). It is possible that MacDonnell's charity toward a creature held in "slavery" grew out of an increasing awareness of the evils of slavery publicized by the growing abolitionist movement in England and the United States. Caliban's captivity also associates him with slaves, particularly with victims of colonial oppression.

Both Robert Browning and Elizabeth Barrett Browning had close ties to the West Indies and strong feelings about Britain's colonial venture there. (There have been repeated attempts to make either Browning or Barrett descendants of black, Jewish, or Creole heritage, and although some scholars call these assumptions "logically unsound and morally vacuous," no final consensus has been reached [Maynard 1977, 394 n. 1]). At the age of twenty, Robert Browning's father went to the West Indies "where his mother's family had plantation holdings on the island of St. Kitts," some eight hundred miles east of Jamaica (23); it is clear that Robert Browning Sr. was to have a hand in the management of the colonial enterprise. The father, however, was repelled by the whole notion of colonialism as well as the slave trade that supported it. Robert Browning, the poet, would later write to Elizabeth that his father "'conceived such a hatred to the slave-system in the West-Indies' . . . that he relinquished every prospect" of advancement or gain there (Browning 1969, 2:1005–6). Barrett Browning was also extremely concerned about the issue of slavery, as E.B.B.'s family owned plantations in Jamaica as well. Further, Barrett Browning published works on the topic of slavery, including "The Runaway Slave at Pilgrim's Point," composed in 1846 and first published in 1848, and "A Curse for a Nation" published in 1860.[17] Browning's Caliban absorbs these cultural charges that were transforming Shakespeare's creature, and his Caliban, in turn, becomes a much more agreeable creation, as we are allowed to see colonization through the oppressed's instead of the oppressor's eyes. Once we sympathize with Browning's more sophisticated Caliban, Browning's mission of appropriation has begun. Without specific physical descriptions to limit our imagination, Browning's Caliban grows more and more human. Just as Caliban creates Setebos in his own image, so readers create Caliban in theirs. It is here, then, that we see the contest of wills, with Browning trying to wrest control of Caliban and the poem from the overbearing presence of "Shakespeare the Playwright" by characterizing his Caliban as a more sympathetic and more topically interesting creature than Shakespeare's creation.

A second influence on Browning's composition, and one that would also add to his empathetic reading of Caliban, comes from Charles Darwin's *On the Origin of Species* (1859). The notion of the "missing link" suggested by Darwin's work was being constantly debated by intellectuals during the time Browning was composing the poem, and Browning's conception of Caliban seems to borrow from the anthropomorphism championed by writers such as Theodore Parker, a writer Browning probably read (Melchiori 1992, 104). Parker argued:

> A man rude in spirit must have a rude conception of God. . . . If a buffalo had a religion, his conception of deity would probably be a buffalo, fairer limbed, stronger, and swifter than himself. . . . (qtd. in Melchiori 1992, 100)

Parker's ideas suggest that any creature, even a "missing link," would create a god in his or her own image. A creature such as this would seem much more human, and therefore, more sympathetic. This "missing link" Caliban also gained currency in stage productions. For instance, in Charles Kean's 1857 production at the Princess's Theatre, Caliban is covered with "bushy brown fur," and exhibiting "long toenails and fingernails," demonstrates that the "era of the apish Caliban had begun" (Vaughan 1992, 199).

Significantly, stage portrayals such as Macready's (1838) and Kean's (1857) may have influenced Browning's characterization of Caliban. Although there is no direct evidence that Browning witnessed the productions, he had a close relationship with Macready, and, as we saw earlier, he wrote *Colombe's Birthday* for Kean. Browning, therefore, would have been aware of their stage interpretations, particularly since he was composing a poem on the same subject. The more important point, however, is that Browning elects himself to re-create and further the evolution of Shakespeare's character. In this way, Browning gains the authority of Shakespeare's past significance and combines that with the current cultural meaning in order to create a more complex character.

Browning endows his Caliban with a sophistication lacking, as he saw it, in Shakespeare's original conception. Browning portrays Caliban as an evolving creature whose idea of God/Setebos—like the reader's, perhaps—is evolving as well. In Shakespeare's play, Caliban learned language from Miranda, who "pitied" him, and took "pains to make [him] speak, taught [him] each hour / One thing or other" (*The Tempest* 1.2.356, 357–58). Shakespeare's Caliban acknowledges her role in his acquisition of language, admitting that he was taught "how / To name the bigger light, and how the less, / That burn by day and night" (lines 337–39), but concludes angrily, "You taught me language, and my profit on't / Is I know how to curse" (lines 366–67). In Browning's version, Caliban also learns speech from his masters, but employs it to contemplate the nature of Setebos, "whom his dam called God" ("Caliban upon Setebos," line 16). These thoughts bother Caliban, however, "[b]ecause to talk about Him, vexes" (line 17).

While the confusing nature of language is highlighted here, it is clear that Browning's Caliban uses his language in a more philosophical—and, by extension, more profitable—manner than Shakespeare's Caliban. Browning's Caliban exclaims that now, "[w]hen talk is safer than in winter-time" (line 19), he will allow "the rank tongue [to] blossom into speech" (line 23). Moreover, his words reflect his sophisticated description of the isle, as well as the "sea which sunbeams cross / And recross till they weave a spider-web" (line 12–13). Although Shakespeare imparts some poetical language to his Caliban, Browning's creature employs language to contemplate existence rather than to curse his captors. Perhaps Browning's appropriation also cheats Shakespeare out of his mastery, just as Caliban finds it "good to cheat the pair" of Miranda and Prospero (line 22).

The question of "mastery" remains one of the fundamental issues in *The Tempest;* authoritative control also plays an important role in Browning's relationship to Shakespeare. The first scene of the first act of the play raises this central question when the mariners on Alonso's ship cry out, "What cares these roarers for the name of king?" (1.1.15–16). In both works, authority and submission are constantly called into question, and the tension between Shakespeare's Caliban and Browning's Caliban reflects the intertextual struggle for dominance in poem and play, and the interpretive control in both remains complicated.

As recent critics have increasingly read Shakespeare's Caliban as a sympathetic victim of colonization, we should also consider the implications of the connection between playwright and colonizer, an implication that also fits appropriating poets such as Browning. Terence Hawkes cleverly connects colonists and playwrights:

> A colonist acts essentially as a dramatist. He imposes the "shape" of his own culture, *embodied in his speech*, on the new world, and makes that world recognizable, habitable, "natural," able to speak his language. (Hawkes 1973, 211)

Looking at it from the other direction, "the dramatist is metaphorically a colonist. His art penetrates new areas of experience, his language expands the boundaries of our culture, and makes the new territory over in its own image" (212). One might argue, then, that Browning is "colonizing" Shakespeare by taking control of Shakespeare's island and re-creating creatures such as Caliban who reside there. Further complicating this idea is the role of the reader. In other words, "[i]f reading makes any difference at all, an author does not guarantee conclusive meaning" because reading "is partially mastery and partially conformity" (Dupras 1986, 81, 77). The reader, therefore, like the Caliban of either work, is caught between dominance and submission in interpreting the poem's "meaning."

If the poem is on one level about "man's inveterate tendency to create God in his own image" (Loucks 1979, 252), it is worth exploring how Browning reshapes Shakespeare in his (Browning's) own image. The poem catches this notion in a number of places as Browning projects on to Caliban his own awe in the presence of Shakespeare. In this reading, where Browning stands for Caliban, Shakespeare is not only a Prospero but also a Setebos. Like Shakespeare who produces all types of worlds in his plays, Setebos also "made . . . the sun, this isle, / Trees and the fowls here, beast and creeping thing" ("Caliban upon Setebos," lines 44–45). Caliban also recalls the creativity of Setebos, who, like Shakespeare, "[m]akes this a bauble-world to ape yon real" (line 147). Further, Caliban/Browning concludes that Shakespeare/Setebos "made all these and more, / Made all we see, and us" (lines 55–56). (If this argument sounds far-fetched, we only need to think of Harold Bloom's recent book where he claims that "Shakespeare invented the human as we continue to know it" [Bloom 1998, xviii].) Perhaps these lines also suggest Browning's struggle with his predecessor. Caliban admits that while Shakespeare/Setebos "could not, Himself, make a second self" because he may "as well have made Himself," the deity could have in "sport" made a lesser poet: "Weaker in most points, stronger in a few, / Worthy, and yet mere playthings all the while, / Things he admires and mocks too" ("Caliban upon Setebos," lines 57, 58, 63–65). This, of course, leads to a Caliban who "strives hard" but "always, above all else, envies Him" (lines 264–65). Yet Browning continues to resist this impulse by re-creating Prospero's island.

Like Caliban, who "[p]lays thus at being Prosper in a way" (line 168), Browning plays at being Shakespeare. Browning's "Caliban upon Setebos," which concerns the evolution of man, also reveals the evolution of an appropriating poet, Robert Browning. Even the epigraph for the poem may reveal Browning's anxiety about appropriating Shakespeare: "Thou thoughtest that I was altogether such a one as thyself" might signal the reader that Browning is confronting his dominant predecessor, addressing those who might believe that Browning is "altogether such a one as" Shakespeare. While the epigraph obviously works on numerous levels, including, of course, the biblical one, as an intertext with Shakespeare's play, it may respond to the prior, powerful authority of Shakespeare. Whatever the case, Browning considered the epigraph an essential part of the poem. For example, in the collected edition of 1868, editors omitted the epigraph; but "when Browning's attention was called to it by Mr. T. J. Wise, he said it was a mistake and the edition of 1889 restored the motto, which helps to a comprehension of the poem" (DeVane 1955, 299). Before the poem even begins, then, Browning hints at the issue of appropriation.

Browning's second method of mitigating influence, therefore, is to write a prequel to Shakespeare's play, and to replace Prospero with Caliban. This move allows the auditor to "see" through Caliban's eyes, the goal of the "objective" poet, and to sympathize with a creature held captive against his will. At the same time, however, Browning competes with Shakespeare: If Caliban is as much a philosopher as Prospero, then perhaps Browning, the poet whose empathy transforms Caliban into an intelligent being, is superior to Shakespeare in his understanding. In this way, Browning also insists on his own "genius," the hallmark of the "subjective" poet. Although intellectually Browning is committing himself to dramatic poetry, the influence of the same romantic models that inform Bloom's account of literary influence have their place in Browning's relation to Shakespeare.

THE SHAKESPEAREANIZATION OF ROBERT BROWNING

Although a somewhat muted reception greeted "Childe Roland" and the other poems collected in *Men and Women* (1855), a shift in critical response at this time demonstrates Browning's successful appropriation of Shakespeare and his cultural authority. Following the publication of *Men and Women,* Browning's name was often evoked with Shakespeare's by the critics as well as by Browning himself. Some reviewers even began to equate Browning's art with Shakespeare's. Defending Browning against the charge of "obscurity," William Morris writes: "Now, I know well enough what [the critics] mean by 'obscure,' and I know also that they use the word wrongly; meaning difficult to understand fully at first reading, or, say at second reading, even: yet, taken so, in what cloud of obscurity would 'Hamlet' be!" (Morris 1856, 172). Defending Browning's alleged obscurity by yoking it with the "obscurity" of the author of *Hamlet*, Morris establishes the movement to Shakespeareanize Browning, and even restates his thesis again in the conclusion of the review: "Yes, I wonder what the critics would have said to 'Hamlet Prince of Denmark,' if it had been first published by Messrs. Chapman and Hall in the year 1855" (172).

John Forster, friend to both Browning and Dickens, while admitting some obscurity, also attempted to defend Browning against the charge. Arguing that "obscurity proceeds from fullness" and not "emptiness," Forster believes that the "perceptions of a poet, when applied to thoughts of more than common subtlety, will often necessarily outrun his reader's" (Forster 1855, 757). Other critics, such as George Eliot, also began to answer the charge of obscurity. Defending Browning in the *Westminster Review,* Eliot argues that in Browning's work, a reader "will find no conventionality, no melodious commonplace, but freshness, [and] originality" (Eliot 1856, 161). By employing "dramatic indication" to fashion a new form, instead of the "didactic laying-out of a subject," Browning's poetry represents a new poetic form (161). Some of the more perceptive critics, then, noticed Browning's attempt to dramatize his poetry, and Eliot concludes that reading Browning is well worth the effort:

> To read Browning [a reader] must exert himself, but he will exert himself to some purpose. If he finds the meaning difficult of access, it is always worth his effort—if he has to dive deep "he rises with his pearl." Indeed, in Browning's best poems he makes us feel that what we took for obscurity in him was superficiality in ourselves. (161)

Swinburne agreed, claiming that the charge of obscurity was "never mis-applied more persistently and perversely than to" Browning; he concludes that Browning was, in fact, "the reverse of obscure" and, in fact, "too brilliant and subtle" for many readers (Swinburne 1925d, 12:145). What Forster, Eliot, and Swinburne are intimating, of course, is that the true artist, say Browning or Shakespeare, is a more complicated thinker than most of his readers, and therefore perplexity should be expected, if not embraced.

In private, Browning also positioned himself as a misunderstood artist, an heir to other complex artists such as the creator of *Hamlet*. In a letter to John Ruskin (10 December 1855), Browning first defends his lack of critical acclaim, stating, "A poet's affair is with God,—to whom he is accountable, and of whom is his reward; look elsewhere and you find misery enough" (qtd. in Woolford and Karlin 1996, 258). Then Browning participates in his own Shakespeareanization:

> Do you believe people understand *Hamlet?* The last time I saw it acted, the heartiest applause of the night went to a little by-play of the actor's own—who, to simulate madness in a hurry, plucked forth his handkerchief and flourished it hither and thither: certainly a third of the play, with no end of noble things, had been (as from time immemorial) suppressed, with the auditory's amplest acquiescence and benediction. (258)

Browning, therefore, as well as critics such as Morris, Eliot, and Forster, begins to position the poet as a Victorian Shakespeare—objective, dramatic, and, like Shakespeare, difficult to comprehend on occasion.

In favorable reviews, poems such as "Caliban" were also used to demonstrate Browning's relationship to Shakespeare. The *Athenaeum*, which had not exactly been Browning's ally in the past, wrote that "Caliban" is a "striking example" of Browning's creativity. Adding that the "revelation of what 'Caliban' 'thinketh' would have delighted Shakspeare himself," the reviewer concedes that "[o]nly a great dramatic poet could have written this poem" (Review of *Dramatis Personae* 1864, 766). Twenty-six years later, Oscar Wilde fashioned a similar connection between Browning and Shakespeare. Contending that Browning created "men and women that live" from "ignoble clay," Wilde proclaims that Browning "is the most Shakespearian creature since Shakespeare" and "from the point of view of a creator of character [Browning] ranks next to him who made Hamlet" (Wilde 1890, 127). Unlike Shelley, Browning writes dramatically about real "men and women." In his irrepressible manner, Wilde also adds: "If Shakespeare could sing with myriad lips, Browning could stammer through a thousand mouths" (127). The equation between Browning and Shakespeare confirms Browning's successful positioning of himself in the Shakespearean poetic line.

Ironically, the private Browning began to chafe at the invasion of privacy brought on by the enormity of his success, an accomplishment due in great measure to his effective Shakespearean appropriation.[18] In the poem "House" we see Browning's new use of Shakespeare, this time to defend rather than to extend his public image. It appears that Browning, like many artists, desired the recognition of others, but disdained the attendant celebrity. In one of his last appropriations of Shakespeare, Browning returns to the theme of the "Essay on Shelley," arguing that Shakespeare is the central dramatic and objective poet; more importantly, in this same poem, Browning seems to identify himself with Shakespeare completely. As John Maynard points out, "on the rare occasion when he used a poet as an image for himself," such as in the poem "House," it was "Shakespeare, not Shelley, with whom Browning would identify" (Maynard 1977, 232). To the degree Browning successfully redefined himself as the objective poet, relinquishing the ambitions of the romantic, subjective poet who wanted to supplant Shakespeare as a literary authority, he achieved greater resemblance to Shakespeare and gained greater cultural authority.

In "House" (1876), Browning denounces subjective poetry such as that of the romantics, while maintaining a poet's right to privacy. Although James F. Loucks detects in this poem a "rather shrill defense of the author's right to privacy" (Loucks 1979, 415 n. 1), I believe instead that the poem emphasizes Browning's choice of Shakespeare as his poetic model at the expense of his Shelleyan connection; this alignment would culminate in Browning's refusal to preside over F. J. Furnivall's Shelley Society and willingness to accept the presidency of the New Shakspere Society, a decision that further distanced him professionally and personally from Swinburne's more radical aesthetics.[19]

The idea that a house could provide important clues about the author's state of mind finds its comically exaggerated conclusion in Browning's poem. Employing the image of the open house on display for all to see, Browning asks:

> Shall I sonnet-sing you about myself?
>   Do I live in a house you would like to see?
> Is it scant of gear, has it store of pelf?
>   "Unlock my heart with a sonnet-key?"
>
> ("House," lines 1–4)

In the last line of this first stanza, Browning paraphrases Wordsworth's poem, "Scorn not the Sonnet," which chastises those critics who have "frowned" on the sonnet form, "[m]indless of its just honours" (lines 1–2).[20] Yet Wordsworth, like many romantic poets, believed that the sonnet was the "key" with which "Shakespeare unlocked his heart" (lines 2–3). In "House," however, Browning continues to resist the pull of confessional poetry, wondering whether he should "[i]nvite the world, as [his] betters have done" to view his "private apartment and bedroom too" (lines 5, 8). "No," he responds, "thanking the public, [he] must decline" (line 10). While he may grant "a peep through [his] window, if folk prefer," Browning pleads for his privacy: "But, please you, no foot over threshold of mine!" (lines 11–12). This disturbing image of the author's life laid bare obviously troubled Browning, and the poem articulates his plea for personal privacy.

Browning begins the conclusion of "House" by again paraphrasing Wordsworth: "'*With this same key / Shakespeare unlocked his heart,*' once more!" (lines 38–39). In Wordsworth's poem, it was suggested that Shakespeare, like many other poets, had revealed himself in his sonnets. But Browning challenges Wordsworth's assertion, exclaiming, "Did Shakespeare? If so, the less Shakespeare he!" (line 40), for if Shakespeare were revealing himself, it would completely undermine Browning's depiction of Shakespeare as the dramatic, purely objective poet, one central argument in the "Essay on Shelley." It is clear that Browning stubbornly refused to equate Shakespeare with any romantic display of autobiographical poetry, particularly in relation to the sonnets.

The debate concerning the homoerotic quality of Shakespeare's sonnets began to intensify at about the same time as Browning's "House," and in part this debate compelled Browning's more ardent followers to begin disassociating Browning's image from Shakespeare's. The controversy had, however, been ongoing for some time. George Stevens, for example, writing on Sonnet 20 in the late eighteenth century, had claimed: "It is impossible to read this fulsome panegyrick, addressed to a male object, without an equal mixture of disgust and indignation" (qtd. in Pequigney 1985, 30). In the very same year that Browning was composing "House," other writers were delicately distancing both Robert and Elizabeth Barrett Browning's works from those of Shakespeare. As Tricia Lootens has convincingly argued, the Brownings' marriage came to be considered as a kind of corrective to troubling questions regarding sexuality in the last part of the nineteenth century (Lootens 1996).[21] While Browning resisted the biographical reading of Shakespeare's sonnets—"if so, the less Shakespeare he"— Browning's contemporaries began to promote him as a more masculine and sanitized bard than Shakespeare himself.

Browning's appropriation of Shakespeare granted him such cultural authority that he began to crowd Shakespeare himself at the center of the English literary canon. A final example of the success of Browning's Shakespearean appropriation concerns his appointment to the presidency of the New Shakspere Society in 1879, three years after "House" was published, and one year before Swinburne's attack. A year later, F. J. Furnivall, the founder of the New Shakspere Society, joined Emily Hickey to found the Browning Society.

The society's prospectus carefully explains its purpose: "This society is founded to gather some, at least, of the many admirers of ROBERT BROWNING, for the study and discussion of his works, and the publication of Papers on them, and extracts from works illustrating them" (Browning Society [1881–84] 1966, 1:19). Following these statements, the initial shaping of Browning's new status as the Victorian bard begins. After the writers of the prospectus cite a paragraph-long analysis by Professor Spalding on Shakespeare, they immediately begin to outline similarities between the two poets, claiming that Browning possesses not only the same "leading note" as Shakespeare—which Spalding defines as "a spirit of active and inquiring thought" that can be seen "on every object which comes under his notice"—but that Browning also enjoys an "imagination [that] is active, powerfully and unceasingly" (19). In addition, both Shakespeare and Browning possess an "'active and piercing understanding'" (19). The prospectus concludes that Browning is "profound enough in thought, noble enough in character and feeling, eloquent and interesting enough in expression, to deserve more thorough study, and a far wider circle of readers, than he has yet had" (20). The justification for Browning's ascendancy to Shakespearean status had now begun in earnest.

Throughout the Society's existence, Shakespeare and his works are almost always the primary touchstones for measuring Browning's achievement, and there are comments comparing both on the topics of reason, thought, and characterization. Yet the Society goes one step further in the process of appropriation by elevating Browning *above* Shakespeare, because, for them, Browning is not only more religious in belief than Shakespeare but also more masculine in his writing. The "Introductory Address" for the first meeting of the Browning Society, given by the Rev. J. Kirkman at University College, London, formalizes the effort to Shakespeareanize Browning. Kirkman proclaims that "Browning is undoubtedly the profoundest intellect, with widest range of sympathies, and with universal knowledge of men and things, that has arisen as a poet since Shakespeare" (Browning Society [1881–84] 1966, 1:172). Adding that Browning's "truly Shakespearian genius pre-eminently shines in his power to throw his whole intellect and sympathies into the most diverse individualities" (172), Kirkman concludes that "Browning is our nearest to Shakespeare" (172). James Thomson, at the third meeting, puts Browning in the company of those who "have learned everything and forgotten nothing," including Chaucer, Shakespeare, and Goethe (239). At the eighth meeting, Hiram Corson, speaking on "The Idea of Personality," comments: "[T]he range of thought and passion which [Browning's poetry] exhibits is greater than that of any other poet, without a single exception, since the days of Shakspere" (293).

Another similarity between the two authors involves their portrayal of dramatic character. In the notes on Browning's poems contained in the Society bibliography for 1881, Furnivall suggests that Browning "culminated in characterization in that Second-Period work, as Shakspere did in his Second-Period *Henry IV*. But *Dramatis Personae* and *Ring and the Book* are greater than *Men and Women*, as *Hamlet* is greater than *Henry IV*" (Browning Society [1881–84] 1966, 1:157). At the twenty-fourth meeting, J. Cotter Morrison makes a number of connections between Shakespeare's Caliban and Browning's "Caliban upon Setebos." The forty-fourth meeting features a paper entitled "Browning's Jews and Shakespeare's Jews." Arthur Symons ponders the question "Is Browning Dramatic?" at the twenty-ninth meeting. In this essay, Symons makes a slight distinction between the two: "Shakspere makes his characters *live*; Browning makes his *think*" (2:6). A respondent disputes even this difference at the eighty-third meeting, arguing that Browning's characters are as "living and real as Richard II., or Hamlet," and further concludes that "Shakspere's characters seem quite as full of thought as any of the creations of Browning" (3:141).

More significantly, the Society attempted to distinguish the two poets from one another, usually at Shakespeare's expense. E. D. West, as early as the fifteenth meeting of the Browning Society, claimed that "Shakspere, innately a positivist, can let any phenomenon be to him as an ultimate fact, which he does not care to go beyond. Browning, born a speculator, cannot and will not forgo the attempt to get at what lies behind the visible things of the world's order" (1:417). Just as Browning's character Caliban had outshone Shakespeare's Prospero as a philosopher, Browning becomes even more philosophical than Shakespeare. In comparing the subjectivity of the two, according to W. A. Raleigh, one also sees a distinction: "If we try to form some idea of the personality of William Shakespere, we are checked, and find it difficult to get further than the characters of his creations" (1:479). On the other hand, "in trying to reach the personality of Browning," we get "a sense of personal acquaintance with him" (479). The author concludes that Browning's sympathy keeps this "intense subjectivism perfectly free from egotism" (479). Here perhaps we most clearly see the effect of the "Essay on Shelley," as Browning, at least for this critic, embodies the two kinds of poet, combining the dramatic poet with one who also gives us glimpses of his or her own nature. Therefore, Browning displays an ability to retain "subjectivism," although one free from egotism, even in the presence of Shakespearean "objectivity."

The Browning Society members considered religion to be a major difference between Shakespeare and Browning as well. Although the Society itself was composed of a wide range of members, including both "pious spinsters" and "militant agnostics" (Peterson 1969, 6), many of the members believed in Browning as a spiritual teacher. We note this religious fervor as early as the Society's inception, as the cofounder Hickey championed Browning "as a religious poet whose ethical teachings were of supreme value" (19). At a time of challenges to traditional Christianity, many writers, including Browning, became secular prophets. Some members clearly saw Browning as a means of salvation, or in one member's case, a means of rediscovering his faith. A Dr. Berdoe, who had dismissed Christianity after his medical training, later, while a member of the Society, found a reaffirmation of his faith through Browning's works. In his book on Browning, he wrote, "[T]he feeling came over me that in Browning I had found my religious teacher, one who could put me right on a hundred points which had troubled my mind for many years, and which ultimately caused me to abandon the Christian Faith" (Berdoe 1896, viii–ix). Even Browning's name was deified, as the Browningites always capitalized Browning's nickname: Master (Peterson 1969, 64), and the religiosity surrounding Browning played an important role in his literary canonization.

Obviously, Browning's cultural currency was taking on new value, becoming at the very least equal to Shakespeare's in some people's eyes. Most importantly, for the Browning Society and Victorian society at large, Browning came to represent a more decorous, less coarse Shakespeare, a Victorianized Bard. Shakespeare was a bit vulgar for some Victorian tastes. Emily Hickey, for example, read Browning's poetry in part because her father absolutely forbade her to read Shakespeare (Peterson 1969, 17). Unlike Shakespeare and his "unwholesome" sonnets, Browning and his works began to symbolize the perfect, "normal" heterosexual poet. Browning also became an antidote to the "femininity" of French writers and English poets such as A. C. Swinburne and the Pre-Raphaelite Brotherhood. Furnivall believed that a "poet should be strong, manly, unpretentious, and Browning was all these" (qtd. in Peterson 1969, 26). And Furnivall was not alone. Another prominent member of the Society, the poet James Thomson, had praised Browning as a poet "[w]ith a masculine soul for passion, a masculine intellect for thought, and a masculine genius for imagination" (Browning Society [1881–84] 1966, 1:247). Browning himself seems to have bought partly into this idea, and a letter to Isa Blagden proves particularly revealing:

> Yes,—I have read Rossetti's poems. . . . [Y]ou know I hate the effeminacy of his school,—the men that dress up like women, —that use obsolete forms, too, and archaic accentuations to seem soft. . . . Swinburne started this with other like Belialisms. (Browning 1951, 336)

Anxiety over homosexuality was beginning to spread in England at this time, and Browning, because of his highly publicized union with Elizabeth Barrett Browning, represented a safer, more traditional "saintly" poet than even Shakespeare.

By 1888, Browning societies in Britain and America were growing in popularity, sometimes at the expense of Shakespeare study groups. One writer in America observed that "the Shakespeare clubs have been gradually elbowed to the wall" by the Browning societies (Hersey 1890, 543). Browning's literary reputation was also "elbowing" Shakespeare out of the center of the Victorian literary canon. This movement resulted at least in part from Browning's appropriation of Shakespeare, which began with the "Essay on Shelley" and continued through the poem "House." As early as the "Introductory Address" to the Browning Society, Kirkman had stated that while Browning and Shakespeare were equal in thought and reason, "[i]n knowledge of many things [Browning] is necessarily superior as being the receptive child of the century of science and travel" (Browning Society [1881–84] 1966, 1:172). In essence, Browning's Shakespearean appropriation worked all too well. Like the sacred literary monument of Shakespeare, Browning was likewise sanctified as a poet-saint of England. By the close of the century, Browning became even more Shakespearean than Shakespeare himself, so that pseudoreligious Bardolatry gave way to an even more infectious "Browning Fever."

4

"An Eminently Practical Father": Dickens, *Hard Times,* and the Family

On a blustery day in January 1854, Charles Dickens sat in his room and composed a letter describing the "indescribable lassitude" of his oldest son, Charley. Addressed to his close friend Angela Burdett-Coutts, the letter complained that Charley was "not aspiring, or imaginative" and had "less fixed purpose and energy than I could have supposed possible in my son." He ends the letter by asking for her advice, and by voicing similar concerns about another son, Walter, whom he hoped would "do his duty steadily, anywhere" (Dickens 1965–, 7:245–46). Exactly two weeks later, Dickens traveled to Preston, Lancashire, to observe at first hand a strike by workers for a 10 percent increase in wages, an event on which he would draw in his next novel, *Hard Times.* Writing from Preston to his associate John Forster, Dickens noted a similar lassitude in the workers, who allegedly "sit at home and mope" instead of challenging the mill owners. He ends his letter in a lighter mood by describing some diversion from the dreariness: "At the theatre last night I saw *Hamlet,*" but due to the poor performance, Dickens concludes that he "should have done better to 'sit at home and mope' like the idle workmen" (7:261). These letters, I will argue, express central concerns in Dickens's life and career: the failure of his family to meet his expectations, his heightened sense of the dramatic, and his preoccupation with Shakespeare's works.

The "dramatic" quality of Dickens's novels is now a critical commonplace, and a number of critics have examined the relationship between Dickens and Shakespeare. Other recent scholarship has focused on Dickens's troubled marriage and domestic life vis-à-vis the sometimes idealized family found in many of his earlier novels.[1] No one, however, has considered the way these ideas intersect. What I will suggest is that in *Hard Times,* Dickens appropriates Shakespeare to portray the Gradgrind family, although

Dickens may be revealing much about his own troubled familial relationships as well. While arguing that Mr. Gradgrind represents a Polonius figure and that his two children, Tom and Louisa, resemble Laertes and Ophelia, respectively, I will also demonstrate that Dickens's actions during this time are also Polonius-like in many respects. The criticism Dickens levels at the "eminently practical" Gradgrind may be, ironically, applicable to Dickens's own shortcomings as a parent and husband.

Dickens's appropriation of Shakespeare is unique in one important way. Unlike Eliot, who negotiated between page and stage in her writing, Dickens accomplished this same feat literally by performing scenes from his novels on stage. He also acted and directed amateur theatrical companies, and George Henry Lewes, Eliot's companion, performed with him on a number of occasions; Browning attended and praised one of them. Like Swinburne and Eliot, Dickens also felt a tension between public and private life; unlike them, however, Dickens embraced his public performances in order to make up for failures in his private life.

DICKENS AND SHAKESPEARE ON THE STAGE

One might argue that Dickens wanted to rescue the Victorian stage nearly as much as he wished to rescue Victorian "fallen" women.[2] Aligning himself with George Henry Lewes, William Charles Macready, John Forster, and others, Dickens took up arms against a sea of talentless, melodramatic, and shabby productions. As James Redmond asserts, "Dickens played a leading role in the long, energetic attempt to reconnect the London stage with dramatic literature, and among his personal friends he acted out the conflicts that were central to the vigorous and at times violent debate" (Redmond 1989, 125).

One article in particular traces this fight to preserve the theater. Writing in 1851, Dickens points out how Sadler's Wells Theatre had recently had as "ruffianly an audience as London could shake together" (Dickens 1851, 25). The "Theatre, by night, was like the worst part of the worst kind of Fair in the worst kind of town," Dickens exclaimed. "Within, it was a bear-garden, resounding with foul language, oaths, catcalls, shrieks, yells, blasphemy, obscenity—a truly diabolical clamour" (25). Although appalled, Dickens conceded that under the more recent management of Samuel Phelps at least the melodramas had given way to Shakespeare. But even this charge was not enough to "rescue" the playhouse, where the players had to compete with a sideshow of audience distractions. Later in the same essay, Dickens provided this eyewitness account of a production of *Macbeth:*

[P]erformed amidst the *usual* hideous medley of fights, foul language, cat-calls, shrieks, yells, oaths, blasphemy, obscenity, apples, oranges, nuts, bis-cuits, ginger-beer, porter, and pipes. . . . Cans of beer, each with a pint measure to drink from . . . were carried through the dense crowd at all stages of the tragedy. Sickly children in arms were squeezed out of shape, in all parts of the house. Fish was fried at the entrance doors. Barricades of oyster-shells encumbered the pavement. (26, italics mine)

As the passage makes clear, Dickens considers this a *usual* occurrence at Sadler's Wells, compelling him to rail against such chaos in both print and public proclamations. Yet Dickens does grant some praise to Phelps for continuing to take measures to "purify" the theater by casting out the "friers of fish, vendors of oysters, and other costermonger-scum accumulated round the doors" (26). After the banishment of the "noisy sellers of beer," the "[c]hildren in arms were next to be expelled" to prevent the "shrill inter-ruptions consequent on the unrolling of dozens of these unfortunate little mummies" during the course of the plays (26).

Going on to detail step-by-step Phelps's success at purging the play-house of distractions, Dickens makes a number of observations that reveal his preference for the tidy page rather than the noisy stage. After a few seasons of predominantly Shakespearean productions, Sadler's Wells in 1851 was so orderly that Dickens is happy to report that even "[t]he pit . . . is constantly filled by respectable family visitors," and a father may sit "there with his wife and daughters, as quietly, as easily, as free from all offence, as in his own house" (Dickens 1851, 27). More importantly, the "audience have desired to show their appreciations of such care, and have studied the plays from the books, and have really come to the Theatre for their intellectual profit" (27). Perhaps even more telling is the language Dickens used in a public speech praising Phelps five years later, when he referred to the Sadler's Wells audience as an "intelligent and attentive . . . body of students" (Dickens 1960, 231). This movement to connect private family reading— and the attendant educational value—with public perfor-mance obviously functions for Dickens in a number of ways. Although at first glance it seems to negotiate between the page and stage, it ultimately tends to make a successful dramatic Shakespeare dependent on an initial studentlike encounter with the playwright on the page. It also elevates read-ing aloud at home to a reproduction of a drama. Because so many families read aloud from both Shakespeare and Dickens, this maneuver by the Vic-torian author makes him, in effect, a kind of nineteenth-century Shake-speare.[3]

Dickens established a second front to restore the stage by managing, organizing and appearing in amateur theatrical productions. We know, for example, that as early as 1833, Dickens both produced and acted in a three-play production entitled *Private Theatricals*. Twelve years later, we have both playbills and portraits of Dickens's performance in Ben Jonson's *Every Man in His Humour* (see illustrations 36 and 37 in Kaplan 1988). In this particular production, the participants, including Forster, divided the ten-pound cost among themselves. Performed in front of an invitation-only crowd of some five hundred spectators, the play was praised by prominent audience members such as Tennyson and Browning. In between these events, Dickens acted and promoted many onstage enterprises. On occasion, his interest in the theater, Shakespeare, and charity all merged, as when his amateur acting troupe, now christened the "Society of Amateurs," expanded their repertoire to include *The Merry Wives of Windsor*. Performing in Liverpool, Edinburgh, and Glasgow, the company earmarked the proceeds to fund a down-on-his luck author and to install him as the newly created director for the Shakespeare museum in Stratford; Sheridan Knowles became the first recipient (Kaplan 1988, 233). We also know that Dickens composed, directed, and acted in an Irish burlesque of *Othello*, which he entitled the *O'Thello*. In fact, his amateur acting/directing career even earns its own chapter in a number of scholarly monographs, such as Valerie Gager's *Shakespeare and Dickens: The Dynamics of Influence*.

DICKENS AND SHAKESPEARE ON THE PAGE

Dickens was particularly concerned with the production of his beloved Shakespeare, and perhaps because of his veneration for the Bard, we are on safe ground in asserting that he reproduced Shakespeare more often on the page in his novels than on the stage. This would accord with the romantic notions of inwardness and the trend, according to Jonathan Arac, initiated by Coleridge and Hazlitt.[4] Dickens was also an associate of the English translator of Schlegel and other romantics, including Charles Lamb, who also championed this shift in critical thinking.

Dickens's esteem for Shakespeare's texts is evidenced in a number of ways. As Dickens prospered, he began to collect valuable Shakespearean editions. G. H. Lewes, who first visited Dickens's home around 1839, had been depressed to find the library filled with "nothing but three-volume novels and books of travel . . . with none of the treasures of the bookstall" (Lewes 1961, 70). In 1841 when Lewes made another visit, however, he was pleased to discover that "the three-volume novel no longer vulgarised the place; a goodly array of standard works, well-bound, showed a more respectable and conventional ambition" (70). One of these works was an edition of Malone's *Plays and Poems* edited by James Boswell the younger, and published posthumously in 1821. We know that Dickens was particularly proud of this acquisition, for he also wrote in 1841 to the scholar John Payne Collier, founder of the Shakespeare Society (1840–53): "I am the proprietor," Dickens boasts, "of a Boswell's Malone" (Dickens 1965–, 2:433). This was, of course, not the only edition he owned. In a letter to John Forster the next year, Dickens reports that his talisman while on his tour of America had been a copy of the playwright's works: "I constantly carry in my great-coat pocket," he writes, "the *Shakespeare* you bought for me in Liverpool. What an unspeakable source of delight that book is to me!" (3:165). He also owned copies of Shakespearean criticism by Hazlitt, Lamb, Johnson, and others.

As most readers and critics are aware, many of Dickens's works draw from Shakespeare, an author whose works he revered second only to the Bible. Gager's work is helpful here again, as she produces an appendix over one hundred pages long, citing references, allusions, parodies, and so on in nearly all of Dickens's novels, and she includes a detailed discussion of *Dombey and Son* and *David Copperfield*. Some critics see David Copperfield as a Hamlet-like protagonist, a distinction also conferred on the title character of *Little Dorrit*. While a few of these connections are more tenuous than others, perhaps we "must take the fat with the lean," as a character in *David Copperfield* asserts (Dickens 1962, 729).[5] Other writers, of course, comment on the echoes of *Hamlet* in *Great Expectations*, including Edward Said, who deconstructs the *Hamlet* production viewed by Pip. Countering those who see Dickens's retelling as merely parodic, Said claims that Dickens's "montage" exposes the "venerated masterpiece to its own vulnerability," allowing this "monument" of literature to produce a number of variant readings (Said 1983, 198). Said astutely concludes that "each time [*Hamlet*] is performed the performance is a substitute for the original," and in this instance the "old and the new can cohabit," because "Dickens puts the two together and lets them happen together in his text" (198–99). On the one hand, we find Dickens stuffily asserting reverence for the Bard; on the other, he challenges that very authority in his texts, collapsing the distinction between highbrow and popular culture, a division that would also affect his decision to perform public readings of his novels. One work, however, that particularly speaks to connections not only between texts, but also between text and context, is his mid-Victorian novel, *Hard Times*. Due to its time of composition as much as its subject matter, this is the text that speaks most clearly to Shakespeare, Dickens, and the family.

"An Eminently Practical Father": *Hard Times*

Although some critics have noted the connection between *Hard Times* and Shakespeare, they generally trace the influence of *King Lear* or *Coriolanus* on Dickens's novel.[6] Yet the text of *Hard Times* proves particularly useful in showing how acts of Shakespearean appropriation are much more complex than simply demonstrating influence. By focusing on another dysfunctional family, who have a great deal in common with Polonius and his children, I will suggest that the text mediates between Shakespeare's work, Dickens's art, and the novelist's own family life.

Early in the book, the narrator suggests that while Thomas Gradgrind, the Utilitarian patriarch, is "an affectionate father, after his manner," he would "probably have described himself . . . as 'an eminently practical' father," one concerned with his children, but only in the most pragmatic way (Dickens 1990, 14).[7] While the father's influence in the novel is suspect, the mother's is nonexistent. Mrs. Gradgrind is described even in the first book of the novel as a symbolically absent mother, completely uninvolved in the education of her children; she even claims that she really "wish[es she] had never had a family" (45). After spouting nothingness to the children and realizing how little she matters to them in the first book, symbolically "she once more died away," according to the narrator, "and nobody minded her" (19). Moreover, "whenever she showed a symptom of coming to life, [she] was invariably stunned by some weighty piece of fact tumbling on her" (17). In the second book, she literally dies, and Gradgrind quickly "burie[s] her in a business-like manner" (154). Not unlike Polonius's offspring, then, both children are left with an overbearing father and no real maternal figure.

Gradgrind's relationship with his children highlights the Shakespearean connection; it is a kinship strengthened by verbal and visual details that continually remind us of Polonius's dealings with Ophelia and Laertes. Similar to Polonius, who chastises his daughter for being a "green girl" (*Hamlet* 1.3.101),[8] Gradgrind refers to his daughter, Louisa, as "'childish'" (Dickens 1990, 16), and also like Ophelia's father, he is glad he has exerted control over her education: She "[w]ould have been self-willed (he thought in his eminently practical way), but for her bringing-up" (16). Both fathers are also concerned about society's view of their daughters at the expense of the girls' feelings. When Gradgrind catches Louisa peeping at the Circus, a place where "Shaksperean quips" echo alongside barkers and horse-riding commands (14), he demands to know, "What would your best friends say, Louisa?" He concludes by asking Louisa what "Mr. Bounderby [would] say" (16). This encounter calls to mind at least two scenes in *Hamlet* in which Polonius expresses anxiety about Ophelia's reputation. The first scene occurs when Polonius is berating his daughter for her feelings toward Hamlet, claiming she does "not understand" herself "so clearly" as she thinks she does (*Hamlet* 1.3.96); more importantly, he points out that her "most free and bounteous" attention toward Hamlet (line 93) is not consistent with behavior that "behoves [his] daughter and [her] honour" (line 97). The second instance takes place when the king questions Polonius about Hamlet and Ophelia's relationship, wondering "[H]ow hath she / Received his love?" (2.2.128–29). Polonius tellingly responds, "What do you think of me?" (line 129). The semantic shift here is important, for it is the way in which her actions reflect on his fatherhood, and by extension his own character, that most concern him. While both fathers want to reproduce perfect images of themselves, they are both shaken when anything challenges their narrow worldview of the way to educate children or the effect on their own offspring, an issue that was not lost on Dickens.

Louisa, "fifteen or sixteen," represents a nineteenth-century Ophelia, and it is interesting that in a book focused on "Facts" the narrator is not even sure of her age (Dickens 1990, 15). Significantly, the first detailed description of her reminds us of the seemingly empty cipher that Polonius's daughter has become under his guidance, for in Louisa's countenance, "there was a light with nothing to rest upon, a fire with nothing to burn, a starved imagination keeping life in itself somehow" (15). This eerie light, however, burns "[n]ot with the brightness natural to cheerful youth, but with uncertain, eager, doubtful flashes, which had something painful in them" (15), descriptions that might apply to Ophelia as well. With no will and even less ambition, Louisa becomes a useful Utilitarian pawn moved about by the men in her life. While Polonius refuses to allow his daughter to marry the man she seems to love, Louisa's father forces her instead into a loveless marriage to Mr. Bounderby—seemingly opposite actions by the fathers, but ones that produce strikingly similar results: psychological or physical death. Orchestrated by her father and encouraged by her brother, this arranged marriage certainly recalls Polonius's alleged "fishmongering" of Ophelia.

The closeness of the siblings also resembles Laertes and Ophelia's bond, as Louisa and Tom suffer from their stern Utilitarian training, while Laertes and Ophelia are likewise warped in many ways by their father's strict guidance. Brought up together with few outside influences or pleasures, both pairs of siblings turn to each other for comfort and counsel. Tom insists that he does not know where he "would be without" Louisa, while Louisa constantly worries that she cannot provide solace for her brother by providing any "angel in the house" comforts usually associated with a husband and wife: "I can't play to you, or sing to you" nor "reconcile you to home better" (Dickens 1990, 43). This sibling attachment is so close that it appears almost unnatural, echoing the potential incest in the Laertes/Ophelia relationship. We remember, for example, that Laertes has warned Ophelia not to open her "chaste treasure" (*Hamlet* 1.3.31), and her response that Laertes alone "shall keep the key of it" (1. 86).[9] Significantly, Tom commits a robbery with a "false key," a point made twice by the narrator (Dickens 1990, 135, 137), and this symbolically foreshadows a later scene that will test the emotional and physical boundaries of the relationship. While Daniel P. Deneau claims that "[i]solated and schooled as they are, Tom and Louisa experience an abnormal brother-sister" bond, he stops just short of claiming a physical relationship. He does admit, however, that in this scene (which we will examine next), "sexual overtones hover over" the two, and the "mental intimacy" established in the encounter "has the atmosphere of a seduction" (Deneau 1990, 363, 366). The text suggests as much when Mr. Gradgrind admits that there are "qualities in Louisa, which—which have been harshly neglected, and—and a little perverted" (Dickens 1990, 178). The closeness reveals itself in the language of the pair, as in Shakespeare's characters, but unlike Laertes and Ophelia, Tom and Louisa express their intimacy in physical action as well.

After the robbery that Tom secretly commits, Louisa anxiously awaits his return in her bed, restlessly listening for the sound of "her brother's coming home" (Dickens 1990, 141). Upon his late arrival, at least "an hour past midnight" (141), Louisa puts on a "loose robe" and silently makes her way to his room, "approaching his bed with a noiseless step." She "kneel[s] down beside" his bed, "pass[es] her arm over his neck," and gently draws "his face to hers" (142). She then proclaims that if he ever "loved" her in his life, he should now confess his crime in this intimate moment; she vows to never "reproach" him, because she is "compassionate and true" to him only, clearly favoring the brother over her husband whose bank Tom has robbed (142). When Tom pretends not to understand, she leans down, and "her hair flow[s] over him as if she would hide him from every one but herself" (142). To show her intimacy, and to expose herself to him in love, she lays her "head down on his pillow," and confesses that she is "barefoot, unclothed, undistinguishable in darkness." But even when "she turns her ear to his lips," with the "energy of her love," Tom continues to deny any wrongdoing. Although Tom still refuses to confess, he sits "up in bed and kiss[es] her," and before she leaves he "kiss[es] her again" (142–43). Not long after this visit, feeling as forsaken as Ophelia, Louisa mentally turns to the same escape as Shakespeare's "poor wretch" who suffers a "muddy death" because she is "incapable of her own distress" (*Hamlet* 4.7.153–54,

149). Louisa felt, we are told, "like one who was floating away upon some great water, all resistance over, content to be carried down the stream" (Dickens 1990, 149).[10] Like Laertes grieving over Ophelia's grave, Tom realizes his loss too late, throwing "himself upon his pillow . . . tearing his hair, morosely crying, [and] grudgingly loving her" (143). Although Louisa does not physically die, both her spirit and her capability for love and happiness are so crippled that by the end of the novel, she stares into the fireplace, silently watching the "the ashes" of her life "turn grey and cold" (219).

PLAYING THE ROLE

Besides critiquing Utilitarianism, Dickens was also chastising overbearing fathers in *Hard Times*, suggesting ways in which such loveless and cruel sins of the father might be visited on the sons and daughters. Paradoxically, however, while Dickens was satirizing such fathers, his behavior toward his own children was often just as harsh. Similar to both Gradgrind and Polonius, Dickens demanded perfection from his children, sometimes severely punishing any failing; he rigorously oversaw their education as well. Although he constantly pestered the headmasters about the children's progress, he also "made certain that their instruction would not embrace opinions he could not approve of" (Adrian 1984, 38). He even went so far as to compose a prayer for them to recite at bedtime, because he was not satisfied with traditional Anglican forms of worship. Unfortunately, all the boys except for Harry showed little facility for academic learning, and so Dickens turned to practical education as a final resort.[11]

The girls were educated by tutors, but the results were equally disappointing to Dickens. Mamie, often described as a female image of her father, was encouraged to improve her voice, while Katie was to develop her drawing ability. Yet Mamie seemed to fixate on Dickens and, not unlike Louisa or Ophelia, never married, nor had children. When asked to explain why his beautiful sister never found a suitable husband, her brother Harry wrote: "I think it was because she was absolutely devoted to my father" (qtd. in Adrian 1984, 93–94). Her own writings confirm this attachment: "My love for my father" she wrote, "has never been touched or approached by any other love," because she held him in her "heart of hearts as a man apart from all other men, as one apart from all other beings" (Dickens 1897, 8).[12] Katie did somewhat better, having a semisuccessful career as an artist.

Sometimes both male and female children suffered under a similar domestic regime, often in connection with Dickens's theatricals. One prominent example of his perfectionism occurred each year in the Christmas pageants that the children always performed. His oldest son's birthday, in fact, fell on Twelfth Night, and as soon as the children were old enough to participate, they were cast in roles that Dickens chose for them. Dickens served as both prompter and director, helping them not only to learn their lines but also to act convincingly. Yet, as Arthur Adrian points out, preparations "were serious affairs, and all knew there must be no trifling." Later, Charley complained that the month of December consisted of one "long rehearsal" (Adrian 1984, 33).

As the number of children increased, Dickens seems to have grown weary of both fatherhood and marriage. By March 1852, just two years before the first installment of *Hard Times*, he confessed to Burdett-Coutts that while he was "happy to say that Mrs. Dickens" had given birth to his seventh son, he could not "afford to receive him with perfect cordiality, as on the whole [he] could have dispensed with him" completely (Dickens 1965–, 6:627). Almost the same wording is used three days later in a letter to William Howitt: "I am happy to say that Mrs. Dickens and her boy are in a most blooming condition," although he is unsure that he "particularly wanted the latter" (6:629). Dickens even began to blame his wife for the children's failures. Writing again to Burdett-Coutts, he complained that Charley's "indescribable lassitude of character—a very serious thing in a man—" must have been "inherit[ed] from his mother" (7:245). He was more concerned, it seems, with how this behavior reflected on him, and we may even hear Polonius's words "What do you think of me?" echoing in the back of his mind. Certainly, he was becoming increasingly alienated from his wife and somewhat embarrassed by his children.

As we now know, other factors also played a role in his discontent, and again the world of theater served as both a catalyst and as an escape for his restlessness. The previous August, during one of the amateur acting tours, Dickens had hired three professional actresses to shoulder some of the grind of constant performances and to relieve his daughters of their roles in the amateur charity performances. On the recommendation of the manager of the Olympic Theatre, he selected Frances Eleanor Ternan and two of her daughters to act in his drama *The Frozen Deep*. The Ternan family had deep roots in the Shakespearean stage of the time; Frances and her husband, Thomas Lawless Ternan, had costarred in a number of provincial performances of Shakespeare, including stints in Edinburgh, Liverpool, and Birmingham, where they starred opposite one another in *Othello, Macbeth,* and *The Merchant of Venice.*

Dickens probably met Mrs. Ternan a decade earlier when she performed with W. C. Macready in *Hamlet, King Lear,* and *Macbeth* at the Princess's

Theatre. Because we know from Macready's diary entry that he and Dickens attended the Royal Academy during this time, it is safe to assume that Macready mentioned his leading actress to Dickens. Later that same year, in Dublin, Mrs. Ternan played Pauline in *The Winter's Tale*, and her youngest daughter, seven-year-old Ellen, played Mamilius. After the death of her husband, Eleanor Francis toured continuously as "Mrs. Ternan and her Daughters." Now, in 1857, Ellen was about to play a role for which she never publicly auditioned.

On 14 September 1857, the female Ternans traveled with Charles Kean's company from the Princess's Theatre to inaugurate the Theatre Royal in Doncaster, and Dickens also made his way there, allegedly to work on an article for *Household Words*. Before leaving, he consulted Forster again about plans to end the marriage:

> [T]he years have not made it easier to bear for either of us; and, for her sake as well as mine, the wish will force itself upon me that something might be done. . . . I claim no immunity from blame. There is plenty of fault on my side . . . in the way of a thousand uncertainties, caprices, and difficulties of disposition; but only one thing will alter all that, and that is, the end which alters everything. (Dickens 1965–, 8:434)

Dickens and Wilkie Collins visited the theater and made an impression on the cast as well as the audience; when the curtain fell, the pit stood up and yelled, "Three cheers for Charles Dickens Esquire!" The actors came back, and the whole house joined in the chant. Dickens was trying to keep at least a part of his life from public view, and this moment prefigures the collapse between his public and private lives that would haunt Dickens even more in the months to come. His attraction for Ellen, perhaps one of the "caprices" mentioned in his letter, now became obvious to a number of colleagues. Rumors of his liaison finally reached Catherine as well.

The next month, Dickens had the master bedroom divided into two separate rooms, the emotional separation becoming a physical one. Even this arrangement failed, however, and the crises reached a breaking point in early May 1858 when, the speculation goes, a gift of jewelry intended for Ellen was mistakenly delivered to Catherine (Kaplan 1988, 377). Now, neither could avoid the issue. Finally, on 10 May 1858, Dickens explained to Charley that he and Catherine would separate.

The household would never be the same, and Dickens was guilt-ridden for causing the breakup, a remorse similar to Gradgrind's when Louisa leaves Bounderby and returns home, collapsing in "an insensible heap" (Dickens 1990, 163). Dickens's daughter Katie later recalled how the separation affected her father and the family: "My father was like a madman when my mother left home. . . . [T]his affair brought out all that was worst— all that was weakest in him. He did not care a damn what happened to any of us. Nothing could surpass the misery and unhappiness of our home" (Storey 1971, 94).[13]

The swirling scandal forced Dickens into making a bold move, a move against which even his closest friends advised. Thinking that the public deserved to be told, Dickens published a "personal" statement in *Household Words*. In this statement, published on 12 June 1858, we see most clearly the tension between the private and public life of the artist, a contradiction that would come to affect the novelist's future work as well, as he began to perform public readings of his work. We also see in the statement a Gradgrindian emphasis on "facts," combined with a Polonius-like pompousness and hyperbole.[14]

Under the heading "PERSONAL," Dickens begins by acknowledging that it has been twenty-three years since he first "entered on [his] present relations with the Public," and then declares that in all that time he has "tried to be as faithful to the Public, as they have been" to him. The word choices here seem particularly ironic, as his lack of *faithfulness* in his relationship with his wife may have precipitated the whole affair. He then attempts to explain why he is making his case public, but nearly contradicts that idea by stating that the "domestic trouble" is of a "sacredly private nature." He also claims that for "the first time" in his life, and, he "believe[s] for the last" time, he will "deviate from the principle" of not presenting himself in his "own Journal" in his "own private character" (Dickens 1858, 601). Dickens adds that he must now begin "circulating the Truth," the real "facts," that is, of the situation. Yet, instead of providing any details or facts, his rhetoric becomes more exaggerated and more like a speech by Polonius. Compare, for example, one of Polonius's famous speeches with Dickens's language. Polonius declaims,

> [T]o expostulate
> What majesty should be, what duty is,
> Why day is day, night night, and time is time,
> Were nothing but to waste night, day, and time.
> Therefore, since brevity is the soul of wit,
> And tediousness the limbs and outward flourishes,
> I will be brief.
>
> (*Hamlet* 2.2.87–93)

Dickens's convoluted rhetoric is no less inflated or obfuscatory:

By some means, arising out of wickedness, or out of folly, or out of incon-
ceivable wild chance, or out of all three, this trouble has been made the
occasion of misrepresentations, most grossly false, most monstrous, and
most cruel—involving, not only me, but innocent persons dear to my heart,
and innocent persons of whom I have no knowledge, if, indeed, they have
any existence. (Dickens 1858, 601)

We can almost hear exasperated readers of Dickens's statement echoing
Gertrude's "more matter with less art," and recent readings of the personal
statement sound as if it could be describing a set speech by Polonius: "The
hyperbolic style is created by an extraordinary preponderance of superla-
tives, emotive expressions and exclamatory protestations" (Waters 1997,
5). This hyperbole begins to reach an even higher pitch as Dickens makes
a direct appeal to the audience, entreating all his "brethren (as they deem
that they have reason to think well of me, and to know that I am a man who
has ever been unaffectedly true to our common calling), to lend their aid to
the dissemination of my present words" (Dickens 1858, 601). He then declares the rumors to be "abominably false," threatening that "whosoever
repeats one of them after this denial, will lie as wilfully and as foully as it
is possible for any false witness to lie, before Heaven and earth" (601).

Dickens was so convinced that his private life had become public knowledge, and that his personal affairs were of such great concern to the public,
that he "doubt[s] if one reader in a thousand will peruse these lines, by
whom some touch of the breath of these slanders will not have passed, like
an unwholesome air" (Dickens 1858, 601). Besides drawing on the image
of pollution he had recently employed in *Bleak House*, Dickens also seems
to have overestimated his notoriety. In fact, most of his contemporaries
agreed with Percy Fitzgerald's assessment that people were "bewildered
and almost stunned," because they were in "supreme ignorance of what the
document could possibly refer to" (Fitzgerald 1971, 190). As one can imagine, the obliqueness of the statement raised more questions than it answered.
And his motive for publishing it has raised speculation from his associates
then to his biographers now. Edmund Yates, his friend, claimed it was because of Dickens's "theatrical ostentation" that the novelist felt compelled
to reveal this "little drama" to the public (Yates 1884, 2:98). More recently,
Kaplan refers to the statement as "hollow at best, cowardly at worst, an
excess of protestation" (Kaplan 1988, 396). When public and private iden-
tities collapse, however, the turn to a dramatic mode, in all senses of that
word, may have made rhetorical sense.

Indeed, this "turn to the dramatic" was commented on by Dickens's
contemporaries. In John Ruskin's review of *Hard Times* in 1860, he claimed

that he wished that Dickens would "limit his brilliant exaggeration" when he "takes up a subject of high national importance" like the critique of Utilitarianism in the most recent novel. Yet, Ruskin continues, even though the characters are "dramatic" instead of "characteristic," we should "not lose the use of Dickens's wit and insight, because he chooses to speak in a circle of stage fire," an accurate assessment of Dickens's personal life as well (Ruskin 1860, 159). This point was supported by even his closest friends, for when Forster read the assessment, he knowingly wrote that the comment by Ruskin had "a wider application" to Dickens's life in the late 1850s than "its inventor supposed" (Forster 1874, 2:146). While Ruskin's comment about "stage fire" and drama was only intended to describe the novelist's creations, it was apparent to a number of Dickens's intimates that the description could be aptly applied to his personal life as well.

FATHERING FECHTER

Dickens and his view of the family also played an important role in an overlooked aspect of the connection between Dickens and Shakespeare: the novelist's almost intimate relationship with Charles Albert Fechter, an actor of French and German descent, who overwhelmed audiences in London with his interpretation of Hamlet.[15] Not only did Dickens embrace him as a close friend, but he also wrote laudatory reviews and even became Fechter's "confidential advisor and semiprofessional impresario in London" (Kaplan 1988, 492). While Dickens consistently explored both the idealized and destructive family in his art, his own family life, as we have seen, reflected the latter more than the former.[16] Yet in the bond between Dickens and Fechter, the lines are blurred not only between public and private life but also between reality and fiction; just as his association with his own children was most strained, he "adopted" Fechter as the motivated and artistic child he never fathered.

When Dickens first saw Fechter in Paris in 1859, he was overwhelmed by the performance, later claiming that he had "studied" his acting and "admired it highly" (Dickens 1869, 242). After witnessing Fechter's portrayals, specifically his more natural delivery than earlier nineteenth-century Hamlets, Dickens claimed that it was as if he were seeing the stories for the first time. A meeting was arranged when Fechter came to London in 1861, and Dickens became his confidant.

If the search for lost parents informs much of Dickens's earlier artistic work, now he seemed instead to be searching for his lost "children," associating with a number of men some twenty years younger than himself. In

Fechter, perhaps, Dickens found both the symbolic son he could support and the daughter figure he could protect, and he was called on to perform both roles in his association with the actor. Whether or not Fechter's acting style had an immediate bearing on this personal feeling is uncertain, but Dickens clearly sensed both feminine and masculine traits in Fechter's character, while others noted it in his acting. Trying to explain Fechter's personality to a friend, Dickens claimed the actor possessed a unique spirit: "He has the brain of a man, combined with that strange power of arriving, without knowing how or why, at the truth, which one usually finds only in a woman" (108). G. H. Lewes made a similar point while commenting on Fechter's somewhat feminized portrayal of Hamlet: "Fechter is lymphatic, delicate, handsome, and with his long flaxen curls, quivering, sensitive nostrils, fine eye, and sympathetic voice, perfectly represents the graceful prince" (Lewes 1878, 119).[17] In spite of his "delicateness," however, Fechter was much more intense than other Hamlets, more sorrowful toward the Ghost, more passionate toward Ophelia. As Gager explains, this almost androgynous quality was unique for the time, particularly on the London stage: "Fechter possessed a greater tenderness, intuition, and sensitivity than was to be found in English actors" (Gager 1996, 132).[18]

Hamlet was Fechter's most famous role in London, and his "natural" acting caused an outpouring of praise not only from playgoers and the press but also from Dickens himself. The inveterate theater critic Clement Scott argued that Fechter had a "mission to perform" in England:

> He had to break down the unnatural, stilted, artificial barriers that the Macready school had left. He had to be the pioneer of natural acting in this country. People were sick and tired of the groaning, grunting, guttural school. They wanted someone to talk in the voice that God had given him, and in the manner that appealed to human nature. (Scott 1891, 16–17)

Dickens hyperbolically added this assessment: "Perhaps no innovation in Art was ever accepted with so much favor by so many intellectual persons, pre-committed to and preoccupied by another system, as Mr. Fechter's *Hamlet*" (Dickens 1869, 244). His portrayal had a run of 115 performances at the Princess's Theatre in 1861, from 20 March to the end of August. This Hamlet's duty, it seemed, was not only to revenge his father's ghost but also to humanize the prince: "to discard the black velvet, the bugles, and the funereal feathers" of earlier Hamlets, "to make Hamlet a man, and not a mouthing mountebank" (Scott 1891, 18). Scott concludes his praise in words that echo Dickens's: "I sat spell bound under Fechter, and seemed to understand *Hamlet* for the first time" (18). The *Athenaeum* agreed: "Mr.

Fechter does not act; he is Hamlet" (Review of Charles Albert Fechter's *Hamlet* 1861).

Now estranged from his wife and tired of his own children's "failures" in life, Dickens strengthened his association with Fechter, including their collaboration on a drama, *No Thoroughfare*, which enjoyed a successful run at the Adelphi in 1861. The two also traveled together to Paris to coproduce the French version of the play entitled *L'Abîme*. As the actor perfected his art, Dickens began to idealize Fechter as the dynamic and creative son he had yet to sire. But even he may have not have realized what was in store, for Fechter began to display a hotheadedness in life that one associates more with a Hotspur than with a Hamlet.[19]

In a memorial book to Fechter, Kate Field published recollections of the actor by a number of his friends. According to Edmund Yates, Fechter "had a most unhappy knack of quarreling with people,—often those with whom he had been most intimate" (Field 1882, 149). His temper got him into trouble not only in London but also in America, so much so that Herman Vezin, a fellow actor, could claim that Fechter's "ungovernable temper was the primary cause of his downfall" (153). If any one challenged his ideas, he would fly into a rage and "ruthlessly insult his best friends so grossly as to make all reconciliation impossible" (153). On occasion, as we shall soon see, it was left for the paternal Dickens to smooth things over.

Another close associate, Wilkie Collins, made similar claims about Fechter's temper. Collins knew Fechter well, as he had also collaborated on *No Thoroughfare*. Yet, in a memorial essay, Collins went so far as to claim that Fechter's temper was one of two "serious defects" in his character that led to his financial and personal undoing (Field 1882, 162). In London, Fechter had offered Phelps a contract to work with him at the Lyceum. After not being cast for three months, however, Phelps suspected Fechter had merely hired him away from Sadler's Wells to eliminate the competition. When Fechter finally cast him as the deceased King Hamlet, Phelps refused to "play the Ghost to a blasted Frenchman," and a feud began that would involve Dickens as well (qtd. in Staples 1956, 75). Shortly after, Fechter took his Hamlet to America, where he received enthusiastic praise in New York and Boston. Apparently, Fechter made a deal with an entrepreneur in Boston to manage a new theater and to share in the proceeds, a sum that would have provided ample income for the rest of his life. Because of a vicious but trivial quarrel with the patron, however, the project never took shape, and he lost all hope of an easy retirement. Still, Dickens remained on the best of terms with Fechter, leaving Vezin to state that it was a "wonder he never quarreled with Dickens" (Field 1882, 153).

The other "serious defect" of Fechter, according to his associates, was his complete lack of financial acumen. Fechter remained constantly in debt, and when he needed money, he borrowed it carelessly. Yet he was also generous to a fault, loaning money when he had it, and even when he did not; if one friend needed money, Fechter would borrow it from a third friend and hand it over gladly to the friend in need. This practice also led to numerous quarrels with intimates. In fact, Fechter lost most of his gains and died a broken man on a secluded farm in Pennsylvania.

As we have seen, Fechter was extremely hot-blooded and contentious, yet Dickens continued to provide paternal protectiveness. At this point in time, they were "inseparable," according to most sources, "to the mystification of Dickens's friends" (Staples 1956, 71). In the Fechter/Phelps dispute, for example, Dickens was asked by both parties to mediate, and at first he defended Fechter, accusing Phelps of being at fault as well as of being discourteous and rude. Later, however, Dickens played the stern father, telling Fechter he had two choices: allow Phelps starring roles or tear up the contract. Fechter, still miffed and behaving like an angry child, chose to nullify the agreement. Dickens also helped out in a fatherly way with Fechter's finances. The story goes that Fechter was unaware that one of his productions in London was £3,000 in debt. When told by his manager, Fechter refused to believe it and became belligerent, storming off into the night. He later met Dickens at Covent Garden and related the story. Although Dickens did not offer assistance at the moment, the next morning when Fechter arrived at the theater he discovered that Dickens had come by at midnight and handed the manager £3,000 cash on Fechter's behalf. Later, Dickens wrote a fatherly letter of introduction for Fechter's American tour.

In this article in the *Atlantic Monthly* (August 1869), Dickens introduced his "intimate" acquaintance, emphasizing his "personal regard" for Fechter. Once more highlighting how Fechter's passionate acting produced a "fresh atmosphere of the story," Dickens credits Fechter's "intensely fiery" portrayals for this effect. Dickens continues in the manner of a boasting and verbose father for three pages, praising Fechter's "remarkable power" (Dickens 1869, 242) and his "passionate vehemence" (243), and commending Fechter's *Hamlet* by applauding its "great and satisfying originality." Dickens ends his article with hyperbole that would do any parent proud. Fechter's "romance and picturesqueness," he exclaimed, "are always united to a true artist's intelligence, and a true artist's training in a true artist's spirit." Dickens concludes that he "cannot wish" the American public "a better actor" than Charles Fechter, a "son" in whom Dickens seems very well pleased (244).[20]

Blurring the boundaries between fact and fiction, Dickens performed the role of the older and allegedly wiser father figure. Always in complete control when involved with stage productions, Dickens quite likely counseled Fechter on his portrayal of Shakespearean roles. The most oft-cited discussion of this connection is contained in a review by Sir Theodore Martin of Fechter's acting in *Othello*. In a backhanded compliment, Martin first ridicules Fechter for his "series of monstrous perversions" in the play, wherein Fechter repeatedly "thrust[s Desdemona] back into bed" with an unnecessary "violence." Dismissing the scene as overly exaggerated, he concludes that the action makes one "think rather of the murder of Nancy by Bill Sikes, than of Othello and Desdemona" (Martin 1861, 783), a jab not only at Dickens's sensationalism, but also his popularity: How dare someone such as Dickens presume to influence Shakespeare? At just about this same time, however, Dickens was wooing new audiences by performing public readings of his works. Later, when he added the scene with Bill and Nancy, he not only brought down the house but also, according to many contemporary reports, undermined his own health.

PERFORMING RECONCILIATION

Although Dickens began to read for charitable causes as early as 1853, he enjoyed the performances so much that he began to do them professionally in 1858, a practice that consumed him right up until the year of his death in 1870. The motivation for touring both England and America, as we shall see, was both public and private. By combining his own novelistic talents with Shakespearean-like dramatic performances, Dickens attempted to control and compose the final chapter of his own life story.

Ironically, if Dickens seemed to valorize the private, domestic reading of Shakespeare over the "vulgarized" public performances of the playwright before Macready and Phelps, he chose the opposite path with his own art, taking private, domestic novels and performing readings of them in public.[21] His decision to do so, however, did not come easily, as his debate with close associates such as John Forster shows. In a letter to Forster written on 5 September 1857, Dickens revealed that he was "very strongly tempted" to revive "that old idea of some Readings from [his] books" (Dickens 1965–, 8:435). Forster ardently opposed the plan based on a division he perceived between art and spectacle; he responded that the readings would be "a substitution of lower for higher aims; a change to commonplace from more elevated pursuits." Moreover, Forster felt it would taint Dickens's artistic integrity. In his strongly worded warning, Forster concluded that the readings had "so much of the character of a public exhibition for money" that they would raise the "question of respect for his calling as a writer, . . . [and] a question also of respect for himself as a gentleman" (Forster 1874, 2:246–47). The division between high and low, public and private, however, caused little concern for Dickens at this time, as he was attempting to satisfy a personal need.

This need is partly explained in a letter Dickens wrote earlier in the same year, in which he speaks of his feelings on directing and acting in *The Frozen Deep*, a play he had co-authored with Wilkie Collins: "As to the Play itself; when it is made as good as my care can make it, I derive a strange feeling out of it, *like writing a book in company*. A satisfaction of a most singular kind, which has no exact parallel in my life" (Dickens 1965–, 8:256, italics mine). If we consider the way in which a community of players helped to balance the solitary life of the writer, we may understand more fully Dickens's desire to expand that "satisfaction of a most singular kind" by reading in public, another way of "writing a book in company."

The difference from his earlier productions was that in the reading tours, Dickens was a "one-man show"—sole author, director, and actor. Although part of the success of the tours was due to an emerging cult of personality,[22] Dickens's own will to win back his adoring public family, while also providing income for his estranged family, seems the primary motivation for the readings that eventually contributed to the writer's death. In this sense, D. W. Winnicott's object-relations theory of the family may be helpful, as the relationship between audience and speaker was clearly symbiotic and dyadic.[23] Dickens needed the audience's attention and adulation as much as they desired his presence among them.

Performing with minimal props, Dickens stood in the center of the stage behind a reading desk, about waist high, with a side shelf for a small pitcher of water, a glass, and a handkerchief. The desk was just short enough so that all his features could be seen, and he sometimes used it like a stage prop to pound out exclamatory phrases. Usually covered in maroon velvet, an oblong box stood on top to Dickens's left side; on it he could rest his book. While the lack of stage devices enabled Dickens to perform at many smaller locations, he may have also been subtly commenting on the overblown Shakespearean productions of the time. Charles Kean's history plays, for instance, were often chastised by critics for their extravagant settings, sometimes at the expense of Shakespeare's poetry.[24] Character and not scenery, Dickens seemed to imply, was the key to a good performance. Dickens did, however, make one theatrical concession. The desk was enhanced by a set of gaslights placed three feet in front of the desk and also above the desk. The whole effect was like a stage performer framed in brilliant light, set off against a dark background, an arrangement that allowed all audience members a good view of his facial expressions and physical gestures. In fact, the visual quality of the performances was so essential to Dickens that a gas man, responsible only for the lighting, accompanied him throughout the tours.

The provincial reading tour, the first full-blown for-profit enterprise, began in August 1858 in Clifton at the Bath Hotel in the West Country; it continued through Exeter, and then on to Liverpool. From there he sailed to Ireland and read at Dublin, where people battled for tickets and where he had to fight his way through a mile of disappointed customers who had been turned away. In fact, the hall at the Rotunda was so crammed that scores of women chose to stand during the entire performance, pressed up against the platform. When he traveled on to Belfast, the reactions were the same. When he read *Little Dorrit*, grown men wept without shame, as he reported to Georgina: "They made no attempt whatever to hide it, and certainly cried more than the women" (Dickens 1965–, 8:643). The women, however, were also caught up in the frenzy, entreating his manager for the flower fastened in Dickens's buttonhole; one night, according to Dickens, they even "mounted the platform after [he] was gone" to pick up the scattered leaves of his geranium "as keepsakes" (643).

Returning to London to rest briefly, he was shocked to find the marital controversy had flared anew, with comments appearing in the London papers on Saturday, 4 September. Although Dickens anticipated a setback in his popularity, he decided against postponing the tour. Four days later he departed on the second leg of the tour, traveling through York and Leeds, and then on to Manchester, a city that had welcomed him years earlier as an actor in his amateur productions. Worried about the negative publicity, Dickens was elated that over twenty-five hundred tickets were purchased; not only did he sell out the auditorium, but he was also greeted with a standing ovation before reciting a single line. He wrote to Forster that the "welcome they gave me was astounding in its affectionate recognition of the late trouble," a reference to the fact that they turned out to see him in spite of his ongoing marital problems (668).

Scotland was next on the tour, and when Dickens read the first night in Edinburgh and the audience was less than he expected, he felt as if the separation from his wife and the alienation from his children were finally taking their toll on his reputation. By the third night, however, hundreds of potential auditors were turned away without tickets. On the last night, in fact, when he was scheduled to read *A Christmas Carol*, he was so concerned with crowds that he posted notices the morning of the show notifying the public that the performance was sold out. It seemed not to matter, however, as the crowds were so huge that the police were called in to keep order. He wrote to W. H. Wills that Edinburgh was his greatest victory, due to the initial apathy, if not anger, he felt had been directed towards him due to his personal life: "There was certainly . . . a coldness, beforehand, about the Readings. I mention it, to let you know that I consider the triumph there, by far the greatest I have made" (Dickens 1965–, 8:674). As was becoming increasingly clear, if he took his marital "case" to the court of public opinion through his readings, he would regain a measure of his popularity, which had begun to wane. The tour concluded at Brighton, where he gave three readings in the town hall. Most amazingly, the tour was completed in less than four months, from 2 August through 13 November, and although the profits were remarkable for the time, for Dickens the personal reconciliation with his public "family" was worth much, much more.

The power of such performances astonished many auditors accustomed to more sedate Victorian readings. Thomas Carlyle even elevated these readings over most dramatic productions of the day. Before "hearing Dickens read," he asserted, he had "no conception . . . of what capacities lie in the human face and voice. No theatre-stage" he added, "could have had more players than seemed to flit about [Dickens's] face, and all tones were present" (Wilson 1929, 505). According to some contemporary observers, even celebrated actresses such as Fanny Kemble paled in contrast.[25] Comparing the two, Annie Fields concluded that Dickens is "so much the greater artist! You can never mistake one character for another, nor lose a syllable of his perfectly enunciated words," while with Kemble "one cannot be sure always if Jessica or Nerissa be speaking" (Fields 1922, 223).

This facility for reading had been cultivated for some time. As early as 1838, after reading aloud parts of a play he had written, Dickens was so powerful that Macready claimed the novelist "reads as well as an experienced actor," and he concluded by pronouncing Dickens to be "a surprising man" (Macready 1912, 1:480). His facility for recitation also sprang partly from his technique of composition, once again blurring the lines between novelistic and theatrical art. In an oft-related incident, Mamie was sitting in his study one day while Dickens was writing the story of the "eminently practical father," *Hard Times*. This intimacy was a special treat, as the children were usually forbidden entrance when Dickens was writing. Sitting contentedly on the floor, Mamie suddenly watched in excitement as her father ran to the mirror, making "some extraordinary facial contortions," often combining this "facial pantomime" with speaking "rapidly in a low voice"; just as suddenly, he flung himself back down at his desk and continued writing (Dickens 1897, 47). This movement, of course, is the literal version of the novelist blurring the distinction between page and stage. Later, when he prepared to deliver the readings, he rehearsed some pieces over two hundred times before he performed them. Philip Collins even refers to his reading texts as "prompt-copies," for they varied from the actual texts, abbreviating some scenes, exaggerating others. They also contained such stage directions as "Mystery," "Action," or "Cheerful Narrative" (Collins 1975, xxx).

The first tour seemed a success at winning back some of the public "family" he felt he had lost. Yet it did not completely distract people from his personal scandal. Just six months later, for example, in March 1859, Elizabeth Gaskell wrote to Charles Eliot Norton: "Mr. Dickens happens to be extremely unpopular just now,—(owing to the well-grounded feeling of dislike to the publicity he has given to his domestic affairs)" (Gaskell 1967, 535). It seems that what offended people such as Gaskell was not so much his actions, but that he turned his domestic tragedy into a public performance.

Because of, or in spite of, this perceived "unpopularity," Dickens continued and even stepped up his public readings. The other major incentives for proceeding were partly financial, partly guilt at his failure as a father. In a letter written during this time, Dickens admits his dismay that he has fathered "the largest family ever known with the smallest disposition to do anything for themselves" (qtd. in Kaplan 1988, 497). Not only was he supporting his nine children, but he was also supporting, in some manner, Catherine, Georgina, Ellen, his own mother, and even his former servant Anne Brown. Perhaps this toil helped to assuage his guilty feelings over the separation from his wife and his liaison with Ellen. Yet the readings began to take a serious toll on Dickens's health as he traveled in unheated trains, spoke in drafty halls, and trudged through knee-deep snow to keep his schedule. Even though he suffered an inflamed left foot, blurred vision, extreme dizziness, and overwhelming exhaustion, Dickens held to his itinerary, not wanting to disappoint his fans or his financial sponsors.

Just before he began his last tour, he once more felt he must explain his motivation to friends such as Forster and George Dolby, who were understandably worried about his failing health as a result of his grinding tour schedule:

> To get that sum in a heap so soon is an immense consideration to me—my wife's income to pay—a very expensive position to hold—and my boys with a *curse of limpness* on them. You don't know what it is to look round the table and see reflected from every seat at it (where they sit) some horribly well remembered expression of inadaptability to anything. (Dickens 1965–, 11:375–77, italics mine)

In one sweeping Gradgrindian indictment, Dickens not only protests his financial obligation to his wife but also attacks the masculinity of the boys, who continued to disappoint him. His public family, however, did not, for the audiences for Dickens grew so devoted that he was able to confess that he sensed a "particular relation (personally affectionate and like no other man's) which subsists between me and the public" (Collins 1975, xxii). As more than one observer noted after a reading, "it was not mere applause that followed, but a passionate outburst of love for the man" (xxii).

After the overwhelming success of the American Tour in 1867 and early 1868 (where he earned the unheard-of sum of twenty thousand pounds), Dickens commenced the Farewell Reading tour on 6 October 1868. Although beset by exhaustion, Dickens demanded that one hundred readings be scheduled instead of the seventy-five his sponsors proposed. During this same autumn, Dickens's youngest, and by all accounts most loved, son was sent to Australia to make his living as a sheep farmer, joining his older brother Alfred, who had been exiled there earlier. The substitution of the public "adopted" family for the private family was now becoming a literal reality. This tour was also a striking success, even though it had to be cut short due to Dickens's health.

Two incidents on the Farewell Tour turn our attention back to the world of Shakespeare and performance. In the first instance, Dickens insisted, in spite of his fatigue, on reading in Cheltenham for his old friend Macready, who was living there in retirement. Although frail and sickly, the aging actor sat in the front row, carefully observing Dickens. When the novelist had finished reading "Sikes and Nancy," Macready rose from his seat and proclaimed, "[I]it comes to this—TWO MACBETHS"; not only had Dickens matched the intensity of a Shakespearean performance, but he had doubled the drama. This story became one of Dickens's favorites during the year of life he had left, for shortly after this reading, Dickens was forced to cancel a number of London and Scotland appearances. After resting, however, he rallied and proposed a dozen more final readings in London. From January though March 1870, Dickens read while his doctors waited in the wings, checking his pulse at the conclusion of every performance. Although he gave his final reading on 15 March, a set of readings earlier in the final days proves noteworthy. Many members of the theatrical community had never had the opportunity to see Dickens read, for they were usually performing on the boards as Dickens was mounting the platform each evening. Solely at their request, which pleased Dickens immensely, the novelist scheduled two afternoon readings. Now the distinction between page and stage was not only erased but in a way reversed, as the greatest actors and actresses of the time watched the novelist perform. He won them over as well, the Bancrofts later claiming, "We all seemed spell-bound under his varying powers," and Dickens himself was moved to tears at the "wonderful reception" the actors lavished upon him (qtd. in Collins 1975, lvii).

Indeed, the reviews for almost all the readings of the Farewell Tour were superb, and one early review of the final readings effusively catches the tone of passion echoed in many similar pieces:

> Hear Dickens, and die; you will never live to hear anything of its kind so good. There has been nothing so perfect, in their way, as those readings ever offered to an English audience. Great actors and actresses—Mrs. Siddons herself among them—have read Shakespeare to us. . . ; eminent authors, like Coleridge, and Hazlitt . . . have read lectures—and many living authors lecture still—but all those appearances, or performances, or whatever else they may be called, are very different from Mr. Dickens' appearances and performances as a reader. . . . His powers of vocal and facial expression are very great . . . and he applies them heartily and zealously to the due presentment of the creations of his own matchless genius. It has been said that an author is generally either greater or less than his works—that is, that in the works we see the best of a man, or that in the man there is better stuff than he is able to put into his works. In Mr. Dickens, as a reader, each is equal to the other. His works could have no more perfect illustrator; and they are worthy of his best efforts as an artist. (Review of Dickens's Public Reading 1868)

This reviewer, then, seems to answer Forster's concerns about the legitimacy of performing in public and also to challenge Forster's artificial division between artistic merit and mere exhibition. The Dickens performances, at least to this critic, were not spectacle but lofty art and therefore equal to the highest calling of the novelist.

I would conclude that the debate over public and private, high and low, lost out to Dickens's love of "family," because by reading aloud, Dickens collapsed the distinction not only between private reading and public performance, but also between his private family, his novelistic family, and his public family—the admiring populace. For if he felt any guilt that he had become like the "bad" father, Thomas Gradgrind, in dismissing his wife and becoming distanced from his children, he assuaged it with an adoring family of fans, who once more thronged to his readings. The negative publicity over the separation finally forgotten, Dickens was restored to his public pedestal to be revered—not unlike his beloved Shakespeare—as a paterfamilias of Victorian society.

Afterword

When we consider the attempts of these four Victorian writers to align themselves with Shakespeare, Robert Browning emerges as the clear victor during the late nineteenth and early twentieth centuries. Today, however, he is mentioned less as Shakespeare's successor than either Dickens or Eliot, while Swinburne's criticism and poetry have been consigned to the dustbin of the British literature survey course. A final glance backward and a quick look forward will not only bring these results into sharper focus, but will also demonstrate the vagaries of canon formation and literary tradition.

At the close of the nineteenth century, Browning was elevated most often to Shakespearean status. In addition to his "institutionalization" as Shakespeare's heir by the Browning Society, other late-Victorian forums continued to connect the two. *Poet-lore*, for example, an American periodical founded in 1889, also promoted Browning as a new Bard. Although created to exalt equally both Shakespeare and Browning, the journal swerved away from the political conservatism of the Browning Society's shaping of the poet's image detailed in chapter 3. Often weighing in on debates over contested literary and political ground, the journal was both feminist and internationalist in bent. Founded by lesbian lovers Charlotte Porter and Helen Clarke, *Poet-lore* not only continued earlier politicized readings of Shakespeare's heroines but also went beyond such critiques. In this journal, according to Tricia Lootens, Shakespeare served as both the herald of the "new woman" and the repository of "race ideals."[1]

Revealing much about the journal's intent, the table of contents of the first volume of *Poet-lore* shows the editors' efforts to dissolve the distinction not only between Shakespeare on the page and stage and but also between a conservative and a more radical Shakespeare. Some of the best-known Shakespearean scholars, such as H. H. Furness, contributed essays on Shakespeare, and new editions of the dramatist's works, including Henry

Irving's *Plays,* elicited reviews in the inaugural publication. The 1889 issue of the journal also attends to various stage productions of Shakespeare, including a version of *Hamlet* at the Comédie-Française and a performance of *Lear* in Munich; Shakespeare's status in Japan and in the Netherlands is also examined (*Poet-lore* 1889, 571, 376, 466, 259). Comments on Browning include an examination of his relationship with Macready (104, 108); his "Idea of Christian Love" (153), "Childe Roland" (91, 104), and Browning's drama *Colombe's Birthday* (464). The volume even chronicles the minutes of Browning societies throughout the world—including those in Boston, Cleveland, Philadelphia, and London—while the proceedings of Shakespeare societies in Oakland, Edinburgh, Melbourne, and Montreal are also included.

The notes detailing the Browning Society meeting in Philadelphia on 21 March 1889, provide a window into the work of the members, while also revealing how literary tradition is constantly challenged. Following the prologue and stanzas from "Fifine at the Fair," a member offers his analysis of the same poem. After a brief musical interlude (many of Browning's poems were set to music for Society performances), a paper by co-founder Porter is presented, entitled "Browning's Shakespeare Poems." Porter argues that "Browning's refusal to call the Sonnets autobiographical was based upon his clear perception of the inherent objectivity of Shakespeare's nature and hence of his art," connecting Shakespeare with Browning again (Porter 1889, 226). Yet, the connections between the two writers, and, indeed, the monolithic Browning image as philosopher/poet, begin to disintegrate almost immediately, for at the same meeting a Judge Wilson stridently opposed the notion of Browning as "the philosopher he is held up to be," concluding that he "would not for a minute *compare* him with Shakespeare. If you look at them both at the same time, you will see only one, and that one is Shakespeare" (228, italics mine). The carefully quilted effort of Browning to equate himself with Shakespeare was already beginning to unravel. Such resistance to Browning's status was, moreover, an omen of things to come.

The most important point here is that the image that Browning had so thoroughly helped to fashion—a more masculine, philosophical, Englishman's bard—is promptly fragmented, as critics challenged the iconic views of many Browning Society members. This early dissent by Wilson also reminds us that "traditions are revised, rewritten, abandoned, and created all the time" (Perkin 1990, 14). We must also be acutely aware, as Robert Weimann asserts, that although "structure is born" early in the artistic creation, later the work "lives in the process of reading and interpretation: it is affected by the social and individual perspectives of its readers and critics"

(Weimann 1982, 8). These shifting perspectives account, in part, for Browning's failure to remain Shakespeare's heir apparent. Although his name is not joined with Shakespeare's as often today, the search for a single reason seems as elusive as Roland's quest for the Dark Tower.

Assigning a reason for Dickens's continued connection with Shakespeare proves much easier. The "dramatic" quality of Dickens's novels, mentioned in chapter 4, as well as his benevolent portrayal of character, has always played a role in his association with the playwright. One of the earliest connections was made by Leigh Hunt in a letter written to Dickens in 1838; Hunt confesses that "[w]hat rejoices" him specifically is that Dickens possesses "so much heart," and he predicts for Dickens "a Shakspearian lot" (qtd. in Gager 1996, 1). While not citing Shakespeare per se in an essay in 1841, Edgar Allan Poe also noted Dickens's sympathy and "dramatic" characterization, arguing that it is "the overflowing kindness of [Dickens's] own bosom" that has caused the novelist to endow "so many of his *dramatis personae* with a warmth of feeling so very rare in reality" (Poe 1961, 21). A review of *Little Dorrit* in 1857 made a similar claim, proclaiming that Dickens's "genius possesses [a] resemblance to that of Shakspeare," due to his "universal sympathy with human nature" (Review of *Little Dorrit* 1857, 617). Defending Dickens against charges of caricature three years later, John Ruskin similarly highlighted the dramatic quality of Dickens:

> The essential value and truth of Dickens's writings have been unwisely lost sight of by many thoughtful persons merely because he presents his truth with some colour of caricature. Unwisely, because Dickens's caricature, though often gross, is never mistaken. . . . But let us not lose the use of Dickens's wit and insight, because he chooses to speak in a circle of stage fire. (Ruskin 1860, 159)

In this backhanded compliment to Dickens and the nineteenth-century theater, Ruskin clearly acknowledges the drama inherent in the novelist's works, but he also intimates that the theater seemed to cater to a lower taste. This comment echoes Forster's concerns regarding Dickens's decision to read from his novels in public, a question considered in depth in chapter 4.

Other critics also debated this distinction between popular and critical taste, another issue that speaks to the notion of canon formation. Referring to Dickens in 1872, G. H. Lewes addressed whether a popular writer can achieve critical acclaim, asserting that "there probably never was a writer of so vast a popularity whose genius was so little *appreciated* by the critics" (Lewes 1961, 57). He goes on to add that while the critics admitted

that his admirers were found in all classes, and in all countries; that he
stirred the sympathy of masses not easily reached through Literature . . .
and [that he] modified the Literature of his age, in its spirit no less than in
its form . . . they nevertheless insisted on his defects as if these outweighed
all positive qualities; and spoke of him either with condescending patron-
age, or with sneering irritation. (57)

What is important in this passage is that Lewes only hints at what was
perhaps the real concern of the critics he chastises: that Literature with a
capital *L* could be read and understood by the "masses." Lewes also cites
Dickens's sympathy and then almost immediately quotes from, but never
directly names, Shakespeare, a subtle pairing of novelist and playwright,
not unlike his method of connecting Eliot and Austen discussed in chapter
1. Dickens, Lewes proclaims, is "gifted" with an "emotional, sympathetic
nature capable of furnishing [his] imagination with elements of universal
power. Of him it might be said with less exaggeration than most of his
peers, that he was of 'imagination all compact'" (58). So often was Dickens
compared to Shakespeare that it should come as no surprise that in the last
letter that the novelist wrote, he quoted from *Romeo and Juliet:* "These
violent delights have violent ends" (2.5.9).[2]

At the turn of the nineteenth century and into the twentieth, Dickens's
name and work were yoked with Shakespeare's, and still are today. Early
in the twentieth century, for instance, Swinburne evoked Shakespeare's
name when discussing *Great Expectations:* "The tragedy and the comedy,
the realism and the dreamery of life, are fused or mingled together with
little less than Shakespearean strength and skill of hand" (Swinburne 1925b,
14:78). In the 1920s, T. S. Eliot argued that "Dickens excelled in character;
in the creation of characters of greater intensity than human beings," and
he concluded that "Dickens's figures belong to poetry, like figures of Dante
or Shakespeare, in that a single phrase, either by them or about them, may
be enough to set them wholly before us" (Eliot 1961, 151–52). In 1953,
Lionel Trilling summed up what many critical reviews of Dickens suggest;
however, even more significantly, Trilling employs Shakespeare as *the* literary touchstone: "With a body of works as large and as enduring as that of
Dickens, taste and opinion will never be done. They will shift and veer as
they have shifted and veered with the canon of Shakespeare" (Trilling 1961,
279). Although Trilling's implied point is that some works by Dickens will
always be canonical, just like Shakespeare's, I would add that Trilling sim-
plifies the comparison, because it may be the critical linkage of the two
writers such as his that keeps Dickens within the canon. In other words, it

is not just an inherent quality, but also an inherited tradition, that secures Dickens's place in the roster of "great works."

Recent criticism of the 1990s and through today also focuses on Dickens's dramatic talent, but his interest in the family and his politics play an increasing role in comparisons between the novelist and playwright. Arguing that Dickens was a "superb stage performer," Harold Bloom posits that Dickens "never stops performing in his novels, which is not the least of his many Shakespearean characteristics" (Bloom 1987, 3). Allan Grant agrees that the novelist's "method is dramatic and his exemplar is Shakespeare," but Grant highlights the fact that Dickens's "preoccupation with the relationship between parents and children is . . . Shakespearean in its mode" (Grant 1984, xi). An essay that appeared as I began writing this afterword provides a more political reading of Dickens. Focusing on race and labor in *A Tale of Two Cities*, it nevertheless details Shakespeare's use of the "bedtrick" in *Measure for Measure* to help explain how the plot of Dickens's work "hinges" on a version of this "bait and switch scam" (Sneidern 2001, 64). If we judge the "winner" of the game of appropriation by the sheer longevity of comparison with Shakespeare, it would be fair to crown Dickens the victor.

George Eliot, on the other hand, seems to be challenging Dickens, even though both her association with Shakespeare and her canonization have waxed and waned. After attaining nearly cultlike status during her lifetime, Eliot's work fell into disregard in the late-Victorian period and into the twentieth century. In fact, it was the mid-twentieth century before Eliot's place in the canon was firmly established. I would suggest that her revival resulted not only from feminist recovery but also from the numerous Shakespearean affinities critics highlighted in her work.

It is not until 1925 that voices praising Eliot began to be heard anew. In an article for *Vogue*, later reprinted in the *Times Literary Supplement*, Virginia Woolf considered the question of why Eliot's reputation had diminished, and four years later, in *A Room of One's Own*, she defended women writers and their concerns, arguing that "the values of women differ very often from the values which have been made by the other sex," and it is the "masculine values that prevail," so that the "feelings of women in a drawing room" are considered 'trivial'" (Woolf 1929, 110). When we remember that Woolf had also included a chapter on Shakespeare's sister in this book, the implication seems clear: important female writers such as Eliot may represent female versions of the playwright.

In 1948, one of the most important works relating to Eliot's canonical status appeared in F. R. Leavis's *The Great Tradition: George Eliot, Henry James, Joseph Conrad*, a work that champions rather than dismisses moral or social criticism. Attempting to revive a so-called lost literary tradition, Leavis equated the best novelists with poets. The major novelists, he argued, "count in the same way as the major poets, in the sense that they not only change the possibilities of the art for practitioners and readers, but that they are significant in terms of the human awareness they promote" (Leavis [1948] 1964, 2). Challenging the popular tradition, he also elevated Eliot's later works, particularly *Daniel Deronda,* to the same status as her earlier novels. Although Leavis's critique may be troubling in other respects,[3] its influence on Eliot's canonicity cannot be dismissed.

Crucial feminist readings of Eliot by later critics such as Barbara Hardy, Elaine Showalter, and Sandra Gilbert and Susan Gubar championed Eliot as an important figure in feminist resistance to the dulling and overwhelming power of the patriarchy in both her life and her work.[4] Yet by far the most significant critical response for my purposes appeared in the mid-nineties, and combined a feminist orientation with a consideration of Eliot's Shakespearean appropriation. In this respect, Marianne Novy's work, particularly *Engaging with Shakespeare: Responses of George Eliot and Other Women Novelists,* sets the standard for discussions of Eliot, feminism, and Shakespeare, and firmly secures Eliot's status as an essential Shakespearean appropriator, if not a Shakespearean author.

Of all the writers I have considered, however, the one who most deserves our renewed attention is Algernon Charles Swinburne. Even though his name is seldom cited today, with or without Shakespeare's, during his lifetime he was considered not only a stellar poet but also a superb critic of Shakespeare. In a symposium in 1895, of nineteen writers queried, twelve nominated Swinburne as their first choice for poet laureate, following the death of Tennyson; Swinburne's critical championing of Blake, Baudelaire, and the Brontës was well ahead of its time; and William Archer considered Swinburne to be Charles Lamb's successor as the single most important dramatic critic of his day. Yet most contemporary Shakespeare scholars are unaware of Swinburne's work.[5] His book on Shakespeare, as noted in chapter 2, however, went through two editions in the first year of publication (the first run was one thousand copies), and was republished in 1895, 1902, 1908, and 1909, a printing history that clearly demonstrates his significance as a Shakespearean critic. The important literary journals of the day, as we have seen, also gave it high marks. Even the noted Shakespearean critic Edward Dowden, at odds with Swinburne over verse tests and other "scientific" criticism of Shakespeare, grudgingly praised Swinburne's book, pronouncing it "something of value" due to its "pieces of bright, penetrating, and original comment" (Dowden 1880, 2).

The recent neglect of Swinburne, as I argued in chapter 2, may have been due at least in part to T. S. Eliot's aversion to the Victorian writer's politics more than to his critical prose. While T. S. Eliot eventually gave Swinburne his due as a textual critic, Swinburne's sexual leanings may have been one of the driving forces for Eliot's dismissal of the Victorian critic's ideas. Eliot's proclamation that Swinburne's "content [was] not, in an exact sense, criticism" (Eliot 1950, 17), followed by the more telling charge that "there was something unsatisfactory in the way in which Swinburne was interested in these people" he wrote about, suggests that Swinburne's personality may have been at the center of Eliot's objections (20). Eliot also sprinkles his criticism of Swinburne's writing with adjectives such as "perverse," and "faulty," condemning Swinburne's critiques as the result of a "disorderly mind" full of "infirmities" (17, 20). As I argued earlier, Eliot's dismissal of Swinburne is complex, so that while he admits that Swinburne "must be read with attention and respect" (17), he ultimately argues that in Swinburne "no conclusions" are reached, except that Elizabethan literature and Shakespeare are "very great, and that you can have pleasure and even ecstasy from" his criticism (21). For Eliot, therefore, Swinburne is a mere "appreciator and not a critic" (19).[6] Kenneth Muir, building on Eliot's argument, continued the assault by pointing out that Swinburne is "sometimes regarded more as a hagiographer than a critic" (Muir 1961–64, 2:283). This pronouncement is also echoed in the final word on Swinburne in the *Cambridge Companion to Shakespeare Studies*. In a single sentence, Harry Levin sweepingly dismisses Swinburne's book (and even gets the title slightly wrong), and sneeringly refers to Swinburne's criticism as no more than "impressionistic rhapsodies" (Levin 1986, 227).

Yet the same claim could be made of Harold Bloom's recent best-seller, *Shakespeare: The Invention of the Human*. Full of rhapsodies to Shakespeare as well as attacks on recent criticism,[7] Bloom's work argues for a return to an aesthetic enjoyment that he claims is now missing in Shakespeare studies. And even some of the more theoretical scholars grant that this stance may be a necessary corrective to postmodern Shakespeare.[8] Still, when Swinburne advances his case, his textual support is always marshaled and documented, while Bloom resorts to scattered generalities and unsubstantiated bombast. Since Swinburne's criticism travels the middle road between the hyperbole of Bloom and the technicalities of textual scholarship, it may ultimately speak to a wider audience than do many other Victorian critics of Shakespeare, such as Walter Pater or even A. C. Bradley.

∽

The category of "winners and losers" is always a construct, of course, whether invoked as a justification for a canonical tradition or a critical summation, so it may be that all my conclusions about Shakespearean appropriation will be modified or superseded by the next generation of scholars. We can only hope so. It may also be true that the greatest appropriator of Shakespeare has yet to be heard from or discovered, and may be rewriting Shakespeare even now from a developing nation or post-colonial view.[9] So much the better. Obviously no single critic or scholarly work could possibly detail all the places where these past and present borrowings have occurred. Nor is it possible to predict with any accuracy where future Shakespearean appropriations may develop. Instead we must be content, to quote from the Duchess of Newcastle with whose words I began this book, to "leave it to those that Read his Playes, and others, to find them out" (Cavendish 1997, 13).

Notes

1. Taylor (1999, 200) claims that recent appropriators, such as Jane Smiley, "now write *against* Shakespeare, either denying his influence altogether, or openly resisting it." He may even be correct when he asserts that Shakespeare's words "are planted in fewer memories than they once were: he has become, like caviar, familiar to the General but arcane in the ranks" (202).

2. Dellamora 1990, Adams 1995, and Dowling 1994.

3. See Altick 1973, for example, or "Introduction to the Victorian Age" in Abrams et al. 2000.

4. Some recent scholarship has now begun on this important topic. Schoch 2002 carefully considers the marginalized world of the burlesque theater vis-à-vis Shakespeare's cultural status.

5. For a more current discussion of this issue, see Pechter 2002.

6. The most helpful discussions include Berger 1989, Osborne 1996, Bulman 1996, and Worthen 1997.

7. See Taylor 1989, Marsden 1991, Novy 1994, Desmet and Sawyer 1999, and Hedrick and Reynolds 2000.

8. *Oxford English Dictionary,* 2d ed.

CHAPTER 1. GEORGE ELIOT AND THE ART OF DRAMATIC REALISM

1. It has "both blemishes and beauties," claimed R. H. Hutton in the *Spectator* (Hutton 1876, 1131), while George Saintsbury stated that it demonstrated the "merits as well as the faults of its writer" (Saintsbury 1876, 253). Following the second installment, the *Athenaeum* wondered if the book "should at last prove to be a novel worthy of the author," because so far it had proved "unpopular with her admirers" (Review of *Daniel Deronda* 1876a, 327). For a thorough overview of the reception of the novel, including the "Jewish question" and the problem of unity in the novel, see J. Russell Perkin's chapter "The Reception of *Daniel Deronda*" in Perkin 1990.

2. I am particularly indebted to Marianne Novy for this section of my work, and I am also thankful for her encouragement on this project. Her ideas suggested other lines of

argument in this chapter as well, including Deronda as a representation of a feminized Hamlet. See Novy 1994, particularly chapter 3 and chapter 6. I've provided, however, much closer textual readings of the connections between *Daniel Deronda* and Charles Knight's version of *Hamlet*, and also examined the dialectical function of Eliot's work, which Novy fails to consider.

3. The influential *Edinburgh Review* in October 1876 made the connection between Deronda and Hamlet, and added that like Hamlet, Eliot's protagonist possessed an "inability to make up his mind what to do or how to do it" (Review of *Daniel Deronda* 1876b, 459). To me, this statement portrays one stereotypical complaint against females, and it may also suggest the notion of a female Hamlet to readers of the review. We will consider the reviews in more detail later.

4. In 1877, Swinburne characterized Eliot as "a type of intelligence vivified and coloured by a vein of genius" (Swinburne 1972a, 190) and in 1902, he referred to her as "the bisexual George Eliot" (Swinburne 1925b, 14:82). Although one of the comments was made in a less-than-flattering context, I believe they demonstrate the perception that Eliot was interrogating gender issues in both her life and her art.

5. Eliot's translation appeared in 1854; the original work was published in German in 1841.

6. Kathryn Hughes seems to be an exception to this rule. In her recent work, *George Eliot: The Last Victorian* (1999), Hughes asserts that without Lewes, there would have been no George Eliot. I am inclined to agree with this statement, specifically regarding the dramatic art of Eliot's novels.

7. This is the title of a collection of Lewes's writings edited by Rosemary Ashton (1992). Lewes published widely, including articles on science, literature, and even metaphysics. These explorations range from "Circulation of the Blood: Its Course and History," to "The Novels of Jane Austen," to "Spirit Rappings and Table Movements."

8. Her readings with Lewes in Weimar and Berlin in 1855 included the following: *Hamlet, Merchant of Venice, Romeo and Juliet, Julius Caesar, Antony and Cleopatra, 1 Henry IV, Othello, As You Like It, Lear, Taming of the Shrew, Coriolanus, Twelfth Night, Measure for Measure, Midsummer Night's Dream, Winter's Tale*, and *Richard III*.

9. Although Novy begins to make this connection, she shies away from crediting Lewes with the influence I feel he had on Eliot, particularly in relation to the dramatic portrayal of character.

10. Citations to Eliot's poems are to Eliot 1989.

11. See Novy 1994, 126.

12. Linda Bamber makes a similar connection in her book *Comic Women, Tragic Men*. She states that the "difference between Deronda and Hamlet is that Hamlet has a powerful sense of free-floating aggression that he uses to heat up the story until it comes to a boil" (Bamber 1982, 89), an aggression that escapes Deronda. In addition, she argues that Deronda "remains trapped in a sexual no-man's-land" and he is "utterly unconvincing as a . . . lover, [and] as a man" (89).

13. All citations are to Shakespeare 1968, edited by Charles Knight. This second edition, published in 1843, is the one that Lewes and Eliot read from and is now in the collection at the Folger Shakespeare Library. Knight generally follows the First Folio, bracketing lines not in F. Departures from F will be signaled in the text with a note. In the general introduction to *William Shakespeare: A Textual Companion*, Gary Taylor and Stanley Wells call Knight's editions "innovative" for breaking the "hegemony" of Malone's 1790 text (Taylor and Wells 1987, 56).

14. This is one of the instances where Knight veers from the Folio, giving these lines to the queen instead of the king. He argues that "the assignment in the [F]olio of so beautiful and tender an image . . . to a man . . . proceeds from a typographical error, which not infrequently occurs" (Shakespeare [1843] 1968, 152).

15. As Showalter (1994) points out, this scene was particularly embraced by the artists of the nineteenth century from the romantics to the Pre-Raphaelites. Novy (1994) also discusses the similarity between Ophelia and Mirah, but she does not provide a close reading of both scenes.

16. Knight chooses the Folio "idle" over the more commonly used "wicked" from the Quartos, arguing that "*wicked* was too strong an epithet for Hamlet to apply to his mother,— inconsistent with that filial respect which he never wholly abandons" (Shakespeare [1843] 1968, 107).

17. I agree with Jenkins, who states, "Evidently the Queen makes as if to depart and is forcibly prevented by Hamlet. The accompanying action is suggested by Q1 at 4.1.8, 'then he throwes and tosses me about'" (Jenkins 1982, 319). Knight follows F in this scene, but regularizes the Folio's "helpe" to "help."

18. Following the famous illustration in Rowe's *Shakspere* (1709), some productions of *Hamlet* use portraits of large oil paintings hung on an upstage wall. Knight includes and comments on the print from Rowe's *Shakspere* at the end of act 3 in his edition (Shakespeare [1843] 1968, 116).

19. As Edward Said argues in a different context but one suitable for my purposes: "[I]t would be quite accurate to say that Shakespeare's play, its text, is there offstage, and what happens onstage [in the novel and outside the novel] is a result of the text's imperfect or insufficient power to command this particular performance" (Said 1983, 198). Said is referring to the mangled performance of *Hamlet* in Dickens's *Great Expectations*, a novel published fifteen years prior to *Daniel Deronda*.

20. In Lodge's novel *Small World* satirizing academia, one of the characters rewrites his thesis so that it examines "T. S. Eliot's Influence on Shakespeare" (Lodge 1984).

21. In our own century, one may also observe the possible effect of Eliot's appropriation of Shakespeare and the subsequent "feminization" of Hamlet. In 1920, for example, a German silent film actress named Asta Nielsen portrayed Hamlet. In the 1940s, Laurence Olivier's film version focused on the feminine aspects of the Prince of Denmark, opening with the caption "a man who could not make up his mind." In this version, Hamlet's flaxen hair is bobbed to copy the hairstyle favored by Hollywood starlets of the 1930s and 1940s. (See Danson 1993, 44 ff.).

22. Comparisons between Eliot and Shakespeare became commonplace. The *Saturday Review* drew this connection between the dramatist and people who inhabit the public house in *Silas Marner*: "We know that these poor are like real poor people, just as we know that the characters in Shakespeare are real men and women." Moreover, the "humour" of Eliot "pervades the representation, just as it does in the comic parts of Shakespeare" (*Review of Silas Marner* 1861, 369). R. R. Bowker in an unsigned review in *International Review* suggested that Eliot was as "unreligious in the personality of her novels as Shakespeare the dramatist" (Bowker 1877, 68). Writing upon the notice of her death, Lord Acton elevated her above the Bard, arguing that in "problems of life and thought, which baffled Shakespeare disgracefully, her touch was unfailing," and he concluded that "[n]o writer ever lived who had anything like her power of manifold, but disinterested and impartially observant sympathy" (Acton 1904, 57). Of course, this notion of sympathy is what was most often cited, as Novy demonstrates in her work (1994).

CHAPTER 2. CHARACTERIZING SHAKESPEARE

1. Besides Sussman, Dowling, and Dellamora, see Adams 1995 and Jenkyns 1980.

2. For the influence of Swinburne on Bloom, see Sawyer 2002.

3. The block quote may also square with the notion of Shakespeare and Hamlet being associated with the alleged feminine trait of being "unable to make up one's mind." For the textual question, see Harold Jenkins, who posits that in Q1 "there is a divergence in the attitude of the Queen, who is shown in league with Hamlet against the King" (Jenkins 1982, 33). Moreover, according to Jenkins, "instead of our seeing Horatio receiving Hamlet's letter, Q1 has Horatio telling the Queen he has received it" (33). Kathleen Irace makes a similar point, stating that the changes in Q1 "make the Queen a more sympathetic character, plotting with her son and his friend against the King" (Irace 1992, 105).

4. This notion is expounded upon in Riede 1993. As paradoxical as the term sounds, it is helpful in understanding Swinburne's appropriation of Shakespeare.

5. Although Johnson's dictionary of 1769 defines the term in less sexual terms, e.g., "to tempt; to corrupt; to deprave," the sexual shading of the word, according to the OED, was current as early as *All's Well That Ends Well* in 1601/2: "Many a maid hath been seduced by them" (Shakespeare 1997, 3.5.19).

6. All citations are to Shakespeare 1997, except where noted.

7. There is an ongoing debate over Shakespeare's revision of the Folio text. The new *Riverside Shakespeare*'s textual notes, for example, agree with Swinburne's assessment, positing that it is "likely" that "the play as it appears in F1 shows some evidence of revision." The notes conclude that "Shakespeare originally intended to include Falstaff among Henry's followers in the French wars and the scenes connected with [Falstaff's] death were later additions" (Evans et al. 1997, 1016). However, Gary Taylor argues that the Hostess's line "look[s] like [an] unauthorized improvement of Henry's character (Taylor 1982, 312). Here I must side with Swinburne against Taylor, as I see no way this line could "improve Henry's character"; if anything, it makes Prince Hal more culpable in the death of Falstaff. Whatever the case, all modern editions include the line: the Cambridge Edition (1992), the Arden Edition (1995), and even Taylor's Oxford Edition of *Henry V* (1982).

8. Patricia Parker argues that Falstaff is one of the original "literary fat ladies" (Parker 1987, 20). She contends that Falstaff's size, as well as his loquaciousness, are characteristics traditionally associated with females. In addition, she posits that Falstaff's own words link him with femininity. As Falstaff claims, "I have a whole school of tongues in this belly of mine. . . . My womb, my womb, my womb undoes me" (*2 Henry IV* 4.2.16–20). Interestingly, these lines fold together two feminine notions. While the womb reference is obvious, the line also positions Falstaff as the garrulous woman, the one "with the proverbially unstoppable female tongue" (Parker 1987, 21). Valerie Traub pushes the feminization of Falstaff one step further, asserting that Falstaff represents the Bakhtinian "'grotesque body'" (Traub 1992, 51), a body she goes on to associate with pregnancy and the maternal. Peter Stallybrass and Allon White elaborate on Bakhtin's notion of the grotesque body. Open and "yawning wide," the body represents "an image of impure corporeal bulk" (Stallybrass and White 1986, 9), a description that calls to mind Hal's of Falstaff when he describes the knight as "sweat[ing] to death, / And lard[ing] the lean earth as he walks along" (*1 Henry IV* 2.3.16–17). All these definitions, I would add, suit Falstaff perfectly. Unfortunately, while feminizing Falstaff, Traub emasculates him in the process, and in turn Traub "heterosexualizes the homosexual." Buried in her critique, however, are the roots of a more Swinburnean reading of Falstaff. Toward the end of her essay, Traub admits that "it is apparent that

homoerotic desire infuses the relationship of Falstaff and Hal" (1992, 59). Yet she polices this homoerotic possibility by suggesting that it is the "feminine" qualities of Falstaff, combined with Hal's "predominant lack of interest in women," that characterize the nature of the relationship (59).

9. The term "imaginary identification" is borrowed from Stephen Greenblatt. His essay entitled "Invisible Bullets" argues that the play "charm[s] us with its visions of breadth and solidarity, 'redeeming' itself in the end by betraying our hopes, and earning with this betrayal our slightly anxious admiration" (Greenblatt 1985, 34). Hence, auditors are "dazzled by their own imaginary identification with the conqueror" (43).

10. There are at least two ways to read this image. If the Prince sees himself as the "sun"—an image of himself he employs on numerous occasions—then it follows, according to Goldberg, that this is an instance of Hal's "cross-dressed" vision of himself. Hal's dissoluteness, we must remember, is hinted at as early as the close of *Richard II,* when his own father describes him as a "wanton and effeminate boy," one who associates "[w]ith unrestrainèd loose companions" (5.3.10,7). Another way of reading this scene is to posit that Hal, as a defense, positions a woman in the space between Falstaff and himself to forestall even the mental image of such an encounter; in turn, this symbolic posturing wards off the potentially homoerotic connection. Another example of a similar dodge by the Prince (or Shakespeare) occurs in the tavern scene in act 3, scene 3 of *1 Henry IV*. In this tender moment of confession, Falstaff declares his love for the prince by claiming, "A thousand pound Hal? a million! Thy love is worth a million; thou owest me thy love" (ll. 125–26). Immediately following Falstaff's declaration, however, the hostess semantically slides between the two and claims that Falstaff is lying: "Nay, my lord," she states, contradicting Falstaff's claim, "he called you 'jack' and said he would cudgel you" (ll. 127–28). Eve Sedgwick also reminds us that this male-female-male triangle is particularly prominent in male homosocial relations. Sedgwick claims that "the bond that links" two males "is as intense and potent as the bond" between the male and the female in a triangular situation (Sedgwick 1985, 21). In other words, the males participate in a routing through women of homosocial desire. Yet Swinburne ultimately intimates that the homosocial relationship between Hal and Falstaff may also be a homoerotic one.

11. Alan Bray points out that "consumptive" behavior often suggests a "self-devouring appetitiveness that could easily take the form of gluttony or thievery" or, in Swinburne's case, excessive drinking (qtd. in Goldberg 1992, 275). In a "Literary Interview" for Frank Leslie's Illustrated Newspaper, Ralph Waldo Emerson "condemned" Swinburne as a "perfect leper and a mere sodomite" (Emerson 1874, 275).

12. These types of behavior are addressed by Eve Sedgwick in what she calls the "problematics of *identification with/identification as*" (Sedgwick 1990, 62).

13. For a perceptive account of another transgressive use of Shakespeare, see Kate Chedgzoy's chapter on Oscar Wilde (Chedgzoy 1995). She argues that in "Wilde's homoerotic appropriation of Shakespeare," he "repeatedly flirts with the popular conception of pederastic homosexuality as the successor to the classical Greek practice of man-boy love as a kind of mentor-disciple relationship (167, 164). Yet Chedgzoy fails to acknowledge Swinburne's role in the transgressive appropriation of Shakespeare.

14. The first one thousand copies were sold almost immediately, and a second edition was quickly printed the same year (1880). New editions appeared in 1895 (the one I am using), 1902, 1908, and 1909.

15. Swinburne wrote to Symonds, telling him that he found the book "delightful" in "the true sense of the word delight-full" (qtd. in Grosskurth 1964, 160).

Chapter 3. The Shakespeareanization of Robert Browning

1. I am indebted to and have borrowed from John Woolford's astute article on Browning and Kean (1989), although he stops short of considering this connection to be a significant early step in Browning's overall appropriation of Shakespeare.

2. Mill wrote that Browning's fictional hero-narrator (and perhaps Browning himself) was "possessed with a more intense and morbid-self consciousness than I ever knew in any sane human being" (qtd. in Maynard 1977, 43). In her chapter entitled "*Pauline* and Mill," Sarah Wood attempts to defend the poem by arguing that Mill's remarks reveal "the severe limitations of readings of *Pauline* as autobiography" (Wood 2001, 33). The reading public must have felt the same as Mill, however, for no copies of the original printing were sold.

3. Many critics have traced the intertextual relationship between *Pauline* and "Alastor," for example. Moreover, Shelley's untimely death is mourned directly in the poem. "Sun Treader," the speaker proclaims, "life and light be thine for ever! / Thou art gone from us" (Browning 1969-c, ll. 151–52). The speaker goes on to lament that "other bards arise, / But none like thee" (ll. 154–55).

4. Citations to *Pauline* are to Browning 1991. Citations to Browning's other poems are to Browning 1969–.

5. George Henry Lewes recalls that during this time when Kean "was sufficiently sober to stand and speak, he could act his part with the precision of a singer who has thoroughly learned his air" (Lewes 1878, 18). Even when drunkenness had ruined his voice, Kean could "become impressively commanding by the lion-like power and grace of his bearing" (15).

6. Byron himself, that unapologetic overreacher, exclaimed when he witnessed Kean's performance, "By Jove, he is a soul! Life—nature—truth without exaggeration" (Byron 1830, 500).

7. For a perceptive account of Browning's "obscurity" see Pearsall 1989, where she argues that this "critical commonplace" had "remarkable generic implications" in the nineteenth century, so that many readers and critics even doubted whether Browning's work could be classified as poetry (43).

8. All citations to *A Blot in the 'Scutcheon* are keyed to Browning 1969–.

9. All citations to *Romeo and Juliet* are keyed to Shakespeare 1997.

10. I am grateful to Frances Teague for pointing out this connection.

11. Of course, other nineteenth-century poets made similar distinctions. In John Keats's famous letter to Richard Woodhouse, he differentiates his poetical "Character" from "the wordsworthian or egotistical sublime; which is a thing per se and stands alone." He claims that he himself is a sort of "camelion Poet" who "has no self—it is every thing and nothing" and has as "much delight in conceiving an Iago as an Imogen" (Keats 1958, 1:386–87).

12. The similarities between Shakespeare's soliloquies and Browning's monologues seem obvious enough: thinking aloud and revealing one's innermost thoughts to an understood or actual auditor. Joseph Dupras, however, suggests that in some poems such as "Caliban" the "interpretive relationship" differs "from the one in the dramatic monologue," as there is no auditor for us as readers to "share the responsibility of deciding meaning and consequence" (Dupras 1986, 75).

13. A number of critics have made convincing comparisons with *King Lear:* Kintgen 1966, Shaw 1968, Shapiro 1975, and Clarke 1962 are among the most perceptive.

14. All references to *King Lear* are to the conflated version in Shakespeare 1997, a

version closer to most Victorian editions of the play, including the Globe edition that Browning owned and that is now in the collection at the Folger Shakespeare Library.

15. Browning's complete response, "Yes, just about that" seems to me to raise more questions than it answers (qtd. in Devane 1955, 231).

16. For a good example of a critical analysis that traces Lear's gradual "self-discovery," see Jorgensen 1967.

17. John Robert Bolton Holloway and Julia Bolton Holloway suggest that the poem was based on a tale told to her "by a part-black Jamaican Barrett cousin" (qtd. in Blain 2001, 64).

18. The publication of *Dramatis Personae* was deliberately delayed for a year because his other works "sold so well" (Litzinger and Smalley 1970, 17).

19. Swinburne and Browning had a curious and contradictory relationship. As an undergraduate at Oxford, Swinburne admired Browning; Rikky Rooksby claims Swinburne "imitated" the other poet's works (Rooksby 1997, 54). But after Browning called Swinburne's poems "moral mistakes, redeemed by much intellectual ability," their relationship became strained (qtd. in Rooksby 1997, 84). The dispute escalated when Browning accepted the position of titular head of The New Shakspere Society in 1879. Swinburne, at odds with the founder, F. J. Furnivall, for years, wrote Browning asking him to resign, but Browning weathered the storm and served out his two-year term. On the occasion of Browning's death, however, Swinburne composed seven laudatory verses, entitled *A Sequence of Sonnets on the Death of Robert Browning*.

20. Citations to Wordsworth's poems are to Wordsworth 1917.

21. See Lootens 1996, which articulates this point concerning the Brownings' marriage.

CHAPTER 4. "AN EMINENTLY PRACTICAL FATHER": DICKENS

1. See, for example, Gager 1996, Harbage 1975, and MacKay 1989. For accounts that focus on Dickens and the family see Waters 1997 and Adrian 1984.

2. Early in 1846, Angela Burdett-Coutts and Dickens decided to open Urania Cottage, an asylum for "fallen women." Dickens spent a great deal of energy in the next ten years promoting this "charitable" cause, believing that "the redemption of a small number of fallen women symbolized the potential for wider salvation" of Victorian society at large (Kaplan 1988, 228).

3. Dickens, of course, was not alone in constructing an image in order to equate himself with Shakespeare. See Novy 1994 as well as the other chapters in this book for other Victorian authors' attempts at self-fashioning and self-promotion.

4. I agree with Jonathan Arac that this distinction developed during the nineteenth century, and he perceptively points out that Samuel Johnson, unlike the romantic and Victorian critics, "praised Shakespeare precisely because his works gave us the typical and general, not the individual or particular" (Arac 1992, 83).

5. The following are representative examples: Arac 1992, Simmons 1995, Dvorak 1984, and Wilson 1985.

6. Hochberg 1993, Smith 1990, and Hochberg 1991 are the most cited. Poole 2000 also proved to be helpful in connecting Dickens and Shakespeare.

7. All citations are to Dickens 1990.

8. All citations of Shakespeare are taken from Shakespeare 1997.

9. Showalter 1994 singles out Trevor Nunn's production in 1970 that "made Laertes and Ophelia flirtatious doubles" and Marianne Faithful's performance in the same period as a "haggard Ophelia equally attracted to Hamlet and Laertes" (236). In the radical feminist Buzz Goodbody's production, Ophelia sat upon the lap of Laertes during the advice scene, playing the role with a "rough sexual" edge (236).

10. Borrowing from Gaston Bachelard, Showalter argues that drowning "was associated with the feminine, with female fluidity," because water is the "profound and organic symbol of the liquid woman whose eyes are so easily drowned in tears, as her body is the repository of blood, amniotic fluid, and milk" (Showalter 1994, 225).

11. The last child, Edward, demonstrated so little aptitude for earning money that Dickens prepared him for sheep training in Australia and sent him to Melbourne in 1868 to join his brother, Alfred, previously "exiled" by his father to the same continent.

12. Later, she tried to further her father's charity work, but she drifted from family to family; lonely and sad, she finally turned to alcohol.

13. In fact, Dickens believed that the shock of the separation is what caused Katie to rush into an ill-advised marriage to a bedridden man, twelve years her senior, a marriage much like Louisa's to an older man. When the wedding was over, and the couple had left for the honeymoon, Dickens made his way to Katie's room, where he buried his anguished face in her wedding gown and told Mamie, "'But for me, Katey [sic] would not have left home'" (Storey 1971, 106). Perhaps if Katie had still been there he may have repeated Gradgrind's words to Louisa: "I must bear the responsibility of [my parenting] failures. I only entreat you to believe . . . that I have meant to do right" (Dickens 1990, 165).

14. For a superb ideological reading of the personal statement, see Waters 1997, 1–12.

15. Although Gager, Kaplan, and others consider Fechter's friendship with Dickens, no one reads the actor as an "adopted" son.

16. For accounts that focus on Dickens and the family, see Waters 1997 and Adrian 1984.

17. For the feminization of Hamlet, see Danson 1993, which comments on the "flaxen" hair style of Laurence Olivier; also see the survey in Novy 1994.

18. Sarah Bernhardt is the most often cited counterexample to the claim about androgyny.

19. There are other parallels, of course. Dickens is like Henry IV, disappointed in his own son and imaginatively wishing that Hotspur is his real heir.

20. Not incidentally, the only English biography of Fechter, first published in 1882 by Kate Field, is dedicated "To the Memory of Charles Dickens," so that even after the novelist's death, the son indirectly keeps alive the memory of a "noble father lost" (*Hamlet* 4.7.25).

21. Deborah Vlock provides a detailed reading of Dickens and the public and private sphere debate, arguing against the Foucauldian notion that the novel represents "the ascendency of the private subject" and the "presumption of a historical evolution from the spectacularity of early modern Europe to the introspectiveness of fully fledged modernity" (Vlock 1998, 8).

22. See Altick 1957, particularly chapter 9. Smiley (2002, 2) makes a similar claim regarding Dickens as a "celebrity" in her new biography.

23. See Winnicott 1971, specifically chapter 7 "The Location of Cultural Experience" (95–103), and the subsection entitled "A Potential Space" (107–10). As Susan Ferguson has recently argued, these readings were "collaborative acts in which writer and reader rel[ied] on one another" (Ferguson 2001). For Winnicott and Dickens, see Sawyer 2003.

24. For the most scholarly reading of Kean, see Schoch 1998.

25. Kemble also took to the reading stage not only to make money but also to elevate her beloved Shakespeare out of the confines of the "despicable" nineteenth-century theater.

AFTERWORD

1. Lootens develops this argument in "Shakespeare, King of What? Gender, Nineteenth-Century Patriotism, and the Case of '*Poet-lore*,'" an essay presented at the 2001 MLA convention in New Orleans. The other essays in this Special Session focused on the following topic: "Re-placing 'King Shakespeare' in the Nineteenth Century."

2. This point is made by Gager in n. 1 to the introduction to Gager 1996. The letter Dickens was composing that includes the quote was addressed to William Charles Kent and was composed on 8 June 1870.

3. For an intelligent analysis of Leavis and the whole reception history of Eliot, see Perkin 1990, particularly chapters 4 and 5.

4. Hardy 1959, 1985, 1983; Showalter, 1977.

5. In the *Cambridge Companion to Shakespeare Studies* (Wells 1986), for example, Swinburne is allotted a mere seven sentences. The first reference refers to mistakes in textual transmission made by Edward Capell's edition from which Swinburne quotes (163), while the second defends him for his claim that Shakespeare did not author *Edward III* (165), an assumption made by many of Swinburne's less astute contemporaries. Even in his essay on the play, Swinburne himself anticipates the point about the attribution of *Edward III*, by claiming that the suggestion by Capell, while "untenable," was certainly not "unpardonable" due to the number of places in the Countess scenes where Shakespeare may have had a hand (Swinburne 1895, 239). Swinburne knowledgeably directs his own readers to Charles Knight's comments on *Edward III,* who also dismissed Shakespeare's authorship, and whose judgment Swinburne calls "not unworthy of a considerate hearing" (Swinburne 1895, 267). To my mind, the essay on *Edward III*, included in *A Study of Shakespeare*, argues for, instead of against, Swinburne's strengths as a critic.

6. Aron Stavisky, as early as 1969, correctly suggested that Swinburne's Shakespearean "criticism is richer and more relevant than the early twentieth century realized" (Stavisky 1969, 16).

7. See Sawyer 2002.

8. While not denying the importance of theory, Charnes 2002 cautions that we should look "very carefully at what we're doing in the academy, and for whom we purport to speak" (265).

9. See, for instance, Loomba and Orkin 1998.

References

Abrams, M. H., et al., eds. 2000. *The Norton Anthology of English Literature.* Vol. 2. 7th ed. New York: Norton.

Acton, Lord. 1904. *Letters of Lord Acton to Mary, Daughter of the Right Hon. W. E. Gladstone.* Ed. Herbert Paul. London: George Allen.

Adams, James Eli. 1995. *Dandies and Desert Saints: Styles of Victorian Masculinity.* Ithaca: Cornell University Press.

Adrian, Arthur A. 1984. *Dickens and the Parent-Child Relationship.* Athens: Ohio University Press.

Altick, Richard. 1957. *The English Common Reader: A Social History of the Mass Reading Public, 1800–1900.* Chicago: University of Chicago Press.

———. 1973. *Victorian People and Ideas.* New York: Norton.

Angelou, Maya. 1985. "Journey to the Heartland." Address delivered at the National Association of Local Arts Agencies convention. Cedar Rapids, Iowa. 12 June.

Arac, Jonathan. 1987. "The Media of Sublimity: Johnson and Lamb on *King Lear.*" *Studies in Romanticism* 26 (summer): 209–30.

———. 1992. "Hamlet, *Little Dorrit,* and the History of Character." In *Critical Conditions: Regarding the Historical Moment,* ed. Michael Hayes, 82–96. Minneapolis: University of Minnesota Press.

Ashton, Rosemary. 1991. *G. H. Lewes: A Life.* Oxford: Clarendon Press.

———. 1992. *Versatile Victorian.* London: Bristol Classical Press.

Auerbach, Nina. 1982. *Woman and the Demon: The Life of a Victorian Myth.* Cambridge: Harvard University Press.

———. 1985. *Romantic Imprisonment.* New York: Columbia University Press.

Austen, Jane. 1980. *Mansfield Park.* Ed. James Kinsley. Oxford: Oxford University Press.

Austin, Alfred. 1970 "Mr. Swinburne." In *Swinburne: The Critical Heritage,* ed. Clyde Hyder, 92–111. New York: Barnes and Noble.

Bakhtin, Mikhail M. 1981. *The Dialogic Imagination: Four Essays.* Ed. Michael Holquist. Trans. Michael Holquist and Caryl Emerson. Austin: University of Texas Press.

Bamber, Linda. 1982. *Comic Women, Tragic Men: A Study of Gender and Genre in Shakespeare.* Stanford, Calif.: Stanford University Press.

Barrett, Dorothea. 1989. *Vocation and Desire.* New York: Routledge.

155

Bate, Jonathan. 1986. *Shakespeare and the English Romantic Imagination*. Oxford: Clarendon.

———. 1989. *Shakespearean Constitutions: Politics, Theatre, Criticism, 1730–1830*. Oxford: Clarendon.

———, ed. 1992. *The Romantics on Shakespeare*. London: Penguin.

Berdoe, Edward. 1896. *Browning and the Christian Faith: The Evidences of Christianity from Browning's Point of View*. New York: Haskell House.

Berger, Harry. 1989. *Imaginary Audition: Shakespeare on Page and Stage*. Berkeley: University of California Press.

Bernhardt, Sarah. 1924. *The Art of the Theatre*. Trans. H. J. Stenning. New York: Benjamin Blom.

Blain, Virginia, ed. 2001. *Victorian Women Poets: A New Annotated Anthology*. London: Longman.

Bloom, Harold. 1973. *The Anxiety of Influence: A Theory of Poetry*. New York: Oxford University Press.

———. 1998. *Shakespeare: The Invention of the Human*. New York: Riverhead Books.

———, ed. 1982. *Falstaff: Major Literary Characters*. New York: Chelsea House.

———. 1987. *Charles Dickens's "David Copperfield."* New York: Chelsea House.

———. 1992. *Caliban: Major Literary Characters*. New York: Chelsea House.

Booth, Michael. 1991. *The Theatre in the Victorian Age*. Cambridge: Cambridge University Press.

Boswell, James. 1887. *The Life of Samuel Johnson*. Ed. G. B. Hill. 6 vols. Oxford: Clarendon.

Bowker, R. R. 1877. Review of *Daniel Deronda*, by George Eliot. *International Review*, January, 68–76.

Bray, Alan. 1991. "'Love among the Muses': Sexuality, Masculinity, and Identity in the Early Modern Period." Lecture, Johns Hopkins University, Baltimore, 24 October.

Browning, Robert. 1950. *New Letters of Robert Browning*. Ed. W. C. DeVane and K. L. Knickerbocker. New Haven: Yale University Press.

———. 1951. *Dearest Isa: Robert Browning's Letters to Isabella Blagden*. Ed. Edward C. McAleer. Austin: University of Texas.

———. 1969. *Letters of Robert Browning and Elizabeth Barrett Browning, 1845–46*. Ed. Elvan Kintner. 2 vols. Cambridge: Harvard University Press.

———. 1969– . *Complete Works*. Ed. Roma A. King Jr. et al. 16 vols. Athens: Ohio University Press.

———. 1991. *Pauline*. First Edition. Reprinted in *The Poems of Robert Browning: Longman Annotated English Poets*, ed. John Woolford and Daniel Karlin. London: Longman.

———. 1997. "Essay on Shelley." In *Robert Browning: The Oxford Authors*, ed. Adam Roberts. Oxford: Oxford University Press.

Browning Society. [1881–84] 1966. *Browning Society Papers*. 3 vols. London: N. Trubner. Reprint, Liechtenstein: Kraus.

Buchanan, Robert. 1866. Review of *Poems and Ballads*, by A. C. Swinburne. *Athenaeum*, 4 August, 137–38.

———. 1869. Review of *The Ring and the Book*, by Robert Browning. *Athenaeum*, 20 March, 399–400.

Bullough, Geoffrey. 1957–73. *Narrative and Dramatic Sources of Shakespeare*. London: Routledge.

Bulman, James C., ed. 1996. *Shakespeare, Theory, and Performance*. London: Routledge.

Byron, George Gordon, Lord. 1830. *Letters and Journals of Lord Byron*. Ed. T. Moore. New York: Routledge.

Carlyle, Thomas. 1966. *On Heroes, Hero-Worship, and the Heroic in History*. Ed. Carl Niemeyer. Lincoln: University of Nebraska Press.

Cavendish, Margaret. 1997. "Sociable Letters." In *Women Reading Shakespeare, 1660–1900: An Anthology of Criticism*, ed. Ann Thompson and Sasha Roberts, 11–14. Manchester: Manchester University Press.

Charnes, Linda. 2002. "The 2% Solution: What Harold Bloom Forgot." In *Harold Bloom's Shakespeare*, ed. Christy Desmet and Robert Sawyer, 259–68. New York: Palgrave.

Chedgzoy, Kate. 1995. *Shakespeare's Queer Children: Sexual Politics and Contemporary Culture*. Manchester: Manchester University Press.

Cixous, Hélène. 1975. "The Character of 'Character.'" *New Literary History* 5:383–402.

Clark, C. C. 1962. "Humor and Wit in 'Childe Roland.'" *Modern Language Quarterly* 23:323–36.

Coleridge, S. T. 1812. *Notes and Lectures*. Edinburgh: John Grant.

———. 1969. *Coleridge on Shakespeare*. Ed. Terence Hawkes. Harmondsworth, England: Penguin.

———. 1992. "Lectures on the Characteristics of Shakespeare." Reprinted in *The Romantics on Shakespeare,* ed. Jonathan Bate, 129–47. London: Penguin.

Collins, Philip. 1975. *Charles Dickens: The Public Readings*. Oxford: Clarendon.

Cross, J. W., ed. 1968. *George Eliot's Life as Related in Her Letters and Journals*. 3 vols. Grosse Pointe, Mich.: Scholarly Press.

Dabbs, Thomas. 1991. *Reforming Marlowe: The Nineteenth-Century Canonization of a Renaissance Dramatist*. Lewisburg, Pa.: Bucknell University Press.

Daily Telegraph. 1879. "Transcript of Shepherd v. Francis." 16 June.

Danson, Lawrence. 1993. "Gazing at Hamlet, or the Danish Cabaret." *Shakespeare Survey* 45:37–51.

D'avanzo, Mario L. 1977. "'Childe Roland to the Dark Tower Came': The Shelleyan and Shakespearean Context." *Studies in English Literature* 17:695–708.

Dellamora, Richard. 1990. *Masculine Desire: The Sexual Politics of Victorian Aestheticism*. Chapel Hill: University of North Carolina Press.

Demaria, Joanne Long. 1990. "The Wondrous Marriages of *Daniel Deronda:* Gender, Work, and Love." *Studies in the Novel* 22:403–17.

Deneau, Daniel P. 1990. "The Brother-Sister Relationship in *Hard Times*." In *Hard Times,* ed. George Ford and Sylvère Monod, 362–67. 2d ed. New York: Norton.

Desmet, Christy. 1990. "'Intercepting the Dew-Drop': Female Readers and Readings in Anna Jameson's Shakespearean Criticism." In *Women's Re-Visions of Shakespeare*, ed. Marianne Novy, 41–55. Urbana: University of Illinois Press.

———. 1992. *Reading Shakespeare's Characters: Rhetoric, Ethics, and Identity*. Amherst: University of Massachusetts Press.

Desmet, Christy, and Robert Sawyer, eds. 1999. *Shakespeare and Appropriation.* London and New York: Routledge.

———. 2002. *Harold Bloom's Shakespeare.* New York: Palgrave.

DeVane, William Clyde. 1955. *A Browning Handbook.* New York: Appleton-Century-Crofts.

Dickens, Charles. 1851. "Shakspeare and Newgate." *Household Words* 4 (4 October): 25–27.

———. 1858. "Personal Statement." *Household Words* 17 (12 June): 601.

———. 1869. "On Mr. Fechter's Acting." *Atlantic Monthly,* August, 242–44.

———. 1960. *Speeches of Charles Dickens.* Ed. K. J. Fielding. Oxford: Clarendon Press.

———. 1962. *David Copperfield.* New York: Signet.

———. 1965–. *The Letters of Charles Dickens: The Pilgrim Edition.* Ed. Madeline House, Graham Storey, Kathleen Tillotson, and K. J. Fielding. 12 vols. Oxford: Clarendon Press.

———. 1990. *Hard Times.* Ed. George Ford and Sylvère Monod. 2d ed. New York: Norton.

Dickens, Mamie. 1897. *My Father as I Recall Him.* New York: Dutton.

Dollimore, Jonathan, and Alan Sinfield, eds. 1985. *Political Shakespeare: New Essays in Cultural Materialism.* Ithaca: Cornell University Press.

Dowden, Edward. 1880. Review of *A Study of Shakespeare,* by A. C. Swinburne. *The Academy,* 3 January, 1–2.

Dowling, Linda. 1994. *Hellenism and Homosexuality in Victorian England.* Ithaca: Cornell University Press.

Dupras, Joseph. 1986. "The Tempest of Intertext in 'Caliban upon Setebos.'" *Concerning Poetry* 19:75–82.

Dvorak, Wilfred. 1984. "On the Knocking at the Gate in *The Old Curiosity Shop.*" *Studies in the Novel* 16, no. 3 (fall): 304–13.

Eliot, George. 1856. Review of *Men and Women,* by Robert Browning. *Westminster Review* (American edition) 65:160–63.

———. 1954–78. *The George Eliot Letters.* Ed. Gordon S. Haight. 9 vols. New Haven: Yale University Press.

———. 1963. "The Natural History of German Life." In *Essays,* ed. Thomas Pinney, 266–99. New York: Columbia University Press.

———. 1988. *Daniel Deronda.* Ed. Graham Handley. Oxford: Oxford University Press.

———. 1989. *Collected Poems.* Ed. Lucien Jenkins. London: Skoob.

Eliot, T. S. 1950. *The Sacred Wood: Essays on Poetry and Criticism.* 7th ed. London: Methuen.

———. 1961. "Wilkie Collins and Dickens." In *The Dickens Critics,* ed. George H. Ford and Lauriat Lane Jr., 151–52. Ithaca: Cornell University Press.

Emerson, Ralph Waldo. 1874. "Literary Interview." *Frank Leslie's Illustrated Newspaper,* 3 January, 275.

Ermarth, Elizabeth. 1985. "George Eliot's Conception of Sympathy." *Nineteenth-Century Fiction* 40:23–42.

Evans, G. Blakemore, et al., eds. 1997. *The Riverside Shakespeare.* 2d ed. Boston: Houghton Mifflin.

Ferguson, Susan. 2001. "Dickens's Public Readings and the Victorian Author." *Studies in English Literature* 41 (autumn). Available online. InfoTrac Onefile.

Feuerbach, Ludwig. 1957. *The Essence of Christianity*. Translated by George Eliot. New York: Harper.

Field, Kate. 1882. *Charles Albert Fechter*. New York: Benjamin Blom.

Fields, Annie. 1922. *Memories of a Hostess*. Ed. M. A. DeWolfe Howe. Boston: Atlantic Monthly Press.

Fitzgerald, Percy. 1971. *Memories of Charles Dickens*. New York: Benjamin Blom.

Ford, George H., and Lauriat Lane Jr., eds. 1961. *The Dickens Critics*. Ithaca: Cornell University Press.

Forster, John. 1855. Review of *Men and Women,* by Robert Browning. *The Examiner,* 1 December, 756–57.

———. 1874. *The Life of Charles Dickens*. 2 vols. London: Chapman and Hall.

Foucault, Michel. 1990. *The History of Sexuality*. Trans. Robert Hurley. Vol. 1. New York: Vintage.

Foulkes, Richard. 1997. *Church and Stage in Victorian England*. Cambridge: Cambridge University Press.

Gager, Valerie. 1996. *Shakespeare and Dickens: The Dynamics of Influence*. Cambridge: Cambridge University Press.

Gaskell, Elizabeth. 1967. *The Letters of Mrs. Gaskell*. Ed. J. A. V. Chapple and Arthur Polland. Cambridge: Harvard University Press.

Gohlke, Madelon. 1983. "'I Wooed Thee with My Sword': Shakespeare's Tragic Paradigms." In *The Woman's Part: Feminist Criticism of Shakespeare,* ed. Carolyn Ruth Swift Lenz, Gayle Greene, and Carol Thomas Neely, 150–70. Urbana: University of Illinois Press.

Goldberg, Jonathan. 1992. *Sodometries: Renaissance Texts, Modern Sexualities*. Stanford, Calif.: Stanford University Press.

Grant, Allan. 1984. *A Preface to Dickens*. London: Longman Group.

Grebanier, Bernard. 1975. *Then Came Each Actor*. New York: David MacKay.

Greenblatt, Stephen. 1985. "Invisible Bullets: Renaissance Authority and Its Subversion, *Henry IV* and *Henry V*." In *Political Shakespeare: New Essays in Cultural Materialism,* ed. Jonathan Dollimore and Alan Sinfield, 18–47. Ithaca: Cornell University Press.

Grosskurth, Phyllis. 1964. *The Woeful Victorian: A Biography of John Addington Symonds*. New York: Holt, Rinehart and Winston.

Harbage, Alfred. 1975. *A Kind of Power: The Shakespeare-Dickens Analogy*. Philadelphia: American Philosophical Society.

Hardy, Barbara. 1959. *The Novels of George Eliot; A Study in Form*. London: Athlone Press.

———. 1983. *Particularities: Readings in George Eliot*. Athens: Ohio University Press.

———. 1985. *Forms of Feeling in Victorian Fiction*. Athens: Ohio University Press.

Hardy, Irene. 1913. "Browning's 'Childe Roland': A Literary Parallel—and Something More." *Poet-lore* 24:53–58.

Hawkes, Terence. 1973. *Shakespeare's Talking Animals: Language and Drama in Society*. London: Edward Arnold.

————. 2002. *Shakespeare in the Present*. London: Routledge.

Hayes, Michael, ed. 1992. *Critical Conditions: Regarding the Historical Moment*. Minneapolis: University of Minnesota Press.

Hazlitt, William. 1818. *Characters of Shakespear's Plays*. 2d ed. London: Taylor and Hessey.

————. 1930. *A View of the English Stage*. In vol. 5 of *The Complete Works of William Hazlitt in Twenty-one Volumes*, ed. P. P. Howe, 169–379. London: Dent.

————. 1992. "On Shakespeare and Milton." Reprinted in *The Romantics on Shakespeare*, ed. Jonathan Bate, 180–88. London: Penguin.

Hedrick, Donald, and Brian Reynolds, eds., 2000. *Shakespeare without Class: Misappropriations of Cultural Capital*. New York: Palgrave.

Henderson, Philip. 1974. *Swinburne: The Portrait of a Poet*. London: Routledge.

Hersey, Heloise E. 1890. "Browning in America." *New England Magazine* 1 (January): 543.

Hochberg, Shifra. 1991. "Mrs. Sparsit's Coriolanus Eyebrows and Dickensian Approach to Topicality." *The Dickensian* 87, no. 1 (spring): 32–36.

————. 1993. "The Influence of *King Lear* on *Bleak House*." *The Dickensian* 89, no. 1 (spring): 45–49.

Howard, Jean E. 1987. "The New Historicism in Renaissance Studies." In *Renaissance Historicism*, ed. Arthur F. Kinney and Dan S. Collins. Amherst: University of Massachusetts Press.

Howard, John. 1963. "Caliban's Mind." *Victorian Poetry* 1:249–57.

Hudson, Derek. 1972. *Munby, Man of Two Worlds*. Boston: Gambit.

Hughes, Kathryn. *George Eliot: The Last Victorian*. New York: Farrar, Straus & Giroux.

Hutton, R. H. 1876. Review of *Daniel Deronda*. *Spectator*, 9 September, 1131–33.

Hyder, Clyde, ed. 1970. *Swinburne: The Critical Heritage*. New York: Barnes and Noble.

————. 1972. *Swinburne as Critic*. London: Routledge & Kegan Paul.

Irace, Kathleen 1992. "Origins and Agents of Q1 *Hamlet*." In *The "Hamlet" First Published (Q1, 1603)*, ed. Thomas Clayton. Newark: University of Delaware Press.

Irvine, William, and Park Honan. 1974. *The Book, the Ring & the Poet: A Biography of Robert Browning*. New York: McGraw-Hill.

Jameson, Anna. 1889. *Characteristics of Women: Moral, Poetical, and Historical*. London: George Bell and Sons.

Jauss, Hans Robert. 1989. "Literary History as a Challenge to Literary Theory." In *The Critical Tradition*, ed. David Richter, 1197–218. New York: St. Martin's.

Jenkins, Harold, ed. 1982. *"Hamlet": The Arden Shakespeare*. London: Routledge.

Jenkyns, Richard. 1980. *The Victorians and Ancient Greece*. Cambridge: Harvard University Press.

Johnson, Samuel. 1768. *The Plays of William Shakespeare*. Vol. 4. London: J. & R. Tonson.

————. [1769] 1819. *A Dictionary of the English Language*. 2 vols. Reprint, Philadelphia: J. Maxwell.

————. 1952. "Notes on the Plays." In *"Rasselas," Poems, and Selected Prose*, ed. Bertrand H. Bronson, 308–27. 3d ed. New York: Holt.

Johnson, Wendell Stacy. 1979. *Living in Sin: The Victorian Sexual Revolution*. Chicago: Nelson-Hall.

Jorgensen, Paul A. 1967. *Lear's Self-Discovery*. Berkeley: University of California Press.

Joyce, James. 1961. *Ulysses*. New York: Random House.

Kaplan, Fred. 1988. *Dickens: A Biography*. New York: William Morrow.

Keats, John. 1958. *The Letters of John Keats, 1814–1821*. Ed. Hyder Edward Rollins. 2 vols. Cambridge: Harvard University Press.

Kintgen, Eugene. 1966. "Childe Roland and the Perversity of the Mind." *Victorian Poetry* 4:253–58.

Lamb, Charles. [1812] 1980. "On the Tragedies of Shakspeare, Considered with Reference to their Fitness for Stage Representation." Reprinted in *Lamb as Critic*, ed. Roy Park, 85–101. Lincoln: University of Nebraska Press.

Leavis, F. R. [1948] 1964. *The Great Tradition: George Eliot, Henry James, Joseph Conrad*. Reprint, New York: New York University Press.

Leverenz, David. 1980. "The Woman in Hamlet: An Interpersonal View." In *Representing Shakespeare: New Psychoanalytic Essays*, ed. Murray M. Schwartz and Coppélia Kahn, 110–28. Baltimore: Johns Hopkins University Press.

Levin, Harry. 1986. "Critical Approaches to Shakespeare from 1660 to 1904." In *The Cambridge Companion to Shakespeare Studies*, ed. Stanley Wells, 213–29. Cambridge: Cambridge University Press.

Lewes, George Henry. 1845. "Shakespeare and His Editors." *Westminster Review* 55:21–41.

———. 1849. "Shakespeare's Critics: English and Foreign." *Edinburgh Review* 40:21–41.

———. 1859. "The Novels of Jane Austen." *Blackwood's Edinburgh Magazine* 86 (July): 99–113.

———. 1878. *On Actors and the Art of Acting*. New York: Henry Holt.

———. 1961. "Dickens in Relation to Criticism." In *The Dickens Critics*, ed. George H. Ford and Lauriat Lane Jr., 54–74. Ithaca: Cornell University Press.

Litzinger, Boyd, and Donald Smalley, eds. 1970. *Browning: The Critical Heritage*. New York: Barnes and Noble.

Lodge, David. 1984. *Small World*. New York: Macmillan.

Loomba, Ania, and Martin Orkin, eds. 1998. *Post-Colonial Shakespeares*. London: Routledge.

Lootens, Tricia. 1996. *Lost Saints: Silence, Gender, and Victorian Literary Canonization*. Charlottesville: University Press of Virginia.

Loucks, James F. ed., 1979. *Robert Browning's Poetry*. New York: Norton.

MacDonnell, Patrick. 1840. *An Essay on the Play of "The Tempest."* London: John Fellows.

MacKay, Carol Hanberry, ed. 1989. *Dramatic Dickens*. New York: St. Martin's.

Macready, Charles. 1912. *The Diaries of William Charles Macready: 1833–1851*. Ed. William Toynbee. 2 vols. New York: G. P. Putnam's Sons.

Marsden, Jean. 1991. *The Appropriation of Shakespeare: Post-Renaissance Constructions of the Works and the Myth*. New York: St. Martin's.

Martin, Theodore. 1861. Review of Fechter's *Othello*. *Athenaeum*, July, 783.

Maynard, John. 1977. *Browning's Youth*. Cambridge: Harvard University Press.

Melchiori, Barbara. 1992. "Upon 'Caliban upon Setebos.'" In *Caliban: Major Literary Characters*, ed. Harold Bloom, 95–108. New York: Chelsea House.

Milsand, Joseph. 1856. Review of *Men and Women,* by Robert Browning. *Revue Contemporaine,* September, 545–46.

Montagu, Elizabeth. 1769. *An Essay on the Writings and Genius of Shakespear.* London: J. & H. Hughs.

Morgan, Thaïs E. 1984. "Swinburne's Dramatic Monologues: Sex and Ideology." *Victorian Poetry* 22:175–95.

———. 1993. "Reimagining Masculinity in Victorian Criticism: Swinburne and Pater." *Victorian Studies* 36:315–32.

Morgann, Maurice. 1972. *Shakespearian Criticism: An Essay on the Dramatic Character of Sir John Falstaff.* Ed. Daniel Fineman. Oxford: Clarendon.

Morley, John. 1866. Review of *Poems and Ballads,* by A. C. Swinburne. *Saturday Review* 4 (August): 145–47.

Morris, William. 1856. Unsigned Review of *Men and Women,* by Robert Browning. *Oxford and Cambridge Magazine* 1:162–72.

Muir, Kenneth. 1961–64. "Changing Interpretations of Shakespeare." In *The Age of Shakespeare*, vol. 2 of *A Guide to English Literature*, ed. Boris Ford, 274–93. London: Cassell.

Novy, Marianne. 1994. *Engaging with Shakespeare: Responses of George Eliot and Other Women Novelists.* Athens: University of Georgia Press.

Osborne, Laurie. 1996. *The Trick of Singularity: "Twelfth Night" and the Performance Editions.* Iowa City: University of Iowa Press.

Parker, Patricia. 1987. *Literary Fat Ladies: Rhetoric, Gender, Property.* London: Methuen.

Pearsall, Cornelia D. J. 1989. "'Is It Poetry?'": The Generic Implications of Browning's Obscurity." *Studies in Browning and His Circle* 17:43–49.

Pechter, Edward. 2002. "Romanticism Lost: Bloom and the Twilight of Literary Shakespeare." In *Harold Bloom's Shakespeare*, ed. Christy Desmet and Robert Sawyer, 145–65. New York: Palgrave.

Pequigney, Joseph. 1985. *Such Is My Love: A Study of Shakespeare's Sonnets.* Chicago: University of Chicago Press.

Perkin, J. Russell. 1990. *The Reception-History of George Eliot's Fiction.* Ann Arbor, Mich.: UMI Research Press.

Peters, Robert L. 1965. *The Crowns of Apollo: Swinburne's Principles of Literature and Art.* Detroit, Mich.: Wayne State University Press.

Peterson, William. 1969. *Interrogating the Oracle: A History of the London Browning Society.* Athens: Ohio University Press.

Poe, Edgar Allan. 1961. *The Old Curiosity Shop.* In *The Dickens Critics,* ed. George H. Ford and Lauriat Lane Jr., 19–24. Ithaca: Cornell University Press.

Poole, Adrian. 2000. "The Shadow of Lear's 'Houseless' in Dickens." *Shakespeare Survey* 53:103–13.

Pope, Alexander. [1743–44] 1969. *Works of Shakespear.* Reprint, 6 vols., New York: AMS.

Porter, Charlotte. 1889. "Browning's Shakespeare Poems." *Poet-lore* 1, no. 5:226.

Redinger, Ruby. 1975. *George Eliot: The Submerged Life.* New York: Knopf.

Redmond, James. 1989. "Action, Character, and Language: Dickens, His Contemporaries, and the Lure of the Stage." In *Dramatic Dickens*, ed Carol Hanberry Mackay, 125–38. New York: St. Martin's.

Review of *A Blot in the 'Scutcheon*, by Robert Browning. 1843a. *Athenaeum*, 18 February, 166.

———. 1843b. *Spectator*, 18 February, 159.

———. 1843c. *The Times*, 13 February, 5, col. 6.

Review of *A Study of Shakespeare*, by A. C. Swinburne. 1880a. *The Examiner*, 10 January, 49–50.

———. 1880b. *Notes and Queries*, 1 May, 368.

———. 1880c. *Saturday Review*, 31 January, 159–60.

———. 1880d. *Spectator*, 3 July, 850–52.

Review of Charles Albert Fechter's *Hamlet*. 1861. *Athenaeum*, 23 March, 725.

Review of *Daniel Deronda*, by George Eliot. 1876a. *Athenaeum*, 4 March, 327.

———. 1876b. *Edinburgh Review*, October, 442–62.

———. 1876c. *Saturday Review*, 16 September, 356–58.

Review of Dickens's Public Reading. 1868. *Scotsman*, 8 December.

Review of *Dramatis Personae*, by Robert Browning. 1864. *Athenaeum*, 4 June, 765–67

Review of *Little Dorrit*, by Charles Dickens. 1857. *The Leader*, 27 June, 617.

Review of *Poems and Ballads*, by A. C. Swinburne. 1866. *London Review*, 4 August, 130–31.

Review of *Silas Marner*, by George Eliot. 1861. *Saturday Review*, 13 April, 369–70.

Richardson, William. 1818. *Essays on Shakespeare's Dramatic Characters, with an Illustration of National Characters*. 6th ed. London.

Richter, David, ed. 1989. *The Critical Tradition: Classic Texts and Contemporary Trends*. New York: St. Martin's.

Riede, David G. 1993. "Swinburne and Romantic Authority." In *The Whole Music of Passion: New Essays on Swinburne*, ed. Rikky Rooksby and Nicholas Shrimpton, 22–39. Hants, England: Scolar.

Rooksby, Rikky. 1997. *A Poet's Life*. Aldershot, England: Scolar Press.

Rooksby, Rikky, and Nicholas Shrimpton, eds. 1993. *The Whole Music of Passion: New Essays on Swinburne*. Hants, England: Scolar.

Rosenberg, Marvin. 1992. *The Masks of "Hamlet."* Newark: University of Delaware Press.

Ruskin, John. 1860. "A Note on *Hard Times*." *Cornhill Magazine* 2:159.

Said, Edward. 1983. *The World, the Text, and the Critic*. Cambridge: Harvard University Press.

Saintsbury, George. 1876. Review of *Daniel Deronda*, by George Eliot. *The Academy*, 9 September, 253–54.

Sawyer, Robert. 2002. "Looking for Mr. Goodbard: Swinburne, Resentment Criticism, and the Invention of Harold Bloom." In *Harold Bloom's Shakespeare*, ed. Christy Desmet and Robert Sawyer, 167–80. New York: Palgrave.

———. 2003. "He Do Redemption in Different Voices: Dickens and the Failure of Atonement." *South Atlantic Review*. Forthcoming, Winter.

Schoch, Richard. 1998. *Shakespeare's Victorian Stage: Performing History in the Theatre of Charles Kean*. Cambridge: Cambridge University Press.

———. 2002. *Not Shakespeare: Bardolatry and Burlesque in the Nineteenth Century.* Cambridge: Cambridge University Press.

Schwartz, Murray M., and Coppélia Kahn, eds. 1980. *Representing Shakespeare: New Psychoanalytic Essays*. Baltimore: Johns Hopkins University Press.

Scott, Clement. 1874. *Some Notable Hamlets of the Present Time*. New York: Benjamin Blom.

———. 1891. *Thirty Years at the Play and Dramatic Table Talk.* London: Railway and General Automatic Library.

Sedgwick, Eve Kosofsky. 1985. *Between Men: English Literature and Male Homosocial Desire*. New York: Columbia University Press.

———. 1990. *Epistemology of the Closet.* Berkeley: University of California Press.

Shakespeare, William. [1843] 1968. *"Hamlet."* In vol. 1 of *The Comedies, Histories, Tragedies, and Poems of William Shakspere,*. ed. Charles Knight. 2d ed. Reprint, New York: AMS.

———. 1997. *The Norton Shakespeare.* Ed. Stephen Greenblatt et al. New York: Norton.

Shapiro, Arnold. 1975. "'Childe Roland,' *Lear*, and the Ability to See." *Papers on Language and Literature* 8:88–94.

Shattuck, Charles H. 1976. *Shakespeare on the American Stage: From Booth and Barrett to Southern and Marlowe*. Washington, D.C.: Folger Shakespeare Library.

Shaw, William David. 1968. *The Dialectical Temper: The Rhetorical Art of Robert Browning*. Ithaca: Cornell University Press.

Showalter, Elaine. 1977. *A Literature of Their Own: British Women Writers from Brontë to Lessing*. Princeton: Princeton University Press.

———. 1994. "Representing Ophelia: Women, Madness, and the Responsibilities of Feminist Criticism." In *"Hamlet": Case Studies in Contemporary Criticism*, ed. Susanne Wofford. New York: St. Martin's.

Simmons, James R. 1995. "Scrooge, Falstaff, and the Rhetoric of Indigence." *English Language Notes* 32, no. 3 (March): 43–46.

Sinfield, Alan. 1985. "Introduction: Reproductions, Interventions." In *Political Shakespeare: New Essays in Cultural Materialism,* ed. Jonathan Dollimore and Alan Sinfield, 130–33. Ithaca: Cornell University Press.

Smiley, Jane. 2002. *Charles Dickens: A Penguin Life*. New York: Viking Penguin.

Smith, Grahame. 1990. "'O Reason Not the Need': *King Lear, Hard Times,* and Utilitarian Values." *The Dickensian* 86, no. 3 (autumn): 164–70.

Smith, Rebecca. 1983. "A Heart Cleft in Twain: The Dilemma of Shakespeare's Gertrude." In *The Woman's Part: Feminist Criticism of Shakespeare*, ed. Carolyn Ruth Swift Lenz, Gayle Greene, and Carol Thomas Neely, 194–210. Urbana: University of Illinois Press.

Sneidern, Maja-Lisa von. 2001. "'An Amazingly Good Jackal': Race and Labor in Dickens's *A Tale of Two Cities.*" *South Atlantic Review* 66:64–90.

Stallybrass, Peter, and Allon White. 1986. *The Politics and Poetics of Transgression*. Ithaca: Cornell University Press.

Stanton, Theodore. 1899. "Sara [*sic*] Bernhardt as Hamlet." *The Critic,* July, 638–40.

Staples, Leslie C. 1956. "The Ghost of a French *Hamlet.*" *Dickensian* 52:71–76.

Stavisky, Aron. 1969. *Shakespeare and the Victorians: Roots of Modern Criticism*. Norman: University of Oklahoma Press.

Storey, Gladys. 1971. *Dickens and Daughter*. New York: Haskell House.

Styan, J. L. 1977. *The Shakespeare Revolution: Criticism and Performance in the Twentieth Century*. Cambridge: Cambridge University Press.

Sussman, Herbert. 1995. *Victorian Masculinities: Manhood and Masculine Poetics in Early Victorian Literature and Art*. Cambridge: Cambridge University Press.

Swinburne, Algernon Charles. 1875. "A Study of Shakespeare." MS. Folger Shakespeare Library. Washington, D.C.

———. 1895. *A Study of Shakespeare*. 2d ed. London: Chatto & Windus.

———. 1896. *Songs before Sunrise*. London: Chatto & Windus.

———. 1925a. "Charles Baudelaire" In *Complete Works*, ed. Edmund Gosse and Thomas Wise, 13:417–27. Bonchurch Edition. London: William Heinemann.

———. 1925b. "Charles Dickens." In *Complete Works*, ed. Edmund Gosse and Thomas Wise, 14:57–88. Bonchurch Edition. London: William Heinemann.

———. 1925c. "Four Plays: *King Lear*." In *Complete Works*, ed. Edmund Gosse and Thomas Wise, 11:232–41. Bonchurch Edition. London: William Heinemann.

———. 1925d. "George Chapman: A Critical Essay." In *Complete Works*, ed. Edmund Gosse and Thomas Wise, 12:136–251. Bonchurch Edition. London: William Heinemann.

———. 1925e. "William Blake." In *Complete Works*, ed. Edmund Gosse and Thomas Wise, 16:50–350. Bonchurch Edition. London: William Heinemann.

———. 1959–62. *The Swinburne Letters*. Ed. Cecil Lang. 6 vols. New Haven: Yale University Press.

———. 1970. *Poems and Ballads & Atalanta in Calydon*. New York: Bobbs-Merrill.

———. 1972a. "The Brontës." In *Swinburne as Critic,* ed. Clyde Hyder, 187–200. London: Routledge & Kegan Paul.

———. 1972b. "On Choice of Subjects." In *Swinburne as Critic,* ed. Clyde Hyder, 146–52. London: Routledge & Kegan Paul.

Symonds, John Addington. 1983. *Male Love: A Problem in Greek Ethics and Other Writings*. Ed. John Lauritsen. New York: Pagan.

Taylor, Gary. 1989. *Reinventing Shakespeare: A Cultural History from the Restoration to the Present*. New York: Weidenfeld & Nicolson.

———. 1999. "The Incredible Shrinking Bard." In *Shakespeare and Appropriation,* ed. Christy Desmet and Robert Sawyer, 197–205. London and New York: Routledge.

———, ed. 1982. *Henry V.* Cambridge: Cambridge University Press.

Taylor, Gary, and Stanley Wells. 1987. *William Shakespeare: A Textual Companion*. Oxford: Clarendon Press.

Thomas, Donald. 1979. *Swinburne: The Poet in His World*. New York: Oxford University Press.

Traub, Valerie. 1992. *Desire and Anxiety: Circulations of Sexuality in Shakespearean Drama*. London: Routledge.

Trilling, Lionel. 1961. *"Little Dorrit."* In *The Dickens Critics*, ed. George H. Ford and Lauriat Lane Jr., 279–93. Ithaca: Cornell University Press.

Vaughan, Alden, and Virginia Mason Vaughan. 1991. *Shakespeare's Caliban: A Cultural History.* Cambridge: Cambridge University Press.

Vaughan, Virginia Mason. 1992. "Caliban's Theatrical Metamorphoses." In *Caliban: Major Literary Characters*, ed. Harold Bloom. New York: Chelsea House.

Vickers, Brian. 1981. "The Emergence of Character Criticism, 1774–1800." *Shakespeare Survey* 34:114–29.

Vining, Edward. 1881. *The Mystery of Hamlet: An Attempt to Solve an Old Problem.* Philadelphia: J. B. Lippincott & Co.

Vlock, Deborah. 1998. *Dickens, Novel Reading, and the Victorian Popular Theatre.* Cambridge: Cambridge University Press.

Waters, Catherine. 1997. *Dickens and the Politics of the Family.* Cambridge: Cambridge University Press.

Weeks, Jeffrey. 1989. *Sex, Politics, and Society: The Regulation of Sexuality since 1800.* 2d ed. London: Longman.

Weimann, Robert. 1982. *Past Significance and Present Meaning.* New York: Routledge.

Wells, Stanley, ed. 1986. *Cambridge Companion to Shakespeare Studies.* Cambridge: Cambridge University Press.

Wilde, Oscar. 1890. "The True Function of Criticism." *Nineteenth Century* 38 (July): 123–47.

Williams, Anne. 1983. "Browning's 'Childe Roland,' Apprentice for Night." *Victorian Poetry* 21:27–42.

Wilson, D. A. 1929. *Carlyle to Threescore-and-Ten, 1853–1865.* New York: Dutton.

Wilson, William A. 1985. "The Magic Circle of Genius: Dickens' Translations of Shakespearean Drama in *Great Expectations.*" *Nineteenth-Century Literature* 40, no. 2 (September): 154–74.

Winnicott, D. W. 1971. *Playing and Reality.* London: Tavistock Publications.

Wood, Sarah. 2001. *Robert Browning: A Literary Life.* New York: Palgrave.

Woolf, Virginia. 1929. *A Room of One's Own.* London: Hogarth Press.

Woolford, John. 1989. "The Influence of Edmund Kean on Browning's *Pauline.*" *Studies in Browning and His Circle* 17:21–31.

Woolford, John, and Daniel Karlin. 1996. *Robert Browning.* Longman: London.

Wordsworth, William. 1917. *The Poetical Works of William Wordsworth.* Ed. Thomas Hutchinson. London: Oxford University Press.

Worthen, W. B. 1997. *Shakespeare and the Authority of Performance.* Cambridge: Cambridge University Press.

Yates, Edmund. 1884. *His Recollections and Experiences.* 2 vols. London: R. Bentley & Son.

Index

Abrams, M. H., 15, 146n
Acton, Lord, 148n
Adrian, Arthur A., 122–23, 153n
Aeschylus, 59, 60, 63
"Alternative-voiced discourse" in
    Swinburne, 51, 65, 66, 67, 76, 81
Altick, Richard, 146n, 153n
Angelou, Maya, 82
Arac, Jonathan, 15, 117, 152n
Archer, William, 143
Arnold, Matthew, 60
Ashton, Rosemary, 25; *Versatile Victorian*,
    24
As You Like It, 30
Athenaeum, 84, 107, 128
Atlantic Monthly, 130
Auerbach, Nina, 22, 23
Austen, Jane: connection with George
    Eliot, 19–20, 26–29, 141; *Mansfield
    Park*, 18
Austin, Alfred, 73

Bachelard, Gaston, 153n
Bakhtin, Mikhail, 51, 74
Bamber, Linda, 147n
Barber, C. L., 75
Barrett, Dorothea, 36
Bate, Jonathan, 16, 22–23, 25, 101
Baudelaire, Charles, 54; *Fleurs du Mal*, 67
Berdoe, Edward, 112
Bernhardt, Sarah, 46–47, 153n; *The Art of
    the Theatre*, 47
Blackwoods Magazine, 27–29
Blagden, Isa, 73, 113

Blain, Virginia, 152n
Blake, William, 54, 143
Bloom, Harold, 66, 100, 105, 142; and
    Falstaff, 70; *Shakespeare: The
    Invention of the Human*, 55, 105,
    144
Booth, Edwin, 48
Booth, Michael, 14
Boswell, James, 71
Boswell, James, the younger, 118
Bowker, R. R., 148n
Bradley, A. C., 15, 144
Bray, Alan, 150n
Bray, Charles, 20, 22
Browning, Elizabeth Barrett, 84, 101–2,
    109, 113
Browning, Robert: "objective" and
    "subjective" poetry, 93–95. Works: *A
    Blot in the 'Scutcheon*, 91–92;
    "Caliban upon Setebos," 100–105;
    "Childe Roland to the Dark Tower
    Came," 95–100, 106, 139; *Columbe's
    Birthday*, 92–93, 103, 139; *Dramatis
    Personae*, 95, 152n; "Essay on
    Shelley," 84, 93–95, 108, 109, 112,
    113; "House," 84, 108–10, 113; *Men
    and Women*, 95, 106, 111; "My Last
    Duchess," 89; *Paracelsus*, 89;
    Pauline, 84–88, 151n; *Return of the
    Druses*, 91; *Ring and the Book*, 111;
    Strafford, 90
Browning Society, 85, 110–13, 139
Buchanan, Robert, 58
Bullough, Geoffrey, 75

Burdett-Coutts, Angela, 114, 123; and
  Urania Cottage, 152n
Butler, Samuel, 44
Byron, Lord (George Gordon Byron, 6th
  Baron Byron), 87, 151n

"Caliban upon Setebos," 100–105
Capell, Edward, 154n
Carlyle, Thomas, 50, 55–56, 80, 82, 134;
  *On Heroes, Hero-Worship and the
  Heroic in History*, 52, 53–54
Cavendish, Margaret, duchess of
  Newcastle, 13, 14, 16, 17, 145
Characteristics of Women (Jameson), 23, 31
Charnes, Linda, 154n
Chedgzoy, Kate, 150n
"Childe Roland to the Dark Tower Came"
  (Browning), 95–100, 106, 139
Cixous, Hélène, 70
Clark, C. C., 98
Clark, Helen, 138
Claudius, 33
Coleridge, Samuel Taylor, 16, 22, 39, 57,
  64, 78, 117, 137; *Kubla Khan*, 100
Collier, John Payne, 118
Collins, Philip, 135, 136, 137
Collins, Wilkie, 124, 129, 132
Cordelia, 59, 64
Critic, 47
Cross, J. W., 20
Cushman, Charlotte, 47

Dabbs, Thomas, 62
Daily Telgraph, 84
Daniel Deronda (G. Eliot), 18–24, 30–45,
  143, 146n, 147nn
Danson, Lawrence, 30–31, 45, 153n
Darwin, Charles, 79; *On the Origin of
  Species*, 102
Dellamora, Richard, 60, 61
Demaria, Joanne Long, 44
Deneau, Daniel P., 121
Desmet, Christy, 23, 68, 70, 71
DeVane, William Clyde, 105
Dickens, Charles, 25; member of "Society
  of Amateurs," 117; performer in *Every
  Man in His Humour*, 117; and *Private
  Theatricals*, 117. Works: *Bleak House*,
  126; *A Christmas Carol*, 133; *David
  Copperfield*, 118; *Domby and Son*,
  118; *The Frozen Deep*, 123, 132;
  Great Expectations, 118, 141; *Hard
  Times*, 114, 118–22, 134; *Little Dorrit*,
  118, 133, 140; *No Thoroughfare*, 129;
  A Tale of Two Cities, 142
Dickens, Charles, family of: Catherine
  (wife), 124; Charlie (son), 114, 123;
  Harry (son), 122; Katie (daughter),
  122, 124–25, 153n; Mamie (daughter),
  122, 134, 153n; Walter (son), 114
Dolby, George, 135
Dowden, Edward, 143
Dowling, Linda, 60, 81
Drury Lane, 15
Dryden, John, 77, 78
Dupras, Joseph, 104, 151n

Edinburgh Review, 19, 26–27
Eliot, George, 142–43; on Browning, 106.
  Works: "A College Breakfast-Party,"
  30; *Daniel Deronda*, 18–24, 30–45,
  143, 146n, 147nn; *Middlemarch* 19,
  22; "The Natural History of German
  Life," 21; *Scenes of Clerical Life*,
  29
Eliot, T. S., 141, 144; *The Sacred Wood*,
  49, 82–83
Ellis, Havelock: *Sexual Inversion*, 46
Emerson, Ralph Waldo, 150n
Ermarth, Elizabeth, 20
"Essay on Shelley" (Browning), 84, 93–
  95, 108, 109, 112, 113
Examiner, 76–80

Falstaff, 50, 66–76, 149nn, 150n
Fechter, Charles Albert, 25; and Dickens,
  127–31, 153n
Feminization of Hamlet, 18–48, 149n, 153n
Ferguson, Susan, 153n
Feuerbach, Ludwig: *The Essence of
  Christianity*, 20–22, 44
Field, Kate, 129, 153n
Fineman, Daniel, 69
Fitzgerald, Percy, 126
Forster, John, 106, 114, 115, 117, 118, 124,
  127, 131–32, 135, 137, 140

Foucault, Michel, 14, 46, 47, 81–82, 153n
Furnivall, F. J., 108, 110, 111, 112, 152n
Furness, H. H., 138

Gager, Valerie, 117, 118, 128, 140, 153n, 154n
Gaskell, Elizabeth, 135
Gertrude, 34, 35, 56, 126; and Alcharisi, 40–42
Goethe, Johann Wolfgang von, 27
Gohlke, Madelon, 36
Goldberg, Jonathan, 68, 74–75, 150nn
Goodbody, Buzz, 153n
Grant, Allan, 142
Grebanier, Bernard, 31
Greenblatt, Stephen, 150n
Grosskurth, Phyllis, 150n

Hal, Prince, 73–76, 149n, 150n
Hamlet, 18–19, 30, 50, 55, 59, 63, 66, 97, 106, 114, 118–21, 123, 128–29, 130, 139, 149n; Charles Knight's edition, 34, 40, 147n; and *Hard Times* (Dickens), 118–22
Hamlet, 18–45, 55, 57, 59, 66, 68, 118, 129, 149n; romantic Hamlet, 30; Fechter's portrayal of, 127–29
Hard Times (Dickens), 114, 118–22, 134
Hardy, Irene, 96
Hawkes, Terence, 79, 104
Hazlitt, William, 20, 28, 30–31, 88–89, 100–101, 117, 137; and sympathy, 22–23
Hennell, Sara, 21
1 Henry IV, 50, 66–75, 149n–150nn
2 Henry IV, 149n
Henry V, 73–74
Hersey, Heloise E., 113
Hickey, Emily, 110, 112
Hogarth, Georgina, 135
Holinshed, Raphael, 75
Holloway, John Robert Bolton, and Julia Bolton Holloway, 152n
Homer, 62
Homosexuality (or "sexual inversion"), 46, 48, 50; and Shakespeare's sonnets, 109; anxiety about, 113
Honan, Park, 90
"House" (Browning), 84, 108–10, 113

Household Words, 124, 125
Howard, Jean, 17
Howitt, William, 123
Hudson, Derek, 76
Hughes, Kathryn, 147n
Hugo, Victor, 72–73
Hunt, Leigh, 25, 140
Hunt, Thornton, 25
Hutton, R. H., 146n
Hyde Park riots, 13
"Hymn to Proserpine" (Swinburne), 54

Irace, Kathleen, 149n
Irvine, William, 90
Irving, Henry, 45, 48, 138–39

Jameson, Anna, 22, 37, 39; *Characteristics of Women*, 23, 31
Jauss, Hans Robert, 16
Jenkins, Harold, 33, 41, 148n, 149n
Johnson, Samuel, 50, 66–68, 71, 72, 149n, 152n
Johnson, Wendell Stacy, 63, 64
Jonson, Ben, 117
Joyce, James: *Ulysses*, 46
Jowett, Benjamin, 60, 71
Julius Caesar, 53

Kaplan, Fred, 117, 126, 127, 135, 152n
Karlin, Daniel, 107
Kean, Charles, 92–93, 102–3, 124, 132, 153n
Kean, Edmund, 22, 24–25, 31, 36, 85–89, 151nn, 153n
Keats, John, 22, 151n
Kemble, Fanny, 134, 154n
Kemble, John, 22, 31
King Lear, 50, 59–66, 119, 123, 139, 151nn; and "Childe Roland" (Browning), 95–99
Kintgen, Eugene, 96
Knight, Charles, 18, 33
Knight, G. Wilson, 59
Knowles, Sheridan, 117

Laertes: and Tom Gradgrind, 115, 119–22
Lamb, Charles, 15–16, 26, 56, 117, 143
Lear, King, 59, 96, 97, 98, 100, 152n

Leavis, F. R., 142–43, 154n
Leverenz, David, 33
Levin, Harry, 144
Lewes, George Henry, 18, 19, 24–29, 117, 128, 140–41; on Charles Albert Fechter, 128; on Edmund Kean, 151n; *On Actors and the Art of Acting*, 24
Litzinger, Boyd, 152n
Lodge, David, 45, 148n
London Review, 62
Lootens, Tricia, 109, 138, 152n, 154n
Loucks, James F., 104, 108

Macbeth, 87, 115–16, 123
Macready, W. C., 86, 89–91, 101, 103, 115, 123–24, 128, 131, 134, 136, 139
Malone, Edmond, 118
Marlowe, Christopher, 62
Married Women's Property Act, 13
Marriott, Alice, 31
Martin, Sir Theodore, 131
Marylebone Theatre, 31
Maynard, John, 87, 108, 151n
Mazzini, Giuseppe, 53
Melchiori, Barbara, 102
Measure for Measure, 142
Merry Wives of Windsor, The, 25, 74, 117
Merchant of Venice, The, 25, 123
Midsummer Night's Dream, A, 79, 92
Mill, John Stuart, 84–86, 151n
Milsand, Joseph, 94
Montagu, Elizabeth, 68–69
Morgan, Thaïs, 50, 58, 75–76
Morgann, Maurice, 67, 68, 69–72
Morley, John, 58, 61
Morris, William, 53, 106
Much Ado about Nothing, 92
Muir, Kenneth, 49, 144
Munby, Arthur J., 76

New Shakspere Society: and Algernon Charles Swinburne, 76, 79–80; and Robert Browning, 108, 110
Nielsen, Asta, 148n
Notes and Queries, 78–79
Novy, Marianne, 19–20, 30, 143, 146n, 147n, 152n, 153n
Nunn, Trevor, 153n

"Objective" poet, 93–95
Olivier, Laurence, 148n, 153n
Ophelia, 36–39, 128; and Mirah, 36–39; and Louisa Gradgrind, 115, 119–22
Othello, 87, 91–92, 93, 117, 123, 131

Parker, Patricia, 149n
Parker, Theodore, 102
Pater, Walter, 51, 60, 75, 81, 144; *Studies in the History of the Renaissance*, 14
Pauline (Browning), 84–88, 151n
Pearsall, Cornelia D. J., 151n
Pechter, Edward, 146n
Pequigney, Joseph, 109
Perkin, J. Russell, 139, 146n, 154n
Peters, Robert, 59
Peterson, William, 112
Phelps, Samuel, 115–16, 129, 130, 131
Poe, Edgar Allan, 67, 140
Poems and Ballads (Swinburne), 60–61
Poet-lore, 138–39
Polonius, 41, 123; and Mr. Gradgrind, 115, 119–20, 122; and Dickens, 125–26
Pope, Alexander, 55, 56
Porter, Charlotte, 138, 139
Prospero, 103, 105
Punch (magazine), 73

Redinger, Ruby, 20
Redmond, James, 115
Richard II, 150n
Richard III, 85, 86, 87, 88, 89
Richardson, William, 66, 67, 69
Richter, David, 51
Riede, David, 63, 149n
Romeo and Juliet, 91–92, 141
Rooksby, Rikky, 152n
Room of One's Own, A (Woolf), 142
Rosenberg, Marvin, 48
Rossetti, Dante Gabriel, 113
Ruskin, John, 107, 126–27, 140

Sade, Marquis de, 61
Sadler's Wells, 31, 115–16, 129
Said, Edward, 44, 118, 148n
Saintsbury, George, 146n
Sappho, 61
Saturday Review, 19, 58, 77–81, 83

Schlegel, August, 23, 117
Schoch, Richard, 146n, 153n
"Scorn not the Sonnet" (Wordsworth), 109
Scott, Clement, 48, 128
Second Reform Bill, 13
Sedgwick, Eve, 43, 150n
Shakespeare: The Invention of the Human (Bloom), 55, 105, 144
Shakespeare, William: *As You Like It*, 30; *All's Well That Ends Well*, 149n; *Coriolanus*, 119; *Hamlet*, 9, 18–19, 30, 50, 55, 59, 63, 66, 97, 106, 114, 118–21, 123, 128–29, 130, 139; *1 Henry IV*, 50, 66–76, 149–50nn; *2 Henry IV*, 149n; *Henry V*, 73–74, 149n; *Julius Caesar*, 53; *King Lear*, 50, 59–66, 95–99, 119, 123, 139, 151n; *Macbeth*, 87, 115–16, 123; *Measure for Measure,* 142; *The Merchant of Venice*, 25, 123; *The Merry Wives of Windsor*, 25, 74, 117; *A Midsummer Night's Dream*, 79, 92; *Much Ado about Nothing*, 92; *Othello*, 87, 91–92, 93, 117, 123, 131; *Richard II*, 150n; *Richard III*, 85, 86, 87, 88, 89; *Romeo and Juliet*, 91–92, 141; *The Tempest*, 16, 100–105; *The Winter's Tale*, 124
Shattuck, Charles, 47
Shaw, David William, 97
Shelley, Percy Bysshe, 85–87, 89, 93, 107, 151n
Showalter, Elaine, 153nn
Siddons, Sarah, 18, 22, 31
Sinfield, Alan, 16
Smalley, Donald, 152n
Smiley, Jane, 146n, 153n
Smith, Rebecca, 35, 36
Spectator, 77–78, 80–81, 83, 92
Spencer, Herbert, 25
Stallybrass, Peter, 149n
Stanton, Theodore, 47
Staples, Leslie C., 129, 130
Stavisky, Aron, 154n
Stevens, George, 109
Storey, Gladys, 125, 153n
Study of Shakespeare, A (Swinburne), 49–83

Styan, J. L., 15
"Subjective" poet, 93–95
Sussman, Herbert, 51
Swinburne, Algernon Charles, 112, 143, 154nn; on George Eliot, 147n; on Robert Browning, 107. Works: "Anactoria," 60; "Hymn to Proserpine," 54; *Poems and Ballads,* 60, 61; *Songs before Sunrise*, 53; *A Study of Shakespeare*, 49–83
Symonds, J. A., 14, 46, 60, 81, 150n
Symons, Arthur, 111
Sympathy in George Eliot and Shakespeare, 20–24

Tait's Edinburgh Magazine, 85
Taylor, Gary, 13, 146nn, 147n, 149n
Teague, Frances, 151n
Tempest, The, 16, 100–105
Ternan, Ellen, 124, 135
Ternan, Frances Eleanor, 123
Third Reform Bill, 14
Thomson, James, 111, 112–13
Times Literary Supplement, 142
Tolstoy, Leo, 66
Traub, Valerie, 149n
Trilling, Lionel, 141

Urania Cottage, 152n

Vaughan, Alden, 101
Vaughan, Virginia Mason, 101, 102
Vezin, Herman, 129
Vickers, Brian, 68
Vining, Edward, 44, 45
Vlock, Deborah, 153n

Waters, Catherine, 126, 153n
Watts, Theodore (Watts-Dunton), 71
Weeks, Jeffery, 60
Weimann, Robert, 139–40
Wells, Stanley, 147n, 154n
Westminster Review, 26–27, 106
Westphal, Carl 46
White, Allon, 149n
Wilde, Oscar, 81, 107–8, 150n
Williams, Anne, 99
Wills, W. H., 134

Wilson, D. A., 134
Wilson, J. Dover, 75
Winnicott, D. W., 132, 153n
Winter, William, 48
Winter's Tale, The, 124
Wood, Sarah, 90, 151n

Woolf, Virginia, 142
Woolford, John, 84, 88, 107, 151n
Wordsworth, William, 109

Yates, Edmund, 126, 129